Text &
Presentation,
2014

TEXT & PRESENTATION, 2014

Edited by Graley Herren

The Comparative Drama Conference Series, 11

McFarland & Company, Inc., Publishers

Jefferson, North Carolina

ISSN 1054-724X • ISBN 978-0-7864-9461-3
ISBN 978-1-4766-2025-1 (ebook)

softcover : acid free paper ∞

On the cover: Signature Theatre's 2012 production of *The Golden Child* with, from left, Julyana Soelistyo, Nadia Gan and Jennifer Lim (photograph by Richard Termine)

Printed in the United States of America

McFarland & Company, Inc., Publishers
Box 611, Jefferson, North Carolina 28640
www.mcfarlandpub.com

Acknowledgments

As editor of *Text & Presentation*, I follow in the footsteps of several inspirational predecessors: Karelisa Hartigan (1980–1993), Bill Free (1993–1998), Hanna Roisman (1998–1999), Stratos E. Constantinidis (1999–2008), and Kiki Gounaridou (2009–2011). I have been generously assisted each year by *T&P*'s associate editor, Kevin J. Wetmore, Jr., who served the Comparative Drama Conference magnificently as its director during the Los Angeles years, and by our long-serving book review editor, the indispensable and indefatigable Verna A. Foster. Special congratulations go to Verna, since this is her final year as book review editor. She has been a great pleasure to work with, and I thank her for a marvelous run as both editor and moderator of the annual "Author Meets Critics" series. Kevin, Verna, and I serve at the pleasure of our esteemed colleagues on the CDC board, and our energetic director Laura Snyder, who organized another memorable conference this year on the sparkling Inner Harbor of Baltimore.

Like theatre itself, *Text & Presentation* is a collaborative effort that depends heavily upon many contributors behind the scenes. I wish to thank all those who participated in the 2014 conference, in particular those who submitted their work for possible publication in *Text & Presentation*. The number and caliber of submissions was high, making this year both a gratifying and a challenging one as editor. I wish to thank the editorial board for vetting the submissions, supplying thorough evaluations, and suggesting thoughtful avenues for revision to our authors. The high quality of the present volume is in large measure attributable to their scrupulous service: José I. Badeness, S.J. (Loyola Marymount University), William Boles (Rollins College), Miriam Chirico (Eastern Connecticut State University), Stratos E. Constantinidis (The Ohio State University), Ellen Dolgin (Dominican College), Les Essif (University of Tennessee, Knoxville), Verna A. Foster (Loyola University Chicago), Yoshiko Fukushima (University of Hawaii, Hilo), Kiki Gounaridou (Smith College), Jan L. Hagens (Yale University), Karelisa Hartigan (University of Florida), William Hutchings (University of Alabama, Birmingham), Baron Kelly (University of Louisville), Jeffrey B. Loomis (Northwest Missouri State University), Ian Andrew MacDonald

(Dickinson College), Helen Moritz (Santa Clara University), Elizabeth Scharffenberger (Columbia University), Laura Snyder (Stevenson University), Tony Stafford (University of Texas at El Paso), Kevin J. Wetmore, Jr. (Loyola Marymount University), and Kelly Younger (Loyola Marymount University). My gratitude also goes out to David Krasner (Dean College), Thalia Pandiri (Smith College), Thomas Strunk (Xavier University), and Tyrone Williams (Xavier University) for additional help in manuscript evaluation.

Text & Presentation, 2014 contains more images than any previous volume in the series. I thank Richard Termine for permission to reproduce his photograph from the Signature Theatre's 2012 production of *The Golden Child* on the cover. Thanks to Maximilian Franz and Stevenson University for permission to include photographs from David Henry Hwang's keynote session. I am grateful to the Schomburg Center for Research in Black Culture (New York), the Dance Collection (Toronto), and the Jerome Robbins Dance Division (New York) for permissions to reproduce several images within Elizabeth Cizmar's essay. For Brigitte Bogar and Christopher Innes's essay, I thank Edition Wilhelm Hansen AS (Copenhagen) for permission to use lines from the *Dyveke* score, and Aleksandar Lukac for permission to use a photograph from his production and a passage from his program notes on *Drums in the Night* (Shabac Theater, Serbia, September 2010). I join Vassiliki Rapti in extending my gratitude to Nanos Valaoritis for permission to reproduce passages and drawings from his unpublished plays in her essay. I also thank John Fitzgerald, Melissa Blackall, and Ryosei Kajiwara for contributing production photos for Yuko Kurahashi's essay.

The 38th Annual Comparative Drama Conference owes much of its success to the generous support of Stevenson University. We thank President Kevin Manning for once again leading off our keynote event and warmly welcoming the attendees. Special thanks go to Chelsea Dove, Rachel Lewis, and Brittany Proudfoot-Ginder, the wonderful assistants who were instrumental in pulling off a mammoth undertaking with hospitality, grace, efficiency, and enthusiasm. You are the worker bees who keep our Queen Bee's crown on straight, and the conference couldn't run so brilliantly without your tireless efforts. And no Acknowledgments section for *Text & Presentation* and the Comparative Drama Conference would be complete without expressing the deepest gratitude to our magnificent conference director, Laura Snyder. Her dedication, hard work, organization, generosity, grace under pressure, and leadership made 2014 another banner year and make all of us look forward to returning to Baltimore each spring.

Finally, I owe my greatest debt of gratitude to my wife, Cathy, and our son, Dylan. You are the twin stars that light my way, and your support makes everything I do possible. I love and thank you both.

Contents

Review of Literature: Selected Books

Preface

The Comparative Drama Conference was founded in 1977 by Karelisa Hartigan at the University of Florida. The annual spring gathering has grown considerably over the years. In 2000 the conference moved from Gainesville to Columbus under the directorship of Stratos E. Constanidis (The Ohio State University). In 2005 Kevin J. Wetmore, Jr. (Loyola Marymount University), assumed the helm for a seven-year stint in Los Angeles. We began the latest leg of the journey in 2012 under the leadership of Laura Snyder (Stevenson University) at our new home base of Baltimore. The conference routinely attracts over 150 presenters and some 200 total participants from across the country and around the globe.

Though the size and scope have expanded over the years, certain core principles have remained intact throughout the conference's history. From the start, Karelisa Hartigan fostered an environment of intellectual rigor combined with hospitality and support. The CDC has always facilitated generous exchanges across the entire career spectrum, from graduate students to the most senior experts in the field. The conference also brings together a refreshingly eclectic mix of scholars and practitioners from various disciplines, including Theatre, Classics, Literature, and Languages. In other words, the conference is truly *comparative*, not merely because papers often compare different plays, but primarily because we encourage comparative dialogue among drama devotees who don't often get the chance to compare notes. The CDC also stands apart as a theatre studies venue where texts are still taken seriously. We certainly acknowledge and appreciate approaches to theatre scholarship that emphasize performance. Indeed, we include staged readings of original plays as an important part of the conference, and we warmly receive any number of scholarly presentations each year that take performance-based approaches to studying drama. Nonetheless, in an academic environment where analyzing the language of plays is sometimes dismissed as pedantic or passé, the Comparative Drama Conference continues to value textual criticism as a vital scholarly pursuit. One of the surest signs of this ongoing commitment is the annual publication of our own text, aptly titled *Text & Presentation*.

1

This volume gathers some of the best work presented at the annual conference. Sponsored by Stevenson University, our sessions took place 3–5 April 2014 at the Pier 5 Hotel in Baltimore's Inner Harbor. There were numerous highlights among the sixty-nine panels and plenary sessions, and several deserve special mention. The weekend featured three staged readings of new plays: *Imperial Image* by Alvin Eng, *Revelation of Bobby Pritchard* by Rich Espey, and *Mock Run* by Stuart Stelly, each coordinated by our resident dramaturg and new board member Janna Segal (Mary Baldwin College). On Thursday we were both entertained and informed by a special session on "Cabaret and the Avant Garde" from Brigitte Bogar and Christopher Innes (both of York University, Toronto). Another very popular session on "Teaching Tips and Trade Secrets" was organized by Miriam Chirico (Eastern Connecticut State University) and Kelly Younger (Loyola Marymount University). Thursday evening's highlight was a marvelous performance of Shakespeare's *Twelfth Night* at Baltimore's Center Stage. Friday afternoon included an enlightening plenary session celebrating fifty years of Ariane Mnouchkine's Théâtre du Soleil. This session featured remarks by Allen J. Kuharski (Swarthmore College) and was moderated by Les Essif (University of Tennessee, Knoxville) and Ian Andrew MacDonald (Dickinson College). The conference was buzzing with anticipation for Friday evening's keynote event, and it exceeded our highest expectations. Playwright David Henry Hwang engaged in a public conversation with Kevin J. Wetmore, Jr. (Loyola Marymount University) that was by turns spirited, provocative, hilarious, and profound. Saturday afternoon included a CDC signature feature, the "Author Meets Critic" plenary session. Each year the book review editor of *Text & Presentation*, Verna A. Foster (Loyola University, Chicago), invites the author of a recent book in theatre studies to interact with two critics in the field. This year the spotlight was directed upon Ric Knowles (University of Guelph), author of *Theatre and Interculturalism*. He had a lively exchange of ideas with Ian Andrew MacDonald (Dickinson College) and Christy Stanlake (U.S. Naval Academy).

All of the research papers contained in *Text & Presentation, 2014* began as relatively brief conference papers. Each was subsequently expanded and submitted for consideration before being double blind reviewed by experts in the field. The accepted essays were revised in response to reviewer suggestions. The final versions published here meet the highest standards of scholarship. Along with twelve research papers, *Text & Presentation, 2014* also contains an interview transcript, a review essay, and ten book reviews. The broad range of subjects, methodologies, and perspectives contained between these covers should give anyone unfamiliar with the CDC an indication of our diverse spectrum of offerings every year.

We were honored to welcome David Henry Hwang as our keynote

speaker and to publish a transcript of his conversation with Kevin J. Wetmore, Jr. (Loyola Marymount University), to lead off the 2014 volume. Hwang will surely be remembered as one of the CDC's best keynote speakers ever. It is also a great privilege to bestow our very first Anthony Ellis Prize for Best Paper by a Graduate Student. The 2014 winning essay is featured as the first of twelve research papers in the volume. The award is named in honor of our late friend Tony Ellis, who was not only a wonderful friend, colleague, and scholar, but was also a great supporter of work by graduate students. It is perfectly appropriate that our inaugural winner, Giuseppe Sofo (University of Avignon and University of Rome), shares Tony's interests in comparative drama and Shakespeare in his work "Translating Tempests: A Reading of Aimé Césaire's *Une Tempête* in Translation."

Next, "Telemachos, the *Odyssey* and *Hamlet*" by Bruce Louden (University of Texas at El Paso), presents a compelling argument that Shakespeare drew upon Homer's the *Odyssey* for key plot and character elements in *Hamlet*. In "Cognitive Misappraisal in Oscar Wilde's *Lady Windermere's Fan*," Todd O. Williams (Kutztown University of Pennsylvania) uses cognitive science to account for the faulty appraisals and bad judgment exercised by Wilde's characters. In the following essay, "Primal, Pure or Something in Between? Aida Walker, Dance and Sexuality," Elizabeth M. Cizmar (Tufts University) analyzes photographic evidence and performance history to appreciate the iconic strategies of African American actress Aida Walker. "Mediating East-West Binarisms: A Study of Al-Hakim's Hybrid Plays," provides an overview by Ahmed Mohammed Ghaleb (University of Ibb, Yemen) of ways in which Egyptian playwright Tawfiq al-Hakim combined the dramatic traditions of East and West to produce groundbreaking new hybrid plays.

Regular attendees at the CDC and readers of *T&P* will be familiar with the distinctive voice of Doug Phillips (University of St. Thomas). His most stylistically daring piece to date is "Fragments Shored: Some Remarks on T. S. Eliot's Drama and the Uses of Hugh Grant's Vacancy," an eclectic meditation ranging from the plays of Strindberg, Wilde, and Eliot, through the poetry of Larkin, to Žižek's philosophy and Hugh Grant's films. Two other mainstays of the conference, the delightful Brigitte Bogar and Christopher Innes (York University, Toronto), contribute an essay on "Cabaret and the Avant-Garde." Their essay builds upon the pair's multimedia revue from CDC 2014 to explore the striking artistic and political affinities between these movements. This year's conference included multiple sessions commemorating the fiftieth anniversary of the Théâtre du Soleil, and the present volume features expanded versions of two such papers. Allen J. Kuharski (Swarthmore College) provides a thorough overview of the company as well as a pedagogical primer in how he teaches their work in "Fifty Years of Ariane Mnouchkine and the Théâtre du Soleil: The Director as Dramaturge, Theater Historian and Public Intellectual." In the following essay, "*Norodom Sihanouk*: The "Unfinished" Story of American Global Totalitarianism by Hélène Cixous and the Théâtre du Soleil," Les Essif (University of Tennessee, Knoxville) examines the company's denunciation of devastating U.S. foreign policies in *The Terrible but Unfinished Story of Norodom Sihanouk, King of Cambodia*.

Vassiliki Rapti (Harvard University) introduces readers to the plays of Nanos Valaoritis in "*Oedipus King / Oedipus Pig*: Nanos Valaoritis's Ludic Politics," providing context for the Greek writer's ongoing anti–Fascist political interventions. In the following essay, "Friends Dying Before Our Eyes in Annie Baker's *The Aliens*," Thomas Butler (Eastern Kentucky University) examines Baker's play in the context of postmodern discourses on presence/absence and the relation of friendship to mortality. The final research paper of this volume is "A Comparative Analysis of Three Plays on Disasters: *Omnium Gatherum*, *Carried Away on the Crest of a Wave*, and *Radio 311*," where Yuko Kurahashi (Kent State University) identifies several patterns connecting recent plays about natural and manmade disasters. As always, the volume closes with a selection of book reviews. Doug Phillips (University of St. Thomas) leads off with a review essay covering books on Beckett, Williams, and Pinter. Finally, *Text & Presentation, 2014* concludes with ten shorter reviews of various recent publications in theatre studies.

One more important feature of the Comparative Drama Conference which deserves special mention is the Philadelphia Constantinidis Essay in Critical Theory Award. This award is endowed by former conference director and long-time board member Stratos E. Constantinidis in memory of his late mother. Established in 2006 to encourage research and writing on Greek theatre and performance, the award recognizes the best comparative essay on Greek theatre published in the previous calendar year. Essays may address any aspect or period of Greek theatre, so long as the essay is comparative in nature and published (in English) in a journal or anthology (in any country). Essays and nominations should be emailed by 31 December to lsnyder4990@stevenson.edu. The 2014 winner of the award was Gonda Van Steen (University Florida) for her essay, "The Story of Ali Retzo: Brechtian Theater in Greece under the Military Dictatorship," published in *Journal of Modern Greek Studies* 31.1 (2013): 85–115.

The Comparative Drama Conference seeks original research papers investigating any facet of theatre and performance. Papers may be comparative across cultural, historical, disciplinary, and national boundaries, and may deal with any issue of theory, history, criticism, dramatic literature, historiography, translation, performance, or production. Information and updates are available on our website: http://comparativedramaconference.stevenson.edu. Only papers presented at the annual conference are eligible for consideration in that year's volume of *Text & Presentation*. On behalf of the executive board, I welcome all readers of this volume to come share your latest research with us at a future Comparative Drama Conference and to submit your work to *Text & Presentation*.

Graley Herren • *Xavier University*

A Conversation
with David Henry Hwang

Transcript of Keynote Panel: 4 April 2014
Presiding: KEVIN J. WETMORE, JR.

Abstract

The keynote panel at the 2014 Comparative Drama Conference was a conversation with David Henry Hwang. He is the Pulitzer Prize-winning playwright of M. Butterfly, as well as several other successful plays, including The Dance and the Railroad, Golden Child, Yellow Face, and most recently Kung Fu. In this session Hwang discusses his approaches to playwriting and his position as an iconic Asian-American artist and cultural spokesperson. The interview was conducted by Kevin J. Wetmore, Jr. (Loyola Marymount University).

Wetmore: As a playwright, how do you determine the form of your drama? Looking especially at your early work, everything seems to involve an experiment with form.

Hwang: Yes, I have a strong interest in form. For each play that I do, I feel that I need to have a question that I'm trying to answer; I want to know basically where I'm starting and where I'm ending; and then there's some kind of formal experiment. For example, in *Yellow Face* I made a stage mockumentary or an unreliable memoir. With *Chinglish* I tried to write a play that was about a quarter to a third in Mandarin with projected titles for the translations like in a movie. And now with *Kung Fu* I'm trying to see if martial arts can be incorporated into a play narrative as a sort of "dancical." In order for me to want to do a play, there has to be some formal challenge that I'm taking on. I want to feel, "Is this possible? Can this be done?"

Wetmore: Will you take us through that process a bit? How does a David Henry Hwang play begin? How does it take form?

Figure 1. David Henry Hwang (photograph by Maximilian Franz, courtesy of Stevenson University).

Hwang: I think writers are always trolling for ideas. I'm always thinking, "Maybe that would be a good story." But there are lots of things that could make good stories. The question is what story is important enough, what story means enough to me such that I want to live with it for three, four, five, seven, or however many years it takes to get the thing on. It's very intuitive. It's the story that makes my heart beat faster. It's the thing that makes me go: "I'm really excited to explore this." Sometimes I compare it to falling in love. When you first fall in love, you always want to be with that person, and when you're not with them you're thinking about them. That's the thing to write about. Then it becomes a question of "Am I still in love six months later? Does it still make my heart beat faster?" That's the test.

M. Butterfly is the most convenient example because most people know it. *M. Butterfly* is the story of a French diplomat who falls in love with a Chinese actress, and they have an affair for twenty years. She turns out to be: a) a spy, and b) a man in drag. The diplomat claims that he never knew the true gender of his lover. The question there is pretty straightforward, it's the question everyone asks when they first hear the story. How could he not know? So there's the element of wanting to answer a question.

The second thing is wanting to vaguely know where I'm beginning and where I'm ending. Sometimes I compare writing a play to taking a road trip.

I know I'm going to drive from New York to Baltimore. But I don't know how I'm going to get there. Finding the road between the two places is sort of the metaphor for writing the play. That allows me to keep some sort of balance between form and content, between impulse and craft. To stretch this metaphor a little, let's say I'm driving from New York to Baltimore, but I have this impulse to stop in Philadelphia. I can indulge this impulse because I know in the back of my head that eventually I have to get to Baltimore. That allows me to retain a certain amount of freedom in the writing process while at the same time having a goal in the back of my head, so that it doesn't go way off course.

The third issue is this thing you bring up, which is the question of form. What form is right for this particular story? What variation on that form might I want to experiment with? A lot of the time that involves modeling plays on other plays. For each of my plays I can tell you what other plays I was ripping off form-wise. In the case of *M. Butterfly* it was largely modeled on the Peter Schaffer plays *Equus* and *Amadeus*. The premise is a protagonist toward the end of his life. He starts the play by directly addressing the audience, basically saying, "This very strange thing happened to me. I met Mozart." Or "There's this kid who blinded horses." Or "I met the Perfect Woman." Then it flashes back, and the older actor plays himself as a younger man in those scenes. The formal variation in *M. Butterfly* is that, in the Schaffer play, the protagonist holds on to the narrative for the whole play; Dysart speaks to the audience for the whole play. In *M. Butterfly* Gallimard begins by controlling the whole narrative in Act One. In Act Two there's a struggle for control over the narrative with Song, the Chinese spy. The third act, at least at the beginning, starts with Song in control of the narrative.

Wetmore: Especially early on in your career, you returned to the same pool of actors: John Lone, Victor Wong, Tzi Ma. As a writer, do you write with particular performers in mind? Or do you write with "the actor" in mind, even if you don't know the specific actor?

Hwang: I usually don't write with a specific actor in mind. At the beginning of my career I wanted to experiment with mashing Western naturalistic theater and traditional Chinese opera, or at least some of the tropes of Chinese theater. That has continued throughout my career. At the beginning I didn't know anything about Chinese opera (and I still don't feel like I know a great deal). But coming across John Lone, who was brought up in the Cantonese opera in Hong Kong, was a great boon. John became essentially my first Chinese opera teacher.

The one time I ever wrote a play with actors in mind was *The Dance and the Railroad*, which was my second play to be done in New York. I wrote it specifically for John Lone and Tzi Ma, who were both actors from my first play *FOB*. John had a background in Chinese opera and Tzi had a background in Chinese dance so that we could create this show. But by and large I don't know who I'm going to cast.

This often creates big problems. For *M. Butterfly* we used to joke that we had to find a Chinese transvestite who could sing and dance. For *Chinglish* we had to find a white guy in his forties who spoke fluent Mandarin. A white guy in his twenties who speaks fluent Mandarin is actually not that hard to find nowadays. But a white guy in his forties is pretty tough. We auditioned people on five continents. We auditioned Caucasian actors in China. Does anyone here have a friend or relative who is a Caucasian actor in China? Okay, then I can say this: they're really bad! It was the worst pool of actors I've ever auditioned. And some were really eccentric. It was July in Beijing, and some guy comes in wearing black wool Armani—this was his Bohemian thing—with a parrot on his shoulder! For *Kung Fu* we were looking for someone who could play Bruce Lee. I had no idea who that would be.

In general (knock on wood) my experiences in casting have taught me that, if you create the opportunity, you will find the person. They are out there. They just haven't been given the chance to shine and to show their talents to the world yet.

Wetmore: You brought up the experience in Beijing. *Chinglish* was performed in Hong Kong, *Golden Child* has gone up in Singapore, and several of your plays have been performed in Asia. How have Asian audiences reacted to your work? So much of the scholarship we do focuses on Asian-American drama in America. But I wonder how your plays play in Asia.

Hwang: The first time I had a play done in Asia was *FOB* in Singapore in 1982, so this was fairly early in my career. If you're going to do an English play in Asia, Singapore is a pretty easy place to do it. Everybody speaks English, and they all grew up on "The Mary Tyler Moore Show." So there are those common references. For a long time Singapore became a place where I did a lot of my shows. Eventually, because *M. Butterfly* was successful on Broadway, it got done in most Asian countries—but not China. Oddly enough, for a play that has been done in three or four dozen countries in the world, the two major countries where it has not been done are China (which you might kind of expect) and France—which is really surprising. I guess the French still don't want to think about that this happened to one of their countrymen.

I find that a lot of the Asian-American work (as opposed to the internationalist work that I do) has been interesting to see in Asia because a lot of these kinds of identity issues are not unknown in Asia itself. Think for instance of Singapore in 1989, when there was a pop album by Dick Lee called *The Mad Chinaman*. It became a hit throughout Asia. Dick is essentially talking about identity issues. Am I Western or am I Eastern? With the introduction of Western culture, and particularly the predominance of Western pop culture in Asia, people are dealing with bicultural identity issues. The Asian-American work seems to resonate with these issues.

It's very interested to see *M. Butterfly* in Japan. Here's a play based on an opera by an Italian composer about an American soldier who has an affair with a Japanese woman, which is then turned into a play by a Chinese-American author about a French diplomat and a Chinese spy—and then you watch it in Japan! The mirrors on mirrors are kind of mind-blowing. Whenever I've seen *M. Butterfly* in Japan—and it was surprising when it happened, though perfectly understandable in retrospect—they're really not interested in the Asian stuff. Okay, the guy kills himself: big deal. On the other hand, there's tremendous interest in the Western scenes, the "exoticism" of scenes that take place in France. The focus of the Japanese productions I've seen seems to be much more on that.

And then China—I've never been able to get anything on in China. As recently as four years ago, there was a production of *M. Butterfly* in Shanghai in English, so it was basically for ex-pats. It was in a 200-seat theater for five performances, but it got shut down after three performances. At the same time, however, the script of *M. Butterfly* was published in Chinese by a Shanghai publisher, and that was fine. So either the censors for the published versions don't actually read what they're supposed to be censoring, or there is this idea that theater is more dangerous. Theater, being a social art, being a place where people gather, seems more threatening to the powers that be than sitting at home alone and reading a book. Not until last year, when we brought *The Dance and the Railroad* (the revival that happened at Signature) to the Wuzhen Festival outside Shanghai, did I finally have a play performed in China that wasn't shut down by the government.

Wetmore: Could you speak about *Chinglish*? Correct me if I'm wrong, but wasn't that show inspired by your experiences in China?

Hwang: I've been spending a fair amount of time in China over the past six or seven years. China has become very interested in Broadway-style shows, and I happen to be the only even nominally Chinese person who has written a Broadway show. So I started getting all of these invitations to come over. And it's China, so they've always got these really huge offers. "We're going to build a new theater district!" Nothing ever happens. But it did give me the opportunity to learn more about China and see the amazing changes that are taking place over there.

On a trip in 2005, I was taken to a brand new cultural center. It was gorgeous, with Brazilian wood and Italian marble and everything was perfect, except for the really bad Chinglishy signs. For instance, the handicapped restroom said "Deformed Man's Toilet." I began thinking about using the signs as a jumping off point for a play about doing business in China today, one that would deal with the issue of language. We always duck that as Americans. You see a play about an American in Brazil, and all the Brazilians speak English with a Brazilian accent. That doesn't capture the nature of the experience at all. My model was *Glengarry Glen Ross*. Could I write *Glengarry Glen Ross* set in China, but then also do it bilingually with titles? Then eventually a love story got in there, too, so now it's not much like *Glengarry Glen Ross* at all. But yes, that experience was the trigger for the play.

Wetmore: I want to go back to something you said earlier. A major theme of your work is the value of art to negotiate and determine identity. We find this in *The Dance and the Railroad, Yellow Face, Chinglish, M. Butterfly*, and even in *Kung Fu* that's something Bruce Lee had to deal with. What is the value of art in helping to negotiate and determine identity?

Hwang: I think a people, a nation, a culture often define themselves in terms of their theater. A culture or nation uses artistic products to create a metaphor for their own identity. Therefore, it's unsurprising that you end up with "culture wars." Culture is not just a matter for entertainment. It really is about how we want to perceive ourselves. I came of age and started doing theater in the seventies, writing about Asian-American characters and themes during a period when it was relatively new, when multiculturalism was a cutting-edge idea. This theory that we should be able to define our own identity and create our own characters and not have it dictated to us by someone else felt pretty exciting. That is inherently about using art to find a notion of self and community. Those are really my roots, and I think I've ended up carrying that into all my subsequent work.

Wetmore: How has that changed since you started writing? I would imagine that some of the negotiations have obviously changed since you came of age in the seventies.

Hwang: To some extent that's what *Yellow Face* was about. *Yellow Face* was about trying to look back on thirty years of multiculturalism and create a comedy about the excesses and absurdities of the movement—from the point of view of someone who also believes this process was and is incredibly valuable. It's easy to make a satire about the excesses of multiculturalism if you don't believe in it. But if you believe in it and are still able to laugh at some of the things that are over the top about it, that seemed to me to be a fun experiment. So that's what *Yellow Face* was about.

Now multiculturalism isn't a new idea anymore and it's not as exciting, so I'm moving on to internationalism. But there are still a lot of culture wars going on these days. This has not gone away. Consider the amount of anger that people have been throwing at each other over the past five days over the #CancelColbert controversy. [*Editor's Note: Hwang refers to controversy gen-*

erated over a tweet posted on 27 March 2014 from the Twitter account of Comedy Central's "The Colbert Report." The punchline was deemed racially insensitive and offensive to Asian-Americans. So-called "hashtag activists" led by Suey Park lobbied for "The Colbert Report" to be canceled in response.] It's angrier and hotter than it's been since the mid-seventies. So this is not over. I thought it was over about ten years ago, but it's not. If anything, it arouses even more passions today.

Wetmore: In the introduction to your first collection, FOB *and Other Plays*, you wrote, "In attempting to define my place in America, I have evolved through several different phases, and I imagine many more lie ahead of me." What are the phases you now imagine ahead of you and the generation you've inspired?

Hwang: I've gotten interested in this idea of interculturalism. When I started out, so much of what we were reacting against as Asian-Americans was this notion of being perpetual foreigners. One's forebears could have been in this country for generations, but if you're Asian people would still come up and say, "Oh, you speak such good English!" Therefore, we took the position that we were first and foremost Americans. We didn't write much about root culture because we didn't want to reinforce the stereotype that we were foreigners. But beginning around 2005 or thereabouts, this notion of interculturalism started to become more prominent. You now have a generation who feels perfectly comfortable working in both the United States and Asia, people who are literate, have good language skills, are educated, and who spend a lot of time traveling. Now we don't need to pick; we can acknowledge all the different influences that make us who we are, whether those are root-culture American or root-culture Asian. I think this coincides with the growth of the internet because it dovetails with the notion of having multiple identities. We all have multiple identities. It has become pointless to say "I'm only this" or "I'm only that."

Right now I've really become captivated by this #CancelColbert thing, and the way in which there's this kind of civil war going on in the Asian-American community surrounding Suey Park and "hashtag activism." I'm not sure where I stand on all this because I'm still trying to understand all the sides of the issue. But it feels fertile to me. There's something to write about there.

Wetmore: Have people come to you, as a pioneer in this field, asking you to take a side on the issue?

Hwang: Fortunately, nobody has forced me to take a stand on #CancelColbert. It seems that, whatever side you take, you get pilloried by the other side. And I'm not going to take a stand tonight either!

Wetmore: Then I won't ask. I do want to follow up on what you just said about multiple identities, particularly given your own multiple identities as playwright and prominent Asian-American in the media. There's a definite autobiographical element to your work. Obviously, in *Yellow Face* there's a character named DHH. But it's also evident in some of your other plays: *Family Devotions* for instance, or *Golden Child* which is about your grandfather. How do your own multiple identities play themselves out in your work?

Hwang: I think that all authors create characters who are manifestations of themselves in one way or another. Writing a play is inherently an exercise in creating multiple identities. In order to create a character that's three-dimensional, to feel for that character and understand that character, you have to find a part in yourself that dovetails with him or her. If you have a play with five characters, then these are sort of five different aspects of yourself. Multiple identities—whether it's with me or with any other writer—that's just part of the creative process. In my own case, I guess there are the explicitly autobiographical works. And then there are the works that I know are autobiographical, but I'm not telling anybody else why they are. But they're all autobiographical. They all explore something that I need to work out for myself. That's why, when I thought about writing them in the first place, it made my heart beat faster.

Wetmore: Just out of curiosity, with *Yellow Face* what's it like watching someone play you on stage? Do you think, "I'm a better me than they are"? Or "Wow, they're a better me than I was"?

Hwang: I've frequently said in reference to *Yellow Face* that it's always hardest to write the autobiographical character. I've used as examples Tom in *The Glass Menagerie* and Jamie in *Long Day's Journey into Night*. Now, *Long Day's Journey* is possibly the greatest American play ever written, so it's not like Jamie's that bad. But you could argue that he's less well developed than the other characters. However, this most recent production of *Glass Menagerie* [directed by John Tiffany, with Zachary Quinto as Tom] made me think that maybe I've been wrong about Tom. Maybe *Glass Menagerie* is completely about Tom's journey. But for me in writing the autobiographical play *Yellow Face*, I had done it before in *Rich Relations* and *Family Devotions*. I always thought my autobiographical characters were lousy. In this case, once I actually named the character after myself, it liberated me to make him just a character. That may sound counter-intuitive, but that's how it played out for me. I thought, "Oh, now I really want to make some stuff up about this guy because he's named DHH." In *Yellow Face* DHH is the butt of most of the jokes. He's sort of the stupidest character in the play, and he makes all the mistakes. He's the source of most of the humor. So if anybody plays him ridiculously, I think that's a great thing; that's what's supposed to happen in this play.

I have to say that *Yellow Face* has had a wonderful life since its premiere at the Public in 2007. It's gotten done a lot, and there's this really great YouTube version of it. Somebody once said to me that, in order to have a discussion about race with people of other races nowadays, you have to be willing to make a fool out of yourself. You have to be willing to say things that are stupid and be open to that. Maybe by writing a play about racial issues where my character makes a fool of himself, maybe it allows audiences to breathe a little more easily. People are permitted to laugh at issues of race (which is hard to do right now), and therefore they may become more open to discussion—as opposed to putting up defensive barriers as we so easily do when dealing with heavy subjects.

Wetmore: Along those lines, Qui Nguyen, who is a playwright and the artistic director of the Vampire Cowboys in Brooklyn—if you don't know them, look them up—has written a play, *The Inexplicable Redemption of Agent G*, about the impossibility of writing a play about the Vietnamese boat-person experience. In it he creates an intertext with *Yellow Face*. He puts himself in the play as a character, and then a character named DHH comes on and says, "I did this first." Then DHH and Qui get into a rap battle about being an emblematic Asian-American playwright. The character DHH raps, "There'd be no you if there weren't no me / Or Young Jean Lee or *BFE*" (this last is a reference to Julia Cho's play). And then DHH wins the battle, noting, "I'm gonna make you my bitch like Miss Saigon!" One of the greatest lines ever written. I introduce this in part because, Audience, if you don't know this man's work, please make a point of getting to know it because it's wonderful. But I also bring it up to ask about your challenge of being an icon and of fostering the next generation of young artists. There's this tremendous respect, but also a sense of "We're doing something different—out of the way."

Hwang: First of all, I love *Agent G*. It was originally Off-Off Broadway and they moved it to Off-Broadway. For the Off-Broadway I did a series of promo videos with Qui where he's sort of following me around. I'm supposed to be like, "Who's that guy following me around?" Whereas Qui is talking into the camera saying, "Oh yeah, I'm gonna hang out with David Henry Hwang—we're good friends!" In the third and final video I find him and I beat the crap out of him. So that was really fun, and Qui is great.

Again, that's kind of what *Yellow Face* was about. The play was about tearing down this image of me as an Asian-American icon, or at least having some fun with the idea. We live in a culture where there are so few representatives of different minorities who rise to some level of public consciousness. So when you do, you end up having to be the official spokesperson of your race or culture. I was the official Asian-American for a while, and then Amy Tan became the official Asian-American. There are a bunch of us who have traded this title around. It's silly. Of course, no one person can represent an entire community because any community is diverse and there are multiplicities of views.

Yellow Face is about the absurdity of this situation. DHH participates in protesting the casting of Jonathan Pryce as an Asian pimp in the Broadway musical *Miss Saigon*. Subsequently, he accidentally casts a Caucasian actor as the Asian lead in his own play, *Face Value*. He believes this actor is of mixed race, but when he finds out that the actor is 100 percent white, he tries to cover up his blunder to protect his reputation as an Asian-American role model. One of the things the play is about is how silly it is to try and guard that turf. What does it mean to be "the Asian-American role model"? Marcus G., the guy who's been mistakenly cast as Asian but is really Caucasian, ends up really liking being a member of the community. By the end of the play Marcus is actually doing the work; he participates in community functions and is politically active. Meanwhile, DHH is merely clinging to his reputation, using this title of Asian-American role model to pick up girls on the internet.

Wetmore: I'm not going to ask if that's one of the autobiographical details!

Hwang: The question is if the scene where DHH goes to get free Asian porn—is that true or not?

Wetmore: ...

Hwang: It was sort of true.

Wetmore: You heard it here, ladies and gentlemen: "Sort of."

Hwang: I took some liberties.

Wetmore: Let's turn to your more recent work. In *Kung Fu* you talk about the culture clashes between East and West and the crises of identity that these clashes inspire. I think that can also describe a number of Bruce Lee's films. *Enter the Dragon*, *Fists of Fury*, *The Big Boss*—they're all about these kinds of cultural tensions. I wonder if you could talk about the influence of Bruce Lee. What made you want to write about him?

Hwang: I first started wanting to write a show about Bruce Lee in the early nineties. Even then it was starting to become clear that the power balance between China and the West was shifting. China, which had always been the "sick man of Asia"—a poor, uneducated, dysfunctional country for the previous two hundred years—was on the rise. Bruce Lee became the first pop cultural manifestation of a new China. So that was my original motivation to get into Bruce Lee. I tried to write a musical version of the Bruce Lee story during the 2000s and just couldn't get it right. Eventually I felt the problem was that we were trying to make Bruce Lee sing, which felt very "South Park"-y (and not in a good way). Then after a few years I thought of doing as what I'm now calling a "dancical." The numbers are dance and martial arts and those move the story forward, as opposed to anyone actually having to sing.

Bruce Lee clearly has become a symbol. He's become an icon. Everyone knows Bruce Lee as a name, as an image, that little yell he does. But nobody knows him as a human being anymore. So at that point the task became writing a show that would humanize him. If it was successful, you'd go in knowing Bruce Lee as an icon, but you'd come out more familiar with what his life was like as a human being. It has been very gratifying to me that his widow Linda felt that this was the most accurate Bruce Lee portrayal she's seen, as well as several of the biographers. I think we succeeded in capturing something that felt like Bruce when he was actually around.

However, I also feel at this point, having created a new show and sort of created a new form—being able to mash martial arts and theater and use the dancical to move the story forward—I don't think we're done. I now want to take what we've learned with this form and do another version of the show. In the show as it currently stands, it's basically about Bruce leaving Hong Kong. He has this tempestuous relationship with his father (which he did), and he plans on never going to go back to Hong Kong. He doesn't want to follow in his father's footsteps. He does Kato in "The Green Hornet," and he hits a glass ceiling in the United States Eventually he does decide to return to Hong Kong, and that's where he makes the movies that established him as a superstar.

That's pretty good. But I'm also wondering, "What does he get from America?" There are two things I want to explore in the next iteration. One is to go deeper into the father-son relationship. In a way it's like the story of O'Neill. You know, O'Neill had the dad who played one role his entire life, the Count of Monte Cristo. O'Neill had a lot of contempt for his father. His father made him get involved in theater, but he really didn't like it that much. He eventually had to get to a point where he was willing to follow in his father's footsteps, but he did it in such a way that he elevated the entire form. That's sort of true of Bruce Lee's relationship to Hong Kong cinema as well.

There's also the political question, "What did Bruce Lee get from America?" At the end of the show now, it feels like maybe he got Hollywood production techniques and brought that back to Hong Kong to elevate the field. But I'm very interested in the possibility that what Bruce Lee learned in America was an understanding of racism, that he learned sixties race theory. Even in terms of his relationship with the Black Power movement. That gave him structure to channel the inchoate rage that he felt as a kid growing up in Hong Kong under British occupation. He channeled it into films that are essentially "stranger in a strange land" narratives where he fights back against "The Man." In the first of his own films he is in Thailand and being oppressed by the mob; in the second one it's Japanese occupation in Shanghai; in the third one he's in Rome and being oppressed by the Italian mafia and has to beat up Chuck Norris. I feel there's a relationship between that and what he learned in the

States during the 1960s about race. I think this also accounts for why initially it was African-Americans and Latinos who were the biggest segment of his audience when those films finally came to America. There's a lot of stuff already written about how Bruce Lee influenced hip-hop culture. I want to go into that further in the next iteration of the show.

Wetmore: You could even extend that to *Enter the Dragon* through the presence of Jim Kelly. The film works very hard to establish the mutual sympathy between Kelly's character and Lee's character in the tournament. There's an identification that he doesn't have with John Saxon's character. I have now revealed myself to be an incredible martial arts movie geek! And we can talk about the Wu-Tang Clan later. Certainly there are a number of profound connections between the hip-hop community and this genre of films in the seventies.

I'm going to ask one more and then throw it open to the audience. As you can see before you, you're at a conference of drama scholars. I know you've said that you wish critics would approach your work slightly differently—

Hwang: —That's just because I've not gotten a good review in the *New York Times* in twenty years!

Wetmore: If it's any consolation, almost no one has. What would you like to see scholars do with your work? You have a captive audience.

Figure 2. Kevin J. Wetmore interviews David Henry Hwang (photograph by Maximilian Franz, courtesy of Stevenson University).

Hwang: I'm happy with what scholars are doing with my work. A few years ago I first sat in on a panel of my work at the Inge Festival in Independence, Kansas. I'd never done it before. I thought it was pretty fun. I used to be an English major, so I can see how one comes at it from that point of view. It's a little easier if I think that they're talking about somebody else's work rather than mine because I'm kind of shy. I'm not one of these people who believe that the author is the final authority on the work. I know more than anyone else in the world about how the play got written. But what the play means? I have my own opinion, but I don't know that my opinion is any better than anybody else's. I find it fascinating to see and hear what other people are getting from the work, like in the two panels I sat in on today. Scholarly work is not like drama criticism: "Oh, I hated that" and "That sucked" and "That could have been better." It's really more about trying to grapple with the themes in a work. I think it's pretty pleasant, so I have no complaints. I'd be happy to do this again sometime.

Wetmore: Congratulations everyone, we're doing a good job! I'm sure the audience has a lot of questions, so let's start it up. [*Editor's Note: The questions from the audience were largely inaudible on playback. Therefore, I transcribe only the answers from Hwang, who fortunately began each response by summarizing the question.*]

Hwang: The question is about writing for stage versus film. I think the question is really about the *M. Butterfly* movie? Look, film is a director's medium. There's a reason why the movies are sometimes referred to as "pictures." There's a reason why the form was originally silent. There's a reason why many film directors believe that, if they've done a good enough job in directing the movie, you should be able to turn off the sound and still follow the story. Film is a visual medium. The director controls the heaviest artistic element. This creates a dilemma for all screen writers, because you're not in control of the medium the way playwrights are most of the time, the way novelists certainly are.

When David Cronenberg made the *M. Butterfly* movie—and I don't think I'm betraying him by saying this, because he was very public about this—he said he wanted to make a movie about how all romantic love is self-delusion. That is a perfectly good Cronenbergian theme. But it's not really what my play is about. So, all things being equal, I like my play better. I don't blame David; he should make the movie he wants to make. I think that's why a lot of authors, when you sell your property to become a movie, you kind of have to let it go, because you just don't know what's going to happen. I did write the screenplay, but ultimately I had no control over the final product.

I gave this example in one of the panels today. There's the scene where Song disrobes, where Song turns from a woman into a man, which happens between Acts Two and Three in the play. When I wrote the screenplay, I had this idea that we would see it happen in Gallimard's face. So much of the play is about experiencing something through the reaction of another character. I had this idea that the police would take Gallimard into one of these rooms with a one-way mirror, and Song would be changing from a woman into a man. He would have to watch it. There would be a series of short cuts: he would see the makeup come off; then he would see the nails come off. But David didn't film it that way.

Hwang: The question is about the difference between an Asian-American company and a non–Asian-American company. I'm somewhat anomalous in that I didn't so much come out of the Asian-American theater scene. I worked a lot in the 1980s particularly with San Francisco's Asian American Theater Company. And Mako, who directed my first play *FOB* at the Public, was one of the founders and for many years the artistic director for East West Players in Los Angeles. So I had a lot of exposure, but the people who originally produced me were non–Asian theaters, or so-called mainstream theaters. My experience in Asian-American theaters is primarily with them doing subsequent productions of my work after the premieres. Therefore, it's a little difficult for me to compare the experiences, because I'm never as involved or as invested in secondary productions of my play as I am when I'm still rewriting.

That said, where East West Players in L.A. really did affect me was as a kid. My mom was a pianist and my dad was the bookkeeper. He was an accountant who later became a banker, and he was the first bookkeeper for East West Players. My mom was the rehearsal pianist for a production they did of Menotti's operetta *The Medium*, one of the earliest East West Players' productions that they set in Japan. I was about ten. I had the choice of going to rehearsals where my mom was the pianist or hanging out at my aunt's house, and I decided to go to rehearsal. It seems interesting to me in retrospect that, as a kid, my first exposure to theater was one where there were Asian-American actors and directors and people in charge making the artistic decisions. Maybe that's one of the reasons that it didn't seem so strange to me later on when I started to think about writing my own plays.

Hwang: The question is about the common student question, "Does Song love Gallimard?" To me, the question to ask is, "Does Pinkerton love Cio-Cio San at the end of *Madame Butterfly*?" Whatever your answer is to that should have a huge bearing on whether Song loves Gallimard. I don't think I have the definitive answer. My opinion is yes, I think Pinkerton loves Cio-Cio San, and I think that Song loves Gallimard. But it's a question of your definition of love. Is it agape love? Is it selfless? No, it's not. Romantic love and passion are so enmeshed with personal need and selfishness and desire for power. It is love, but love itself is a rather compromised notion. I would argue that Song was playing at first. But after a while, who you play becomes who you are.

Hwang: The question has to do with balancing my emotions for my characters. I love all my characters. I think you have to love your characters in order to write them well—even if the character is a villain, even if the character does nothing particularly redeemable, even if you're writing Frank Underwood [from the Netflix television series "House of Cards," starring Kevin Spacey]. I know some of the people who write him, and I know they love Frank Underwood. If you don't love the subject of your play then there's no point in writing it. If you don't love a character, I guess sometimes you still have to write that character because they somehow fit into the plot. But probably you're not going to write that character very well. I feel powerful affection for all my characters. It doesn't mean that I like them all the time, the same way that you don't always like your brother or your parents. But I do feel love for them.

Hwang: The question is about the recent production of *The Dance and the Railroad* in China. First, I didn't realize the tickets were so expensive [the questioner brought up the high price of going to theatre in China] —I certainly didn't make any money from that production! I guess *The Dance and the Railroad* ended up being my first play to be done in China for a variety of reasons. First, we'd just done a revival in New York, so there was a production to bring over. Second, the show was relatively inexpensive: two actors and we could hire live musicians over there. Third, there was nothing anyone over there could object to content-wise because it's about bad Americans oppressing Chinese people building the Transcontinental Railroad in 1867. We considered doing it in Chinese. But one of the actors' Mandarin wasn't really good enough to perform in Chinese. The other American productions at the Wuzhen Festival were in English, so we did ours in English as well. I think there is a desire at this point to try and remount it in Chinese, which would be more accessible to local audiences.

As for how the audience reacted to it, I think it went well, but it's really hard for me to tell. It's like doing *M. Butterfly* in Japan. They keep bringing *Butterfly* back there, so I guess it's doing well. But you can't judge on ticket sales or critical response, and the audience reacts differently than I'm used to. I would say the same thing about China: I'm not really sure how it went. But it was really fun to be there.

Wetmore: I wonder if you might say a little more about the Signature season, and the experience of seeing three of your plays—one of your earliest, and a more recent work, and obviously the world premiere of *Kung Fu*. What was it like having that year-long experience and juxtaposing those plays?

Hwang: For those of you who don't know it, Signature is an Off-Broadway theater in New York that was created around the idea of doing a whole season devoted to one writer. For example, they've done seasons of Arthur Miller, Edward Albee, Tony Kushner, and Athol Fugard. It was a great honor to be invited for a season of my work. Going into it, I felt a little apprehensive about doing revivals. I generally don't like to see my plays that much because all I notice are the things that I could still make better. So my question was, "Am I going to feel compelled to rewrite everything?" Would that be a good idea? Or should I just leave the plays alone? Is the me of 2013 qualified to rewrite the me of 1981? With *Golden Child*, I picked that play partially because there were a couple of sections I'd always wanted to rewrite anyway. With *The Dance and the Railroad*, I just let it go. I thought, there's some stuff here I wrote when I was twenty-two that could be better crafted. But it also has a kind of energy and willingness to just follow my impulses which is pretty powerful. I don't know how to do that anymore. So I felt I should respect the me who wrote that play.

Two things are particularly great about working at Signature. First, they commit to a full season of your work, which takes the pressure off any one piece. Relatively speaking, you have to deal with less of the New York crap than normal. Number two, all of their tickets are $25—every seat for every show in the initial run is $25.—which so changes the paradigm. It's like the National Theatre in London. It means that anyone who wants to go, who's just interested in the show, can probably cough up $25 and go see it. They don't wait for the reviews to come out; they don't have to decide if this is worth sending $125 on. I love that!

Wetmore: I have three final rapid-fire questions. Just one-sentence answers please. Here we go! In an interview about *M. Butterfly* you said, "I have never been a transvestite, except for the occasional late-night *Rocky Horror Picture Show*." So I have to ask, did you just go in drag? Or are you a closet Dr. Frank-N-Furter? Riff Raff? Eddie? Janet?

Hwang: I'm pretty sure I went as Frank-N-Furter. I remember looking at myself in the mirror and thinking, "Wow, I'm sort of hot!"

Wetmore: Question Two: What comes after *Kung Fu*?

Hwang: I don't know. I have a couple operas, I have a couple musicals, but I don't have another play. Maybe it's because *Kung Fu* isn't finished yet.

Wetmore: And last but not least, what is the best thing about being David Henry Hwang?

Hwang: I've gotten to spend my adult life doing mostly things I love, and even the bad days haven't been so bad.

Translating Tempests: A Reading of Aimé Césaire's *Une Tempête* in Translation

Giuseppe Sofo

Abstract

This essay is an analysis of Césaire's rewriting of Shakespeare's The Tempest *and its translation by Richard Miller,* A Tempest, *published in 1986 and revised in 1992. Rewriting and translating share the opportunity of giving new versions of canonical texts, disrupting the authority of the "original" text and culture, and favoring the construction of a multifaceted reality rather than a clear-cut one. By looking at the patterns of interpretation and misinterpretation of this fluid text, in the double passage from the Western canon to postcolonial Martinique and back to the English language of the colonizer, this essay will try to reach a better understanding of the changes the play has undergone and of the paths of sense construction and deconstruction it has followed through the centuries.*

A history of the relationship between translation and colonial domination informs us that this practice is far from innocent in allowing, and at times enhancing, the strategies of colonial domination and cultural assimilation that have helped shape the "asymmetrical relations of power that operate under colonialism" Niranjana has written about (2). "Translation has indeed been used as a tool of colonial dominance," as Robinson has suggested in his *Translation and Empire* (88), and thus needs to be considered as a very influential political and cultural process in the colonial environment, rather than a simply

---

2014 Winner of the Anthony Ellis Prize for Best Paper by a Graduate Student

linguistic practice. We cannot forget, in fact, that language and translation have played a fundamental role in the imperialistic project, and that "the processes of translation involved in making another culture comprehensible entail varying degrees of violence, especially when the culture being translated is constituted as that of the 'other'" (Dingwaney 4).

To study the translation of a rewriting of the canonical text *The Tempest* involves unveiling several degrees of postcolonial revision. Lefevere has defined translation as "the most obviously recognizable type of rewriting," and "potentially the most influential because it is able to project the image of an author and/or (series of) work(s) in another culture" (9). It is exactly this opportunity of projecting a new image of cultures that had to find a way out of colonialism which has made translation and rewriting two of the most powerful means for constructing new identity in the postcolonial era. Both are among those "strategies of appropriation" described by Aschroft, Griffiths and Tiffin which "seize the language, re-place it in a specific cultural location, and yet maintain the integrity of that Otherness, which historically has been employed to keep the post-colonial at the margins of power, of 'authenticity,' and even of reality itself" (77).

To use Caliban's words, colonialism has taught its subjects the power of language and translation, and their profit on it is they now know how to turn it to their favor. The "calibanism" and cannibalism chosen by postcolonial writers and translators,[1] who invoke the devouring and the digestion of the great European original, has opened a different understanding of this linguistic and cultural practice. The concept of originality, discussed in deeper detail in the last part of this article, is fundamental for literatures and cultures that were initially perceived as mere imitations of the motherland's example.

This article is a comparative analysis of Aimé Césaire's *Une Tempête*, a rewriting of Shakespeare's *The Tempest*, and the English translations of Césaire's text by Richard Miller, *A Tempest*, published in 1986 and revised in 1992.[2] It is meant neither as a critique of a translation nor of a translator. Rather, I try to understand how the relationship between the original text and its rewriting can influence the translation of the latter. Instead of looking for possible "mistakes" or sways in the translation, I will follow the patterns of interpretation and misinterpretation, both in Césaire's rewriting of Shakespeare and in Miller's translation of Césaire, to shed some light on the relationship between the original Shakespearean text, its francophone rewriting, and the translations of this postcolonial rewriting back into English. In this case the translator himself is a rewriter, for two reasons: he rewrites his translation when he revises it in 1992; and in this second edition he even offers, in the appendix, a second possible translation of the songs he had already translated in the play, a quite unusual choice. Reading how Shakespeare's *The Tem-*

pest has been transformed through rewritings and translations informs us on the possible reasons behind the play's changes and the paths of sense construction and deconstruction it has followed through different authors, settings, and times over the last five hundred years.

A Caribbean Tempest

As an army of cannibal calibans, postcolonial writers have devoured and deconstructed *The Tempest* to be able to reconstruct the image of the world the text represented and to contribute to a cultural translation of the imperialistic world its characters implied. Published in 1969, Aimé Césaire's *Une Tempête* is one of the most clearly political rewritings of Shakespeare's play. For this reason, Ngal has spoken of a "decolonization dramaturgy," and Césaire himself has admitted that his political trilogy (also including *La Tragédie du roi Christophe* and *Une saison au Congo*) is strictly connected to the political uprisings and new claims in the Americas and in Africa at the time of his writing.

For the first part of my analysis, I have selected a short passage as exemplary of the changes happening throughout the text.[3] The passage is taken from the second scene of the first act and is part of the first dialogue between Prospero and Caliban. Here for the first time Caliban claims his independence from Prospero and directly challenges not only Prospero but also Shakespeare's Caliban. In these lines, Shakespeare's monster turns himself into a man, a colonized man, and steps on the scene embracing a new life, wearing a new mask, or maybe finally no mask at all. After a close reading of these lines, the second part of the analysis will touch on more general issues with reference to the whole text.

The most used word in the passage I have selected is the subject pronoun "*je*," with twelve occurrences, followed by the subject pronoun "*tu*" and the direct object pronoun "*te*." In the confrontation between Caliban and Prospero, the distance between "me" and "you" is extremely important for the construction of Césaire's new island. The abundance of pronouns and possessives helps the Caribbean author depict the clash between the two sides and their different ideas of the world. In the English translation this is usually respected, with a few cases more than in the text in French. What is relevant is where the translator has chosen not to translate the possessives and the direct object pronouns. The English translation of "*C'est le sobriquet dont ta haine m'a affublé*" (28) in the 1986 edition was "It's the name given me by hatred" (18); by removing the possessive, the translator effectively altered Prospero's responsibility. The duke of Milan became linguistically less engaged in the naming of Caliban, and therefore less "guilty" for it. Although the translator revised this in 1992, adding the possessive, the same process can also be observed in another sentence left unchanged in the revision: "*La trique, c'est le seul langage que tu comprennes; eh bien, tant pis pour toi, je te le parlerai haut et clair*" (27), rendered as "Beating is the only language you really understand. So much the worse for you: I'll speak it, loud and clear" (17).

A fundamental stylistic mark of theater writing is punctuation, because it is through punctuation that the author suggests to the readers and especially to the actors the way the text should be read and interpreted. In this passage, as in the rest of the play, Césaire makes extended use of exclamation marks (more than six hundred in total). The English translator replaces many of them, removing about a quarter of the total. This choice becomes quite important when we realize that Césaire also uses exclamation marks to signal power relationships in the play. Prospero almost never uses any when talking to his shipwrecked compatriots. He uses almost half of his own to talk to Caliban and most of the rest addressing Ariel.[4]

The lines I have selected for my study see twenty-two exclamation marks in French and just eight in English (about one third); the other fourteen are replaced seven times by a full stop, twice by a comma, twice by a question mark, twice by ellipsis, and once by a comma and a question mark. One of Caliban's lines in particular has every single exclamation mark replaced: "*Bon!* *J'y vais ... mais pour la dernière fois. La dernière, tu entends! Ah! j'oubliais ... j'ai quelque chose d'important à te dire*" (27) becomes "All right, I'm going ... but this is the last time. It's the last time, do you hear me? Oh ... I forgot: I've got something important to tell you" (14). These changes clearly alter the understanding and interpretation of this line by Caliban. In the English version, he appears less verbally aggressive, weaker, and especially more resigned to his enslaved life, instead of using this sentence to mark the beginning of his true rebellion.

Another aspect of translation which is usually overlooked or left to editors is italicization. Yet the use of italics is probably as important as punctuation for staging the play. In this short passage, Césaire italicizes two words: "*Cannibale*" in the sentence "Cannibale *t'irait bien, mais je suis sûr que tu n'en voudras pas!*" (28); and "*volé,*" stolen, in the sentence "*l'homme dont on a* volé *le nom*" (28). Stressing these words, Césaire is clearly proving their importance in the economy of the text, and he is also hinting at the fact that actors should put a special accent on their interpretation. The translator removes the italics for "Cannibal" and keeps them for "stolen" only in the 1986 edition, not in 1992. He also italicizes "telling" in the sentence "I'm *telling* you that from now on I won't answer to the name Caliban" (14), and "isn't" in the 1992 sentence "Well, because Caliban *isn't* my name" (15)—two choices that Césaire had not made. The first one especially puts the accent on the fact that Caliban is *telling* Prospero that Caliban is not his name, rather than on the name given to Caliban by Prospero, and on the colonizer's act of naming the colonized, one of the most common imperialist practices of cultural and linguistic assimilation.

Miller also translates *"je ne serai plus Caliban"* (27) as "I don't want to be called Caliban any longer" (14). It is true that Césaire's Caliban clarifies later that what he means with *"je ne serai plus Caliban"* is that he is not going to answer to that name anymore. However, we cannot ignore that the ambiguity of "I am not going to be Caliban any longer," with its negation of the verb "to be," casts doubt on the existence of the colonized subject, not just his denomination. Put another way, it questions the very existence of an enslaved subject bearing the name imposed upon him by the colonizer. This is quite a strong statement by Césaire which we risk losing in the English translation.[5]

Through these apparently small changes, the tone of the whole dialogue has been modified, to the point that Césaire's Caliban and Prospero in English seem to be closer to Shakespeare's characters than what their new author had wanted them to be. Prospero appears less despotic, more comprehensive, and Caliban suffers an even deeper transformation. His speech loses power, and with his words, the voice of the colonized people given us by Césaire is also weakened.

If we look at the translation on the whole, a discourse of desire seems to be involved in the re-appropriation of Shakespeare, as a sin recovering the original sin of Césaire's transformation of *The Tempest*. The translator writes in his preface to the 1992 edition that "the temptation to quote the Ariel songs, for example, or to paraphrase them, was strong," and he admits that although he has "attempted to avoid temptation," at least once he was "unable to resist." Actually, the direct quotations are definitely more than one, though of very different kinds, especially in the 1986 version.

In some cases, it is Césaire who translates Shakespeare rather than rewriting him, and somehow obliges the English translator to go back to the Shakespearean words. This is the case of simple quotes as Gonzalo's blessing in *The Tempest* "Be it so! Amen!" translated by Césaire as *"Ainsi soit-il. Amen"* (82) and retranslated by Miller as "Be it so! Amen" in 1986 (65). For Ferdinand's and Prospero's comments on the vision of the goddesses, Césaire also uses almost the same words as Shakespeare, forcing the translator to follow him. *"Quelle majestueuse vision! Oserais-je croire que ce sont là des esprits!"* (68) is translated as "What a splendid and majestic vision! May I be so bold to think these spirits?" (47), very close to Shakespeare's "This is a most majestic vision... May I be bold to think these spirits?" (52).

In some other cases, Césaire is close enough to Shakespeare to allow Miller the freedom to use Shakespeare's own words, although that means being closer to Shakespeare than to Césaire. This happens when Prospero frees Ariel, and Césaire's *"tu retrouves aujourd'hui ta liberté!"* (83) is translated as "today thou shalt be free" (66).[6] Another example is offered by the blessings of the goddesses: Juno's *"longue vie et longue lignée!"* (67) is translated with "long continuance and increasing long life" (46) to echo Shakespeare's "long continuance, and increasing" (52). In the same way, Iris celebrates *"une union d'amour pur"* (67) in Césaire's text, and "a contract of true love" in the English translation (46),[7] exactly as in Shakespeare.

Even more interesting is the third case, in which Miller seems to prefer quoting Shakespeare to translating Césaire, as if the original text he was working on was *The Tempest* and not *Une Tempête*. The best example is surely Caliban's freedom song, when he meets Stephano and Trinculo, replaced with Shakespeare's song:

> No more dams I'll make for fish,
> Nor fetch in firing at requiring
> Nor scape trenchering nor wash dish
> Ban Ban Cacalyban
> Has a new master, get a new man!
> Freedom, hi-day. Freedom, hi-day!
> (*As in Shakespeare.*) [1986: 49].[8]

Another interesting example is to be found in the second scene of the second act, where Césaire has Antonio quoting Baudelaire's *Parfum Exotique* to celebrate the beauty of the island and of its people: *"Des hommes dont le corps et mince et vigoureux / Et des femmes dont l'œil par sa franchise étonne"* (40). Miller translates this, but he also adds a quote more familiar to the English-speaking audience, and not just any quote. He has Antonio pronounce the most famous words of Shakespeare's Miranda: "Oh, brave new world, that hath such creatures in it!" (1986: 29).[9]

In his second translation of 1992, Miller revises almost all of the direct quotes, especially those of the second and third kind, further away from Césaire. Of the examples given above, he translates Caliban's song by Césaire, removes Miranda's quote,[10] and replaces Prospero's "thou shalt be free" with "you will be free" (59). The translator seems to go so far in trying to avoid quoting Shakespeare that he even avoids some quotes of the first kind. For instance, "Ainsi soit-il. Amen" (82) becomes in fact "Amen! Amen!" (59). However, some traces of these quotes do remain in the revised edition: the blessing of the goddesses and Ferdinand's and Prospero's words commenting their arrival are among those cited. The Shakespearean original haunts the revision. What is most relevant is that these changes in the second edition show us that the translator was perfectly aware of having quoted Shakespeare much more than Césaire had compelled him to do.

This brought to an English (re)translation of *Une Tempête* which has indeed functioned, at least partially, as a redomestication, a (re)familiarization of Césaire's text, rather than the defamiliarization the postcolonial writer had achieved in his own language. When Shakespeare's words come back to English, after having been lead across the ocean to Martinique, Césaire's work has undergone the same losses migration imposes on all of us, humans or words. The irony is in the fact that this translation of a translation, or this rewriting of a rewriting, not only re-places the text in a cultural context that is closer to the original one, but it also reacquires some of its original characteristics and even some of its original words.

Translating the Great Original

The close reading of this play and its translations, along with Shakespeare's text, has helped us see the influence of the "original" literature and culture on rewriting and translation. These two literary processes are extremely close, as they both function as an interpretation of the original work, as a re-reading and re-writing, which can produce "a decentred, diasporic or global rewriting of earlier, nation-centred imperial grand narratives" (Hall 247). However, if rewriting and translation in postcolonial literatures share the function of giving a new version of the words and of the meanings implied in European colonial literature, the translation of these literatures needs to be done with full awareness of the risk of domestication (or redomestication) implied by paying too much homage to the "great Original" (Bassnett, Trivedi 4). Albertazzi has written that "to choose how to tell a key text of literature is a strongly political act" (121), and we cannot forget that the same is true for translation, which could risk becoming one of those instruments used to "compact and reduce an alien reality into the terms imposed by a triumphant Western culture" (Simon 11).

When this play was performed by New York's Ubu Theatre in 1991, Virginia Mason Vaughan and Alden T. Vaughan observed a work which "despite its overt political purpose [...] seemed the most true in spirit to Shakespeare's original play" (17). The question arises whether or not it is too close to this original spirit. Reading the translator's own words in the preface to the 1992 edition is quite enlightening: "Although Césaire has denied attempting any linguistic echo of Shakespeare, the transposition of his play into English inevitably calls up such echoes, for the literate English/American playgoer cannot help but 'hear,' behind the language of the play, the original text resounding in all its well-known beauty, its familiarity." The translator speaks once again of familiarity and of spirit when he says that he has chosen for Ariel "songs familiar to an English-speaking audience that [he] thought reflected something of the spirit and possible familiarity of the originals." I cannot read these words without thinking about Douglas Robinson's question: "what is the 'true' source text?" (2011: 190).

The translator of this play refers in fact to Shakespeare's work as "the original text," although the original he is working on is *Une Tempête*. And once this question has been asked, Robinson can also inform us of one possible reason for the sway in translation, which he describes as "the influence of the source author (or, in translating certain sacred texts, the divine Source Author), source text, or source culture on the translator" (2011: 189). Probably no other non-religious author is more likely to be seen as a "divine Source Author" than Shakespeare, and we do not need to say much on the possible influence of the source culture on postcolonial literatures and their reception in the former motherland.

"To read existing translations against the grain," as Niranjana has suggested, "is also to read colonial historiography from a post-colonial perspective" (172). Therefore, further knowledge of the choices translators have made and of the reasons behind these choices can advance our reading of postcolonial history. It can also inform us of how postcolonial literatures have succeeded in bringing forth a real process of literary and cultural renewal, how they have been read and interpreted. The deconstruction of the meanings implied in European literature, the first necessary step towards the reconstruction by postcolonial authors of new (is)lands which can account for a new reality, needs to be respected in the "double passage," the voyage of return to the mother(is)lands of postcolonial rewritings. Otherwise, in the complex relationship between writing, rewriting and translation, we risk losing the new version and the cultural translation of the world which writers like Aimé Césaire aimed at with their drama.

UNIVERSITY OF AVIGNON *and* UNIVERSITY OF ROME, LA SAPIENZA

NOTES

1. See De Andrade's *Manifesto Antropófago* and Vieira's article on cannibalism from De Andrade to De Campos.

2. Unless otherwise specified, references to Césaire's text in English will be cited from the revised edition of 1992.

3. The passage includes six lines each for Prospero and Caliban, starting from Prospero's line "Caliban, j'en ai assez! Attention!" (27) and ending after Caliban's line: "Appelle-moi X. Ça vaudra mieux" (28), pages 17–18 in the English translation of 1986, and 14–15 in the revised edition of 1992.

4. To think that Césaire was counting his exclamation marks would obviously mean overinterpreting the author's intentions. But it is surely indicative of the power relationships in the play to note that Prospero and Caliban use almost exactly the same number of exclamation marks, and exactly the same when they address each other.

5. The addition of the italics for "*isn't*" in "Caliban *isn't* my name," could function as a partial compensation for this lack, although nothing indicates that this is the reason of the translator's choice to italicize these words.

6. Shakespeare's original reads: "Thou shalt be free" (65). The fact that the translator does not use this archaic form anywhere else in his translation, makes the direct quote even more easily recognizable.

7. In the 1992 revision, the text reads "a contact of true love," a typo for "contract," correctly transcribed in the first edition of 1986 (51).

8. Although the translator writes "as in Shakespeare," there are some changes in the text, which originally reads: "No more dams I'll make for fish; / Nor fetch in firing / At requiring; / Nor scrape trencher, nor wash dish / 'Ban, 'Ban, Cacaliban / Has a new master: get a new man. / Freedom, hey-day! hey-day, freedom! Freedom, hey-day, freedom!" (37). Césaire's original text was: "*Noir picoreur de la savane / le quiscale arpente le jour nouveau / dru et vif / dans son armure hautaine. / Zip! L'incisif colibri / au fond d'une corolle s'éjouit / fera-t-il fou, fera-t-il ivre / lyre rameutant nos délires. / La Liberté ohé! La Liberté!*" (64).

9. The original words by Miranda are: "O brave new world, / That has such people in't!" (63).

10. In the 1992 version, we read "*Men whose bodies are wiry and strong / And women whose eyes are open and frank ... / creatures in it!*" (25), with the removal of "Oh, brave new world, that hath such" only, and not of the whole line, almost surely a mistake in the editorial process. It could be argued that the mistake consisted in removing the sentence, rather than in leaving only part of it. However, reading the preface and seeing the general tendency to revise these passages in the 1992 version, it seems much more likely that the translator's intention was to remove the whole quote.

Works Cited

Albertazzi, Silvia. "Postcoloniale/Postmoderno." *Abbecedario Postcoloniale*. Eds. Silvia Albertazzi and Roberto Vecchi. Macerata: Quodlibet, 2001. 115–124.

Ashcroft, Bill, Gareth Griffiths, and Helen Tiffin. *The Empire Writes Back*. New York: Routledge, 1989.

Bassnett, Susan, and Harish Trivedi. "Of Colonies, Cannibals and Vernaculars." *Post-Colonial Translation: Theory and Practice*. Eds. Susan Bassnett and Harish Trivedi. New York: Routledge, 1999. 1–18.

Césaire, Aimé. *Une Saison au Congo*. Paris: Éditions du Seuil, 1966.

_____. *A Tempest: Based on Shakespeare's* The Tempest: *Adaptation for a Black Theatre*. Trans. Richard Miller. New York: Ubu Repertory Theater Publications, 1986.

_____. *A Tempest: Based on Shakespeare's* The Tempest: *Adaptation for a Black Theater*. Trans. Richard Miller. New York: Ubu Repertory Theater Publications, 1992.

_____. *Une tempête*. Paris: Éditions du Seuil, 1969.

_____. *La Tragédie du Roi Christophe*. Paris: Présence Africaine, 1963.

De Andrade, Oswald. "Manifesto Antropófago." *Revista de Antropofagia* 1.1 (1928): 3–7.

Dingwaney, Anuradha. Introduction. "Translating 'Third World' Cultures." *Between Languages and Cultures: Translation and Cross-Cultural Texts*. Eds. Anuradha Dingwaney, and Carol Maier. Pittsburgh: University of Pittsburgh Press, 1995. 3–15.

Hall, Stuart. "When Was 'the Post-Colonial'? Thinking at the Limit." *The Post-Colonial Question: Common Skies, Divided Horizons*. Eds. Iain Chambers, and Lidia Curti. New York: Routledge, 1996. 242–261.

Lefevere, André. *Translation, Rewriting and the Manipulation of Literary Fame*. New York: Routledge, 1992.

Miller, Richard. Preface. "Translator's Note." *A Tempest: Based on Shakespeare's* The Tempest: *Adaptation for a Black Theater*. Aimé Césaire. Trans. Richard Miller. New York: Ubu Repertory Theater Publications, 1992.

Ngal, Georges. "Le théâtre d'Aimé Césaire: une dramaturgie de la décolonisation." *Revue des Sciences Humaines* 35.140 (1970): 613–636.

Niranjana, Tejaswini. *Siting Translation: History, Post-Structuralism, and the Colonial Context*. Berkeley: University of California Press, 1992.

Robinson, Douglas. *Translation and Empire: Postcolonial Theories Explained*. Manchester: St. Jerome, 1997.

_____. *Translation and the Problem of Sway*. Amsterdam-Philadelphia: John Benjamins, 2011.

Shakespeare, William. *The Tempest*. 1611. Ed. A. W. Verity. 14th ed. Cambridge: Cambridge University Press, 1927.

Simon, Sherry. Introduction. *Changing the Terms: Translating in the Postcolonial Era*. Eds. Sherry Simon and Paul St-Pierre. Ottawa: University of Ottawa Press, 2000. 9–29.

Vaughan, Alden T., and Virginia Mason Vaughan. "Tampering with the Tempest." *Shakespeare Bulletin* 10.1 (1992): 16–17.

Vieira, Else Ribeiro Pires. "Liberating Calibans: Readings of *Antropofagia* and Haroldo de Campos' Poetics of Transcreation." *Post-Colonial Translation: Theory and Practice*. Eds. Susan Bassnett, and Harish Trivedi. New York: Routledge, 1999. 95–113.

Telemachos, the *Odyssey* and *Hamlet*

BRUCE LOUDEN

Abstract

To flesh out his Teutonic tale of revenge, Shakespeare draws on Telema-chos's circumstances at the beginning of the Odyssey. *In its characters' central circumstances and interrelationships, the epic serves him as a conceptual model, offering paradigms for his own principal characters. Telemachos's skepticism, initial inability to act, and cunning are templates for Hamlet. Athena's repeated appearances and direction of him anticipate the Ghost with Hamlet. The Suitors predict Claudius and his inner court, as Penelope, in her strained relations with her son, does Gertrude. Most surprisingly, Telemachos's interactions with the epic poet Phemios, and Odysseus's with Demodokos, serve up a model for Hamlet's interactions with the Players and the play-within-the-play. The* Odyssey's *use of the Orestes tale to comment on its own plot offers Shakespeare a further example for Hamlet, as the oldest heroic revenge tale. Polonius's son, Laertes, bearing an Odyssean name, is a signpost of Shakespeare's procedures.*

For much of the play, among several heroic responses that he might take, Hamlet hesitates. While central threads of the basic plot spring from primeval, Teutonic sources (the *Prose Edda* and Saxo's *Historiae Danicae*), Hamlet's feigned madness is often linked to the version in Francois de Belleforest's *Histoires tragiques*, itself influenced by Livy's account of Lucius Junius Brutus.[1] Nonetheless, several of *Hamlet*'s best known plot points, defining scenes and relationships, remain unaccounted for. Of eleven such components that Hibbard identifies (12), I propose a new argument for four: the Ghost; the coming of the actors to Elsinore; the play-within-the-play; and the pirates who intercept the ship, taking Hamlet to England. I argue that Shakespeare enriches his play's texture and comments on Hamlet's dilemma by figuring him as a character from classical Greek myth that has escaped attention. This method provides not only these four elements but also some of the play's defining characteristics, including the hero's hesitation. To inform and comment on Hamlet's own potential course of action, Shakespeare evokes Telemachos's situation in the opening books of the *Odyssey*, and, to a lesser extent, Orestes's, as a young man pressed by Apollo to avenge his father.

Why would Shakespeare do this? Reflecting on *Hamlet*'s length and on the consensus that two-hour performance was the Elizabethan norm, Erne concludes that what we have is a text never intended for performance, but a self-conscious literary product aimed at a "readerly audience."[2] The "Prefatory Letter" to *Troilus and Cressida*, in its address to an "Eternal Reader" and in its references to Plautus and Terence, also suggests a reading audience well versed in classical literature (Erne 101). Texts written for a reading audience, never intended for the stage, were a common late sixteenth-century phenomenon. Most intriguing for my argument is *Ulysses Redux*, an academic Latin drama from 1592.[3]

Shakespeare draws on multiple sources for a given play, some of which have become well known, others known only to interested specialists. Sheen serves as an example of more nuanced applications of source criticism in this respect.[4] We could envision a continuum of possible relationships for Shakespeare's use of earlier texts, regarding some as instances of intertextuality, others as "authorial transfer," and others possibly as "public domain" if useful for his purposes.[5] In *Hamlet* he has a larger net of sources than realized and employs classical texts as conceptual models. For his troubled young Dane he taps into the oldest coming-of-age story in Western literature, Telemachos, and the oldest revenge story, Orestes.

Though the interrelationships I am pursuing are larger than what is typically meant by allusion, and I will use the term *subtext* instead, I agree with James's assumption "that allusions underscore meanings in a given play" and that "Shakespeare took seriously the potential of a classical text [...] to prompt audiences to speculate" (38). By building Hamlet's circumstances partly on Telemachos's, Shakespeare amplifies concerns central to his own play, particularly the corresponding characters' relationships with each other. Applying Miola's analysis, James further considers that Shakespeare's likely reasons for using subtexts fall into two broad categories: "Miola sensibly assumes that an allusion should 'shape character and theme' and 'illustrate' the dramatic moment, or reverse that process and underscore dramatic irony" (41). Of Miola's two positions, I argue that the former non-ironic approach applies to Shakespeare's extended use of the *Odyssey* as a subtext in *Hamlet*.

In a broader sense, Shakespeare draws on the *Odyssey* because it confers an epic dimension and seriousness upon *Hamlet*. He appropriates the *Odyssey* not for the passing allusions but as a conceptual model that offers him paradigmatic instances of the central circumstances and the interrelationships between the principal characters that he has in mind for his own narrative. Since his play is set in a roughly contemporary Renaissance court, governed by a Christian worldview, significant differences emerge between how Telemachos and Orestes might act, on the one hand, and Hamlet, on the other, to corresponding sets of circumstances. By employing Greek heroic subtexts Shakespeare may suggest that Christianity problematizes traditional modes of heroic action permissible under the ancient worldview of polytheism. Does it matter if previous audiences have not noticed his engagement of Homeric epic? Again, I agree with James's larger intertextual position: "Many allusions reinforce meanings in a narrative sequence that does not depend upon their recognition," and "not all allusions, even to famous texts, are immediately obvious" (39–40).

Hamlet himself instigates an extensive focus on a hero from Trojan War myth, Pyrrhus. He requests of the Players "Aeneas's tale to Dido [...] of Priam's slaughter," directing the focus to Pyrrhus (2.2.441–509).[6] Hamlet implies correspondences between Pyrrhus and himself. His mother complains earlier about his preference for wearing black: "cast thy nightly color off" (1.2.68). Hamlet's Pyrrhus dresses in corresponding fashion: "He whose sable arms, Black as his purpose, did the night resemble" (2.2.443–4). Pyrrhus's father, Achilles, has been slain by Priam's son. Hamlet thus sees in Pyrrhus a potential model for taking revenge. Accordingly, his Pyrrhus strikes a relevant pose: "Black as his purpose [...] the hellish Pyrrhus / Old grandsire Priam seeks" (2.2.444–55). Then Shakespeare innovatively adds, "So as a painted tyrant Pyrrhus *stood*, / And like a neutral to his will and matter / *Did nothing*" (2.2.471–73, italics mine). Pyrrhus does not pause in Marlowe or Vergil. But this Pyrrhus forecasts Hamlet's own dynamic of hesitation: vengeance before him, within his grasp, he does not act. The scene thus establishes Hamlet himself as an informed reader, engaged in the Trojan War saga in particular, but also demonstrates Shakespeare's larger interest in applying Trojan War myth to his play.

Hamlet continues personal application of Trojan War myth in his focus on Hecuba. Hecuba's iconic sufferings, to which Shakespeare alludes throughout his career (*Titus Andronicus, Troilus and Cressida, Coriolanus, Cymbeline*), continue to move Hamlet at the end of the scene. The depictions of Pyrrhus and Hecuba prompt him to think up his own play-within-the-play device. His assumption that Claudius will be moved by recognizing that a dramatic representation of a story applies to himself (2.2.593–94) further demonstrates that Hamlet sees himself and his mother in the tableau of Pyrrhus, Priam, and Hecuba. The episode reaffirms Shakespeare's interest in applying Trojan War myth to Hamlet's situation.

Telemachos and Hamlet

Trojan War myth occupies Shakespeare's attention in *Hamlet* beyond Pyrrhus and Hecuba. Shakespeare uses two figures as frames and models for Hamlet, whose circumstances are even closer, Telemachos and Orestes. In the *Odyssey*'s first four books Telemachos is heir to the throne but has his position blocked by potential usurpers who will eventually plot his murder. He is pessimistic, paralyzed by ambiguity over his father's circumstances, and presumes him dead (1.166–68). For most of the play Hamlet's situation is much the same. To flesh out the character of Hamlet, Shakespeare thematically applies the situations and relationships the *Odyssey* depicts between Telemachos, Athena, the suitors, and Penelope, to the four characters in *Hamlet* that correspond with them. Telemachos provides the germ for Hamlet, Athena for the Ghost, the suitors for Claudius, and Penelope for Gertrude.[7] *Hamlet*'s correspondences with the *Odyssey* account for four elements unaccounted for by the Germanic materials: the Ghost; the actors coming to Elsinore; the play-within-the-play; the pirates who intercept the ship taking Hamlet to England,[8] as well as specifics of Hamlet's interactions with corresponding characters.

Athena and the Ghost

Until Athena arrives as Mentes, Telemachos is in a kind of stasis: the palace taken over by the suitors, he is unable to act, until Athena provokes him into heroic action (1.88–95). She assumes the guise of a father figure (1.308), providing Shakespeare with some of the dynamics he will instill in the Ghost, who similarly prompts Hamlet to heroic action. Hamlet is also initially in a similar stasis, with Gertrude and Claudius complaining of his excessive, obsessive mourning for his father (1.2).

As Athena first arrives, Telemachos is "imagining, in his thoughts, his noble father" (1.115).[9] Right before Hamlet first sees the ghost, he declares, "methinks I see my father [...] In my mind's eye" (1.2.183). The *Odyssey*'s supernatural means are the gods, the traditional divine apparatus of Homeric epic.[10] In the ghost Shakespeare uses a Christianized form of supernatural agency, operating under the constraints of renaissance Christian assumptions (e.g., 1.5.10–20). Under the *Odyssey*'s larger rubric of hospitality and theoxeny,[11]

Athena comes to Telemachos as a stranger and guest. Shortly before seeing the Ghost, Hamlet figures his father as a god, Hyperion (1.2.139–40).[12] In private conversation, Athena steers their discussion to Odysseus's absence, the problem of the suitors, and Orestes. She recounts to Telemachos how he avenged the murder of his father Agamemnon by slaying his assassin, Aigisthus: "what glory was won by great Orestes [...] when he killed the murderer of his father" (1.298–99). Applying Orestes' circumstance to Telemachos, she continues, "So you too [...] be bold also" (1.301–2). The ghost of Hamlet's father, in private dialogue, away from the others, commands him, "Revenge his foul and most unnatural murder" (1.5.25). Both supernatural agents also stress that their admonitions be remembered. The Ghost commands, "Remember me" (1.5.91), and Hamlet responds, "And thy commandment all alone shall live / Within the *book and volume* of my brain" (1.5.102, italics mine).[13] Telemachos sums up his reaction to Athena's advice, "My guest, your words to me are very kind and considerate, / what any father would say to his son. I shall not forget them" (1.307–8). Both supernatural agents return to further advise and direct the youthful heroes, Athena, later taking the form of Mentor. The larger teamwork between Hamlet and Ghost corresponds to that between Telemachos and Athena.

Because of their meetings with the supernatural agents, there are now, in effect, a new Telemachos and Hamlet, who plot against the corresponding characters, the Suitors and Claudius. For the remainder of the epic, Telemachos masks his real intentions toward the Suitors as he plots against them and acts harshly toward his mother. When Antinoös, the suitors' ringleader, asks who the stranger was (Athena as Mentes), Telemachos suppresses what he learned from Athena (1.405–19). Hamlet, to hide his plots against Claudius, uses cunning to pretend he is mad (1.5.178–88). Telemachos displays corresponding cunning, 47 times receiving the epithet *pepnumenos*, "astute, shrewd, sagacious." Both plot against their opponents for the remainder of their narratives, until, after much maneuvering, they will slay them in corresponding climaxes, the *Odyssey*'s archery contest and *Hamlet*'s fencing match.

Telemachos and Phemios, Odysseus and Demodokos, Hamlet and the Players

After Athena departs Telemachos interacts with the epic singer Phemios (1.325–61), who performs in the palace for the suitors. Phemios provides the germ of Hamlet's interaction with the Players. He sings about the Greeks' painful homecomings from Troy, a self-referential miniature of the *Odyssey* (1.154–55, 325–27). Hearing an epic that reminds her of her own circumstances, her own husband missing and apparently dead, Penelope requests a song less painful for her (1.337–44). Telemachos criticizes her, asserting his prerogative in determining which songs Phemios will sing, reiterating his stance that Odysseus has perished (1.346–63). He declares that audiences prefer the most current songs (1.350–2: *neôtatê*), suggesting literary criticism. He praises Phemios' performance and skills as divinely inspired (1.367–71).

The episode provides Shakespeare with the general dynamic for Hamlet's interactions with the Players (2.2.364–531; 3.2.1–279), with necessary adjustments to the relevant literary genre. In accord with epic norms, Phemios habitually performs in the palace, whereas the traveling Players arrive and so have an entrance. Where Phemios is a solo singer of epics, the Players perform tragedy, as they are designated "the tragedians of the city" (2.2.325), each performing the corresponding self-referential form of the larger work.[14] As noted, Hamlet initially engages the Players in Trojan War myth, Pyrrhus's slaying of Priam. After they finish, he remarks, much as Telemachos does, on their currency: "they are the abstracts and brief chronicles of the times" (2.2.514–17). He then gives them instructions that, as with Telemachos, touch on issues of literary criticism (3.2.1–42). He proposes they perform *The Murder of Gonzago* to display to Claudius and Gertrude circumstances resembling their own. Similarly, in the *Odyssey* Homer has Penelope hear an epic that painfully reminds her of her circumstances.

In Book 8 Odysseus also interacts with the Phaiacians' epic singer, Demodokos, requesting the specific topic of his song. Demodokos's third song, and Odysseus's reaction to it, has the most in common with Hamlet's interaction with the Players in 2.2. Odysseus requests a specific subject, almost the same as the speech Hamlet requests the Player to perform. Odysseus asks him to sing "the wooden Horse [...] full of the men who sacked Ilium" (8.492–95). When he later gives his own account of the Trojan Horse (11.523–37), Odysseus centers it around Pyrrhus, "pleading to go forth from the Horse [...]] intending evils for the Trojans" (11.530–32). Hamlet asks the Player to perform the same topic, Pyrrhus's climactic act after issuing from the Horse.

An extraordinary simile follows Demodokos' performance (8.523–31). Odysseus, weeping as he hears the account of his own role in the Trojan Horse and Sack of Troy, is likened to a Trojan woman weeping over her slain husband. As a traditional Homeric simile, the woman and her slain husband are generic—how many such incidents comprise the fall of Troy? But from the perspective of *Hamlet* and Shakespeare's thematic use of the *Odyssey*, the wife and slain husband are Hecuba and Priam.

The *Odyssey*'s multiple songs with inner audiences, each commenting on the dynamics of the epic's larger plot, provide extensive examples for Shakespeare to refashion, to fit the form of dramatic tragedy and the particulars of Hamlet's circumstances. As Telemachos for Phemios and Odysseus for Demodokos, Hamlet sees to the overall reception and safety of the Players, even suggesting some of the *Odyssey's* thematic concern with hospitality: "Gentlemen, you are welcome to Elsinore" (2.2.365; cf. 2.2.414–21, 2.2.534–35). As Odysseus with Demodokos, Hamlet asks for a particular performance, a subset of the same episode in Trojan War saga that Odysseus requests. His request is less for a dramatic performance and more for an epic recitation: "Aeneas' speech to Dido [...] where he speaks of Priam's slaughter" (2.2.437–39). As with Odysseus to Demodokos, the Player's emotional performance stirs Hamlet: "What's Hecuba to him, or he to Hecuba, / That he should weep for her?" (2.2.546–48).

Hamlet makes a second performance request, switching genres from epic to drama: "Friends, we'll hear a play tomorrow" (2.2.514), "can you play *The Murder of Gonzago*?" (2.2.525–26). His request approved, he proceeds further: "You could [...] study a speech of some dozen or sixteen lines which I would set down and insert in't, could you not?" (2.2.528–30). He effectively inserts himself as author of part of the performance.[15] Hamlet has a specific purpose behind this insertion, seeking to affect a single audience member, Claudius:

> I'll have these players
> Play something like the murder of my father
> Before mine uncle [2.2.583–85)].

At the corresponding point in the *Odyssey*, after his interaction with the epic singer, Odysseus give his own poetic performance of Books 9–12, including his account of Pyrrhus in the Trojan Horse (11.523–33). Odysseus also seeks to affect one member of those in attendance at the palace, Queen Arete.

Before requesting the Trojan Horse and Sack of Troy from Demodokos, Odysseus praises the singer's earlier performances for being κατὰ κόσμον, "orderly, in good proportion" (8.489). Hamlet makes a similar assessment of what constitutes good performance, "Suit the action to the word, / the word to the action [...] that you o'erstep not the modesty of nature" (3.2.1–18). In his epic recitation, Odysseus describes how a series of women, queens, wives, and mothers, approached him in the Underworld, and told him their stories (11.152–332). Odysseus here reaches his specific inner audience, Arete, through his focus on women, especially women who correspond to her own status. He figures himself as a man sensitive to women, respectful of their roles.[16] Both corresponding audiences, Queen Arete, and King Claudius, interrupt the respective performances, when the inserted narrations have achieved the desired results. Arete speaks, recognizing him as her guest, recommending the Phaiacian nobles give him gifts (11.333–41). Odysseus has achieved the inner objective of his inset narrative, securing conveyance across the sea, the final stage of his homecoming.

Interruption of the play-within-a-play occurs at the corresponding point in 3.2. Seeing a scenario corresponding to the Ghost's account of how Claudius murdered him (3.2.239–45), the King stands up, asks for light, and abruptly departs (3.2.249–53). The performance is not resumed, but Hamlet's objective, like Odysseus's with Arete, is achieved.

The Suitors and Claudius

Penelope's suitors take over the palace in hopes of marrying her and replacing Odysseus as king. This provides Shakespeare with precedents for Claudius, who has already accomplished what they intend. While he embodies the suitors' chief traits as a group, he especially replicates defining characteristics of the ringleaders Antinoös and Eurymachus. The combined forces of Claudius, Polonius, and their agents (Rosencrantz, Guildenstern, and Laertes) correspond to the Suitors as a collective. The assembly Telemachos calls, at Athena's suggestion, to deal with the problems the Suitors have caused provides Shakespeare with a paradigm, reconfigured with Renaissance realities, for the court politics and intrigues at Elsinore in general, and Claudius's behavior in particular.

At Athena's bidding, Telemachos calls the Ithacan assembly into session to make known how the Suitors are depleting his father's estate (1.272–74; 2.48–79). Antinoös responds by claiming it is all Penelope's fault, since she has yet to agree to marry any of them and is allegedly leading them on (2.85–133). This is paradigmatic of the Suitors' irresponsibility, blaming others for the consequences of their own acts, and of their thematic tendency to abuse rhetoric. In his opening remarks to Hamlet, Claudius projects a smooth exterior that masks his actual intentions, displaying the same two characteristics and strategies we located in Antinoös. When he chastises Hamlet for his excessive mourning, his irresponsibility is staggering; as with the Suitors, he is in fact the cause of suffering, having murdered Hamlet's father. He engages in sophistry, abuse of rhetoric, and hypocrisy. According to Claudius, Hamlet's lengthy mourning,

> [...] shows a will most incorrect to heaven,
> A heart unfortified, a mind impatient,
> An understanding simple and unschooled [1.2.95–97].

Mourning for one's father is "incorrect to heaven," but slaying one's brother, at least by his reasoning, is not. Claudius claims Hamlet has "an understanding simple and unschooled," a charge the play reveals as utterly baseless, not only harsh, but dishonest.

When Gertrude finds Claudius after a conference with Laertes, he asserts, "How much I had to do to calm his rage! / Now I fear that it will start again" (4.7.167). In fact, they were plotting how to arrange her son's death (4.7.100–37). The exchange approximately matches an episode where Penelope, having heard the Suitors are plotting to murder Telemachos, is reassured by Eurymachus, the Suitors' other ringleader ("a master at offering false assurances"),[17] that no one will harm her son. Eurymachus will look out for Telemachos, since her son is the dearest of all men: "So he spoke in encouragement, but he himself was preparing his destruction" (16.434–48). Telemachos and Hamlet both go on sea voyages, which the Suitors and Claudius attempt to exploit as means for murdering them (4.660–786, 16.363–92; 3.1.169, 3.3.3–26, 3.4.189, 4.1.29, 4.3.8, 41–51, 4.3.66–67, 4.7.64). Failing in their attempts, both plot to murder the princes at home. Claudius makes further progress than the Suitors, employing Laertes (himself a Homeric signpost) as his agent, one who ultimately proves successful.

As the Suitors throughout the *Odyssey*, Claudius is prone to excessive drinking. For both, excessive drinking is intertwined with their deaths. On their final day the Suitors each have at least three goblets of wine (*Odyssey* 20). Though Danish custom may lie behind some aspects of drinking in the play, when Hamlet describes Claudius as "The King doth wassail tonight and take his rouse, / Keeps wassail and the swaggering upspring reels" (1.4.8–9), he matches the Suitors' defining characteristics:

> Set me the stoups of wine upon that table [...]
> The King shall drink to Hamlet's better breath [...]
> 'Now the King drinks to Hamlet' [5.2.214–24].

The Suitors are all slain by Odysseus and Telemachos after drinking three goblets of wine while witnessing the protagonist defeating them in the archery contest, the doors locked so no one may escape (21.380–87). Claudius is slain by Hamlet after consuming multiple glasses of wine while witnessing Hamlet's unexpected defeat of his proxy Laertes in a fencing match, the doors locked so he may not flee (5.2.265). Unable to even string Odysseus's bow, the Suitors do not take part in the archery contest; Claudius also watches passively, drinking on the sidelines.

Penelope and Gertrude

In her strained relations with Telemachos, Penelope anticipates Gertrude's interactions with Hamlet. As noted, when she complains that Phemios's song is painful to her (1.328–63), Telemachos tells her to return to her room. She is startled when he does so: "Astonished, she went back up into the palace, for she stored the shrewd word of her son deep in her heart" (1.360–1). Stanford notes, "Penelope is astonished at Telemachos's sudden tone of authority and strength" (231). In a similar exchange in Book 21, before the archery contest, Telemachos commands her to return to her room, using the same formulaic expression (21.354–55 = 1.360–61: Ἡ μὲν θαμβήσασα πάλιν οἶκονδε βεβήκει· / παιδὸς γὰρ μῦθον πεπνυμένον ἔνθετο θυμῷ). In a third exchange, after Odysseus has slain the Suitors and Penelope remains aloof, Telemachos rebukes her: "My mother, ill mother, having a harsh heart [...] But always your heart is harder than stone" (23.97–103). In response, Penelope utters a similar expression, "The heart in my breast is astonished" (23.105: θυμός μοι ἐνὶ στήθεσσι τέθηπεν). *Hamlet* presents a sequence of corresponding events, with corresponding expressions in Gertrude's reaction to the play-within-the-play. Rosencrantz and Guildenstern report to Hamlet, "The Queen, your mother, in most great affliction of spirit [...] your behavior *hath struck her into amazement and admiration*" (3.2.294–309). Hamlet restates her reaction: "O wonderful son, that can so *astonish a mother*!" (3.2.310, italics mine). Both expressions suggest the Homeric θαμβήσασα (*thambêsasa*), which Cunliffe interprets as "To wonder, be struck with wonder or amazement."

A reader of the *Odyssey* traditionally sees Penelope as an ideal of marital fidelity. However, some studies have emphasized indeterminacy in her character and her possible attraction to some of the Suitors.[18] The relevant scenes again find correspondences in Hamlet's attitude toward Gertrude. To prompt his quick return from his sea voyage, Athena plants doubts in Telemachos about Penelope's larger intentions (15.15–26). She claims Penelope's family is pressuring her to marry Eurymachus, that a woman is more concerned with building up the estate of the man who marries her, forgetting her former children and husband.[19] As Athena to Telemachos, the Ghost implies Gertrude's infidelity to Hamlet (1.5.86–88), and several of Hamlet's comments to her, "I will speak daggers to her, but use none" (3.2.379), are reminiscent of Telemachos's postures. Telemachos identifies so greatly with his father that he slights his mother's own circumstances and needs, as does Hamlet.

Telemachos's meeting with Penelope after returning from his sea voyage (17) provides a rubric for Hamlet's meeting with Gertrude in 3.4.[20] Both meetings are interwoven with the respective sea voyages; Telemachos's immediately follows, while in *Hamlet* it immediately precedes his sea voyage. Aware of the Suitors' plot to kill him, Penelope bursts into tears when she sees that he has returned safely. He tells her not to make a scene since he has escaped danger, but he bids her to wash, change her clothes, and perform hecatombs to Zeus. Throughout, he employs a firm, commanding tone, devoting his final four lines to mention of his mysterious guest, unbeknownst to her, her husband.

Hamlet, in 3.4, employs a similarly forceful tone throughout, "You go not till I set you up a glass / Where you may see the inmost part of you" (3.4.20–1). As Hamlet's charges against his mother grow stronger, she reacts in terms that correspond to Penelope's reactions to Telemachos,

> O Hamlet, speak no more.
> Thou turn'st mine eyes into my very soul,
> And there I see, such black and grained spots
> As will not leave their tinct. [...]
> These words like daggers enter in my ears [3.4.79–83, 87].

In the middle of the scene, the Ghost appears, but visible only to Hamlet (3.4.95–131). At the corresponding point in the *Odyssey* (17.52–56), Telemachos mentions his mysterious guest, Penelope's actual husband, with both wives ignorant of their spouse's proximity. As Gertrude witnesses Hamlet, interacting with something she cannot see, the Ghost observes, "Amazement on thy mother sits" (3.4.104), again suggesting the Homeric *thambêsasa*. The scene concludes with mention of Hamlet's sea voyage to England (3.4.189), the counterpart of which comes immediately before Telemachos's meeting with Penelope.

Hamlet sounds Telemachean tones when he criticizes Gertrude for her speed in remarrying (1.2.138–57; cf. "O most pernicious woman!" 1.5.105). Penelope is under considerable pressure to do the same in the *Odyssey*. Her act of weaving a funeral shroud for Laertes but never finishing it (1.249–50) provides Shakespeare a model of a mother keeping her son in stasis, preventing him from assuming his inherited position. Both mothers' fates are determined by the corresponding events, archery contest and fencing match.

Nestor and Polonius

For Polonius, Shakespeare draws on Nestor, whom Telemachos visits in the *Odyssey* 3, and whom Shakespeare presents as a character in *Troilus and Cressida*. Polonius replicates and exaggerates Nestor's chief functions in the *Iliad* and the *Odyssey*, the supposedly sage elder who dispenses advice that becomes tedious, waxing at length about his own youthful exploits. Where Nestor's exploits are heroic, fit for epic, Polonius's are theatrical and metatheatrical: "And truly in my youth I suffered much extremity for love" (2.2.188); "and was accounted a good actor [...] I did enact Julius Caesar" (3.2.93). Like Nestor, Polonius is part of the executive branch as chief councilor to the king. While the *Iliad* introduces Nestor as a honey-tongued orator (1.247–49), there is considerable irony in his failure to conciliate Achilles and

Agamemnon. Polonius's attempts to manage Hamlet are even less successful. He is wrong about Hamlet's feigned madness, erroneously assuming *eros* is the cause. Polonius gives lengthy advice to his son with the Homeric name (1.3.58–80), as Nestor famously does for Antilochus (*Iliad* 23.303–50). His overuse of rhetoric and tendency toward loquacity are here first on display.

Polonius's interaction with Hamlet and the Players is a tour-de-force set-piece, with key instances of his serving as a victim of unintended irony:

> [...] to expostulate
> What majesty should be, what duty is,
> Why day is day, night night, and time is time,
> Were nothing but to waste night, day and time [2.2.86–89].

If meaningful content is so easily discarded, reasonable length is the next casualty,

> Therefore, since brevity is the soul of wit,
> And tediousness the limbs and outward flourishes,
> I will be brief [2.2.90–92].

However, he has already failed to achieve brevity. His loquacity is also a defining characteristic of the Homeric Nestor. Asked by Telemachos if he knows how Odysseus met his doom (3.3.83–101), Nestor replies at length (3.102–200), only to conclude, "And so I returned, dear child, ignorant, knowing nothing of this" (3.184). Thematic irony at Polonius's expense thus becomes overtly comic when he says of the Player's speech, "This is *too long*" (2.2.486, italics mine). In his speech on dramatic genres (2.2.391–95), he fashions words into rhetorical figures more for their own sake than for expressing an argument, classification for its own sake, irrelevant to what follows.

Throughout, he is the naïve optimist to the melancholic Hamlet, as is Nestor to Telemachos. While Telemachos visits him in Pylos, Nestor correctly deduces that since Athena showed his father such affection at Troy, she will now do so for his son (3.218–24). Telemachos denies that this could ever be (3.226–28), though Athena, as Mentor, stands beside him as his guide. Under the larger impulse of Romance the *Odyssey* moves toward a positive outcome in which moral characters are rewarded and Nestor's view validated. In the overtly tragic *Hamlet*, the protagonist's following assessment of the same character proves more accurate:

> This counselor
> Is now most still, most secret, and most grave,
> Who was in life a foolish prating knave [3.4.193–95)].

His son's unusual name, Laertes, is Shakespeare's overt nod to the *Odyssey*. In the *Odyssey* Laertes carries out the epic's last killing (24.513–25).

Orestes and Hamlet

Trojan War myth provides Shakespeare with another model and frame for Hamlet, the Ghost, Claudius, Gertrude, and Horatio, in the tale of Orestes. As he meets the Players, Hamlet addresses Polonius as "O Jephthah, judge of Israel, what a treasure hadst thou" (2.2.400). The Renaissance recognized the correspondence between Jephthah sacrificing his daughter (Judges 11) and Agamemnon sacrificing Iphigenia in Trojan War myth. Shakespeare thus makes a glancing reference here to the myth of Orestes, Agamemnon's son, Iphigenia's brother, and reveals that he will use it to comment on Hamlet's circumstances. Hamlet's "Jephthah" follows Polonius's mention of Seneca, who wrote an *Agamemnon* and *Thyestes*, two components of Orestes's myth.

The *Odyssey* makes thematic reference to the Orestes myth (1.30, 1.40–43, 1.298–300; 3.253–328; 4.546–7, etc.), as a paradigm for the external audience, and within the epic for Telemachos. Zeus notes how Orestes slew Aigisthus, whom he had earlier warned not to pursue the married Clytemnestra and not to kill Agamemnon on his return from Troy (1.29–43). For the poem's external audience, Zeus's focus on Aigisthus predicts what will happen to the Suitors,[21] who, like Aigisthus, are wooing a married woman whose husband has long been away at Troy. The external audience is meant to perceive these larger, partial correspondences. The Orestes myth presents a possible trajectory *within* the *Odyssey* for Telemachos, since he does not know the future: Athena and Nestor warn him that he may be called upon to avenge the murder of his father. If Shakespeare consciously reacts to the *Odyssey*, he would also see that the epic shows how to use the Orestes myth to comment on and frame the action of its own narrative.

In 1914 Gilbert Murray noted parallels between *Hamlet* and Orestes.[22] But under the sway of idiosyncratic theories, he dismissed any connection between them. Recently, however, Schleiner has made some contributions to the discussion.[23] Orestes's father Agamemnon was killed by his mother Clytemnestra and her lover Aigisthus. Years later, adult Orestes returns to avenge his father by slaying both Aigisthus and Clytemnestra. Shakespeare refracts the Orestes myth throughout *Hamlet*, with Hamlet corresponding to Orestes, his father to Agamemnon, Claudius to Aigisthus, and Gertrude to Clytemnestra. Shakespeare would have had easy access to the larger myth. As Schleiner notes, in 1567 Henri Estienne published a Latin anthology of Aeschylus, Sophocles, and Euripides, by a range of translators including Erasmus (31). Even more immediate, in 1599 the Admirals' Men staged an English version of a two-play redaction of Aeschylus' *Oresteia*, *Agamemnon*, and *Orestes' Furious* or *Orestes' Furies*.[24] In Aeschylus's *Libation Bearers* which offers the greatest correspondence to Hamlet's circumstances,[25] Orestes addresses his dead father at his grave (8–9, 315–22, 345–53, 479–99) and describes how Apollo directs him to take vengeance on Aigisthus and Clytemnestra (276–96, 558, 900–2, 939, 953–56, 985–90, 1029–39). Pylades, Orestes' trusted friend who helps him avenge the death of his father, provides the rubric for Horatio (*LB* 561 ff., 900–2).[26]

Orestes's myth depicts his anguish over having to slay his mother to avenge his father. His guilt and torment are externalized in the Furies, goddesses who hound those who have committed murder that others cannot see. They drive him to madness until Athena helps appease them. They appear in the *Libation Bearers* (1048 & ff.) and throughout the *Eumenides*. Hamlet's ghost combines the functions of three supernatural forces for Orestes: Apollo's oracle, demanding vengeance; Agamemnon's spirit, as Orestes imagines it; and the Furies that drive him mad, invisible to others (*LB* 1048–62). Shakespeare incorporates the Orestes myth most clearly in *Hamlet* 3.4 and 5.1. In 3.4 when the Ghost appears and Hamlet speaks with a figure she cannot see, Gertrude concludes what he, after all, had wanted everyone to think of him: "Alas, he's mad" (3.4.98). His aggressive postures and accusations so alarm her she asks, "What wilt thou do? Thou wilt not murder me?" (3.4.22). Hamlet's own perspective is to obey the Ghost, "Th' important acting of your dread command?" (3.4.101). All the Oresteian versions of the corresponding characters are present, all striking postures in accord with the myth. Hamlet/Orestes seems on the verge of slaying Gertrude/Clytemnesta. For Hamlet, the Ghost is Apollo's demanding oracle, where for Gertrude he is the invisible Furies.

Shakespeare reworks elements from the beginning of *The Libation Bearers* in 5.1, which opens with Orestes and Pylades approaching Agamemnon's tomb to dedicate a lock of hair to his father. Women approach, including Orestes's sister Electra, still mourning her father, to pour a libation on his grave. In the Churchyard scene, Hamlet and Horatio correspond to Orestes and Pylades.[27] Returned from his sea voyage and accompanied by his loyal intimate, Hamlet approaches the grave in ignorance as another party comes to perform rituals. Ophelia, though dead, presents the expected Electra figure, similarly obsessed with her own departed father ["She speaks much of her father" (4.5.4)]. But the biggest new wrinkle is Laertes, who, from the perspective of an Orestes subtext, is another Orestes figure, commiserating with his sister in their desire to avenge his slain father.

Of the two myths, however, Shakespeare clearly found the *Odyssey* more fertile for his larger concerns in *Hamlet*. While both myths present the same five corresponding characters—son, slain or absent father, would-be or actual usurpers, mother, and supernatural mentor—Hamlet's character traits are far closer to Telemachos than Orestes. Telemachos's thematic skepticism (1.216–20, 1.234–51, 1.313–14, 3.226–28) and his recurring epithet *pepnumenos* (which Cunliffe renders as "astute, shrewd, sagacious") emphasize his mental acuity and dexterity. His bildungsroman contours, his transition from inexperienced youth to hero, his use of irony, counter-moves against the Suitors, the sea voyage, all combine to suggest a proto–Hamlet figure. Add the *Odyssey*'s self-referential narratives, Telemachos's and Odysseus's interactions with the singers, and a great deal of what Shakespeare is about in *Hamlet* is here, if in germinal form. The *Odyssey*'s climax in the archery contest, which provides the means for slaying the usurpers, provides a model for *Hamlet*'s finale, the fencing match.[28]

Telemachos and Orestes present two different stages of the same basic situation that unfolds in *Hamlet*. In the *Odyssey*, the correspondences are more in the future as potential events. Telemachos *thinks* his father is dead, learns that the suitors are *plotting* to kill him, and *suspects* his mother will marry one of them. Odysseus is not dead, but Athena, as Mentes, conjures up a version of him to warn Telemachos (1.308). The suitors would attempt to slay Odysseus, but his prolonged absence prevents this. Penelope remains faithful, though Telemachos starts to doubt her. In the *Libation Bearers* Aigisthus slew Agamemnon years before; Orestes knows his mother is unfaithful, an accomplice in his father's murder. Hamlet occasionally projects a perspective close to Orestes's, as in his remarks to Horatio, right after the churchyard scene (5.2.65–68). In the fencing match, Hamlet slays Claudius, Gertrude also dying in the process, but not through his agency.

Clytemnestra, Gertrude, and Penelope occupy three degrees of fidelity: Clytemnestra openly unfaithful, Penelope ideally faithful, and Gertrude in between. Though the Ghost thinks her unfaithful, he urges Hamlet to take no action against her, "nor let thy soul contrive / Against thy mother aught— leave her to heaven, / And to those thorns that in her bosom lodge To prick and sting her" (1.5.85–88). Shakespeare navigates a middle ground between the two Greek myths. The five corresponding characters occupy three degrees in the intensity of the revenge, with the Orestes characters the most extreme, Telemachos the least, and *Hamlet* the middle. Aigisthus and Clytemnestra freely cohabit in Agamemnon's absence, jointly slay him, and openly vaunt over doing so. Orestes slays Aigisthus and his mother. In the *Odyssey* the Suitors plan but do not execute the deaths of Odysseus and Telemachos, Penelope remains faithful, and Telemachos helps slay the would-be usurpers.

Shakespeare presents a Christianized version of the larger dynamic. Orestes and Telemachos receive aid from the gods. Hamlet receives supernatural advice from the Ghost but no actual agency. Christian beliefs, in fact, get in his way, and repeatedly problematize his taking action. He questions whether the Ghost was sent by the Devil to damn him (2.2.587–92) and worries if he slays Claudius at prayers he will he go to heaven (3.3.73–96)—absurd notions for Telemachos or Orestes. By figuring Hamlet through the lens of heroes from classical myth, Shakespeare seems to imply that Christianity problematizes traditional modes of heroic action. With the *Odyssey* and *Oresteia* available to him in Latin translations from 1537 and 1555, and two *Oresteia*-derived plays produced in London in 1599, it is time to reassess Shakespeare's relation to Greek literature.

UNIVERSITY OF TEXAS AT EL PASO

NOTES

1. See Hibbard (6–11) for a useful overview, also Eckert 323.

2. See Erne 1, 48, 49, 159, etc.

3. See Erne 69.

4. See especially Sheen 157–59.

5. Sheen cites Rosenthal to this last effect but questions the validity of the position (159).

6. All quotations and references are to G. R. Hibbard's *The Oxford Shakespeare: Hamlet.*

7. Renaissance translations and renderings of the *Odyssey* include Demetrius Chalcondyles's 1488–89 complete Latin translation; a French translation of the first two books (1547 and 1580), in Jacques Peletier du Mans's *OEuvres poetiques*; and William Gager's academic Latin drama from 1592, *Ulysses Redux.*

8. I do not claim that all aspects of these four elements derive exclusively from the *Odyssey.*

9. Felson-Rubin (143) sees his doing so as his imagining a narrative and thus acting as a poet. Translations from the *Odyssey* are my own.

10. On the larger functions of the gods in classical epic, and Athena's specific role as a mentoring god, see Louden 2005.

11. Theoxeny, the genre of myth in which a God comes disguised as a stranger to test mortal's hospitality. On its importance to the *Odyssey*, see Louden (2011): 30–56.

12. Cf. 3.4.56–63, where Hamlet compares his father again to Hyperion, but also to Jove, Mars, and Mercury.

13. Note how Hamlet immediately thinks of it all in terms of a *text.*

14. On self-referentiality as a recurring feature of Homeric epic, see Martin.

15. Cf. Felson-Rubin (143) on *Odyssey* 1.115–18, where Telemachos imagines a narrative and thus acts as a poet.

16. Discussion in Louden (1999): 12, 119.

17. Louden (2011a): 2075.

18. See Katz, *Penelope's Renown: Meaning and Indeterminacy in the Odyssey* and Felson-Rubin, *Regarding Penelope: From Character to Poetics.*

19. On the episode, see Felson-Rubin: 82–3 and Katz: 59–61.

20. The *Odyssey* lacks a parallel for the slaying of Polonius.

21. See discussion in Louden (1999): 19, 29, and especially 42.

22. "Gilbert Murray's essay, "Hamlet and Orestes," was first delivered as a lecture in 1914 and later included in his well-known *The Classical Tradition in Poetry* (Cambridge, Mass., 1927). (Eckert 321).

23. See Schleiner, "Latinized Greek Drama in Shakespeare's Writing of 'Hamlet.'"

24. See Schleiner 34–5. The plays do not survive, just the record of their performance, with different accounts of the second title.

25. Cf. Schleiner, 39, 42.

26. Cf. Schleiner 40–41.

27. See Schleiner 42.

28. As a romance with a happy ending, Telemachos, Odysseus, and Penelope all survive.

Works Cited

Cunliffe, Richard John. *A Lexicon of the Homeric Dialect*, expanded ed. Norman: University of Oklahoma Press, 2012.

Eckert, Charles W. "The Festival Structure of the Hamlet-Orestes Tradition." *Comparative Literature* 15 (1963): 321–37.

Erne, Lukas. *Shakespeare as Literary Dramatist*. 2d ed. Cambridge University Press, 2013.

Felson-Rubin, Nancy. *Regarding Penelope: From Character to Poetics*. Princeton: Princeton University Press, 1994.

Finkelberg, Margalit. *The Homer Encyclopedia*. New York: Wiley-Blackwell, 2011.

Gager, William. *Ulysses redux: Tragoedia nova: In aede Christi Oxoniae publice academicis recitata octavio idus, Februarii 1591*. Reprint from the University of California Libraries.

Heubeck, Alfred. *A Commentary on Homer's Odyssey*. Vol. 1: Introduction and Books i–viii. Eds. Stephanie West Heubeck and J. B. Hainsworth. Oxford: Oxford University Press, 1988.

Hibbard, G. R. *Hamlet. The Oxford Shakespeare*. Oxford: Oxford University Press. 1987.

Hirsch, Rudolph. "The Printing Tradition of Aeschylus, Euripides, Sophocles and Aristophanes." *Gutenberg Jahrbuch* 39 (1964): 138–46.

James, Heather. *Shakespeare's Troy: Drama, Politics, and the Translation of Empire*. Cambridge: Cambridge University Press, 1997.

Katz, Marilyn A. *Penelope's Renown: Meaning and Indeterminacy in the Odyssey*. Princeton: Princeton University Press, 1991.

Kinney, Arthur F. *Hamlet: New Critical Essays*. New York: Routledge, 2002.

Louden, Bruce. "Eurymachus." *The Homer Encyclopedia*. Ed. Margalit Finkelberg. New York: Wiley-Blackwell, 2011. 275.

_____. "The Gods in Epic." *A Companion to Ancient Epic*. Ed. John Miles Foley. New York: Blackwell, 2005. 90–104.

_____. *Homer's Odyssey and the Near East*. Cambridge: Cambridge University Press, 2011a.

_____. *The Iliad: Structure, Myth and Meaning*. Baltimore: Johns Hopkins University Press, 2006.

_____. *The Odyssey: Structure, Narration and Meaning*. Baltimore: Johns Hopkins University Press, 1999.

Martin, Richard, "Self-Referentiality." *The Homer Encyclopedia*. Ed. Margalit Finkelberg. New York: Wiley-Blackwell, 2011. 787–88.

Martindale, Charles, A.B. Taylor, eds. *Shakespeare and the Classics*. Cambridge: Cambridge University Press, 2004.

Miola, Robert. "Vergil in Shakespeare: From Allusion to Imitation," pp. 241–58 in *Vergil at 2000*, ed. John D. Bernard. New York: AMS Press, 1986.

Russo, Joseph, Manuel Fernandez-Galiano, Alfred Heubeck, eds. *A Commentary on Homer's Odyssey, Vol. III Books XVII–XXIV*. Oxford: Oxford University Press, 1989.

Schleiner, Louise. "Latinized Greek Drama in Shakespeare's Writing of 'Hamlet,'" *Shakespeare Quarterly* 41.1 (1990): 29–48.

Sheen, Erica. "'These are only men': Seneca and Monopoly in *Hamlet* 2.2." *Shakespeare and the Classics*. Eds. Charles Martindale and A.B. Taylor. Cambridge: Cambridge University Press, 2004. 156–67.

Stanford, W. B. *The Odyssey of Homer: Books I–XII*. New York: St. Martin's Press, 1959.

Cognitive Misappraisal in Oscar Wilde's *Lady Windermere's Fan*

Todd O. Williams

Abstract

This essay uses current advances in cognitive science to consider Oscar Wilde's ethical purpose in writing Lady Windermere's Fan *and the aesthetic strategies that he used to achieve his moral aims. Characters in the play make appraisals based on person-schemas and prototypes that human beings commonly rely on to process information. However, as is often the case, these appraisals turn out to be incorrect, leading to bad judgments and rash actions. Wilde was deeply interested in human psychology, and cognitive science offers useful concepts through which to understand his critique of humanity and his approach to challenging his audiences to develop deeper awareness of their cognitive processes.*

In an 1897 letter to Ernest Dowson, Oscar Wilde writes, "Psychology is in its infancy, as a science. I hope, in the interest of Art, it will always remain so" (*Letters* 665). While Wilde is known for his contradictions, this remains a curious statement considering his evident interest in psychology, which recent scholarship by Elisha Cohn has demonstrated dates back at least to his days as a young man at Oxford. Wilde often wrote about his work and of art in general in terms of its "psychological interest." He did not, of course, enjoy the benefit of having late twentieth- and early twenty-first century advances in cognitive science at his disposal, but Wilde was able to intuitively understand modes of information processing in human beings on which cognitive approaches to appraisal and categorization have since shed light. With its emphasis on both mental representations (how the mind represents concepts or information to itself) and meaning making (how humans create meaning from these representations) cognitive science provides a sophisticated and empirically based model that can illuminate patterns of misappraisal found particularly in Wilde's society comedies. Psychology is no longer in its infancy; in cognitive science we now have a model through which to examine psychological tendencies that Wilde noticed in human beings and wanted to challenge the validity of. Wilde seeks to achieve ethical aims by making his characters and audiences more aware of and critical of human nature. A cognitive understanding of human information processing is especially useful for studying Wilde because it allows us to better explain the moral aspect of Wilde's work that has often been viewed in conflict with his aesthetic aims.

In *Lady Windermere's Fan*, Wilde's first dramatic success, he demonstrates the cognitive meaning making processes of his characters and shows where they fall short. In doing so, he critiques the gossiping nature of the late Victorian society that he portrays in the play, while also implicating the audience. Cognitive literary critic Blakey Vermeule discusses human beings' obsession with gossip, which she links to our interest in literature. Vermeule states that "most stories are gossip literature" and that we are "obsessed with the secret motives of other humans" (7). As with many of Wilde's writings, the plot of *Lady Windermere's Fan* revolves around secrets so that characters and audiences are led to infer the truth on their own. This results in a series of misjudgments that end up threatening the Windermeres' marriage. It is not the secrets themselves, however, that Wilde portrays as dangerous. In the end none of the major secrets in the play are even revealed to the characters to which they pertain. What causes problems is the way that Lady Windermere and her society cognitively process information and gossip.

The play begins with Lady Windermere receiving a visit from Lord Darlington whose flirtations make her uncomfortable. They are joined by the Duchess of Berwick who reveals to Lady Windermere the gossip that Lord Windermere has been having an affair with a Mrs. Erlynne. Shortly thereafter, Lady Windermere discovers several checks that her husband has written to Erlynne and decides that the rumors about her husband must be true. When confronted, Lord Windermere denies the affair. He does not tell his wife, but he is actually being blackmailed by Mrs. Erlynne. She is really Lady Windermere's mother, whom she had always thought dead. Erlynne abandoned Lady Windermere and her father long ago to run off with another man. She threatens to reveal this and bring disgrace onto Lady Windermere if Lord Windermere will not use his money and connections to help her reenter London society. In Act Two, Lady Windermere is humiliated at her own birthday party when Erlynne arrives and receives a lot of attention from Lord Windermere.

Absolutely convinced that her husband is having an affair, Lady Windermere accepts an offer from Darlington to run away and elope with him. She leaves a note informing her husband of this, but Erlynne intercepts it and decides she must help her long estranged daughter to avoid the kind of scandal with which she herself has had to live. Shortly thereafter, Erlynne arrives at Darlington's residence where Lady Windermere is waiting and convinces her to return to her husband. Before they can leave, however, Darlington and Lord Windermere arrive at the house with several of their male friends, including Tuppy, who Erlynne is hoping to marry. Erlynne sacrifices her own reputation and her chance at reentering society by appearing to the men in Darlington's rooms while Lady Windermere escapes. Erlynne and the Windermeres meet in the play's final act, but Erlynne does not reveal her identity to her daughter. Lady Windermere decides not to reveal her near elopement to her husband, and Lord Windermere is never called on to explain the nature of his relationship with Erlynne. Erlynne even manages to reconcile with Tuppy in the end. They plan to leave the country and London society together and get married.

In his society comedies and elsewhere, Wilde is always critical of the falsity and hypocrisy of the Victorian upper-classes. In "The Decay of Lying," he writes that "what is interesting about people in good society [...] is the mask that each one of them wears, not the reality that lies behind the mask" (15). While the upper classes wear masks of decorum and propriety, they are susceptible to the same flaws to which all humans fall prey. In *Lady Windermere's Fan*, Wilde portrays a society where adultery is common practice, but where its members are also quick to publicly chastise those other-women who allow for it. Wilde pulls his audience into the play's high-society gossip, as well. Vermeule writes that humans have "a general preference for social information over other kinds of information" (22). We cannot resist gossip for the same reasons that we cannot resist a good story. Vermeule continues, "The human intellect is extremely well-suited to thinking about other people, their problems, and the situations they get themselves into. The problems we care about come packaged in human form. Other people set our puzzles of practical and moral reasoning for us" (23). For this reason, she states, "The attempt to write amoral fiction—like the attempt to be amoral—is doomed because human psychology is inevitably moral psychology and because I too am afflicted by human psychology, I am not going to be able to resist the temptation to moralize" (135). Wilde displays the moralizing of Lady Windermere's society to show that it is not only hypocritical but also often based on false information and assumptions. In doing so, Wilde has a moral purpose of his own. Gregory Mackie describes how Wilde achieved modernity "by dramatizing the limitations of moral language and hence moral judgment, in a social world shaped by the elaborate artifice of decorum" (145–6). High-society concerns itself with maintaining appearances and achieves this, in part, by locating others to ostracize on moral grounds. As Lady Windermere eventually learns, this can prove a dangerous mistake.

Criticism on Wilde has long concerned itself with the balance between ethics and aesthetics in his work (e.g., Anderson; Brown; Ellman, "Introduction"; Mackie). In "The Critic as Artist," Wilde insists that "the critic should be able to recognise that the sphere of Art and the sphere of Ethics are absolutely distinct and separate" (198). Yet what follows serves to clarify: "They are too often confused in England now, and though our modern Puritans cannot destroy a beautiful thing, yet, by means of their extraordinary prurience, they can almost taint beauty for a moment" (198). According to Wilde, Puritanical moralism has no place in quality works of art. However, this does not mean that works of art cannot lead humanity to better ethics. Wilde explains that the artist who makes the facts of life beautiful shows their "true ethical import" (199). In her close readings of Wilde's prose, Julie Prewitt Brown argues that Wilde's work is an attempt to break with the dualism between aesthetics and ethics, which nearly all of the previous, great Victorian prose writers viewed in opposition to each other. Brown writes, "The aestheticism developed in Wilde's writing cannot be reduced to a simple assertion of the predominance of beauty or the autonomy and disinterestedness of art" (xv). She continues by clarifying his use of terminology:

> [H]is animadversions against "morality" refer to the puritan and philistine moralities of the period. Wilde asserted the centrality of the aesthetic imagination, but not as something divorced from moral and spiritual life. His claim that aesthetics is "higher" than ethics [...] is based on definitions of both terms that understand the aesthetic to transform, rather than transcend, the ethical [xvi].

Wilde seeks to transform his audience by showing the flaws in his characters' thinking, and by showing how they come to self-knowledge through a better understanding of human nature in general. Wilde writes, "To know anything about oneself one must know all about others" (*Intentions* 178). Art can teach us about others by aesthetically concentrating our focus on certain elements of human nature—like our modes of processing information—and by providing us with corrective information when appropriate. Wilde explains why art is superior to life in this regard: "Don't let us go to life for our fulfillment or our experience. It is a thing narrowed by circumstances, incoherent in its utterance, and without that fine correspondence of form and spirit which is the only thing that can satisfy the artistic and critical temperament" (173). In *Lady Windermere's Fan*, our attention is focused on faulty appraisals which are corrected by the play's conclusion; in real life, faulty appraisals are common, but are not necessarily corrected. "It is through Art," Wilde explains, "and through

Art only, that we realize our perfection" (174). *Lady Windermere's Fan* leads us to realize the flaws in our information processing and seeks to correct them through aesthetics.

Just as Wilde's characters make inaccurate appraisals based on limited available information, the audience is also led to initially assume that Lord Windermere and Mrs. Erlynne are having an affair. Lady Windermere in particular makes a faulty appraisal of the situation and acts rashly by running off with Darlington, but the audience cannot blame her at first since they are led to a similar appraisal. One aesthetic issue that arose during the early development and performance of the play was the issue of when to reveal to the audience Mrs. Erlynne's identity as Lady Windermere's mother. Wilde initially wanted to save the revelation for the final act, but George Alexander, the manager of St. James's Theatre where the play was originally produced, urged Wilde to reveal it earlier. Before the play's opening on 20 February 1892, Wilde argued adamantly, "had I intended to let out the secret, which is the element of suspense and curiosity, a quality so essentially dramatic, I would have written the play on entirely different lines" (*Letters* 308). He felt that an early revelation of Erlynne's identity would "destroy the last act" of the play and insisted, "I have built my house on a certain foundation, and this foundation cannot be altered" (309). Joel Kaplan explains that Wilde's "strategy caused much friction between Wilde and Alexander during rehearsals. Alexander, appearing in the role of Lord Windermere, complained that a late disclosure put both Lord Windermere and Mrs. Erlynne in 'false positions' for three quarters of the play." Alexander had been venting his frustrations with Wilde on this point to Clement Scott of *The Daily Telegraph* who complained in his review of the play's opening night that the withholding of Erlynne's identity came off as a betrayal of the audience and served only to annoy them (Kaplan, "Puppet's" 60–61). Apparently this review had the desired effect on Wilde, because after the opening performance he revised the play so that the revelation would be hinted at early on and revealed fully in Act Two. Wilde later responded to an article in the *St. James's Gazette* that attributed the change to the influence of critics. He instead attributes the change to a conversation with friends at a dinner party after the performance:

> [A]ll my friends, without exception, were of opinion that the psychological interest of the second act would be greatly increased by the disclosure of the actual relationship existing between Lady Windermere and Mrs. Erlynne—an opinion, I may add, that had previously been held and urged by Mr. Alexander. As to those of us who do not look on a play as a mere question of pantomime and clowning, psychological interest is everything [*Letters* 313].

The psychological interest of the second act and what follows was increased by this change because of the position that the audience would now take in relation to Erlynne's character. This is significant not only in allowing the audience to better understand her motivations but also in creating tension through dramatic irony when the audience learns early on that she has been appraised wrongfully by the other characters in the play and that she is not having an affair with Lord Windermere. Human beings appraise fictional or dramatic characters in essentially the same way that they do people in real life. We make appraisals without having all of the information, and dramatic literature can demonstrate the consequences of this. However, artists can manipulate their audiences to get the optimal effect. There is a difference, as Wilde learned, between not having information in a real life situation and having information purposely withheld by an author, which the audience may perceive as a trick. By having Erlynne's identity revealed in Act Two, Wilde places the audience in a position of knowing early on. Instead of experiencing a shocking surprise in the play's final scene, the audience members become aware of their own faulty appraisals of Mrs. Erlynne at around the halfway point. For the rest of the play they are put in the position of witness to the faulty appraisals of others.

Much of the dramatic structure of *Lady Windermere's Fan* would have been familiar to Wilde's late Victorian audience as he adopted conventions from popular melodramas from earlier in the century. Kerry Powell gives the most thorough account of the various French and English literary works that have been or could be cited as sources for Wilde's play (14–32). These plays contain familiar characters and plot structures involving fallen women, concluding with some form of poetic justice, which generally involves the fallen woman being either punished or redeemed or both. Wilde differs from his nineteenth-century sources by avoiding the kind of moralizing that characterized popular Victorian melodrama where morally "bad" characters are ultimately taken to task. As Francesca Coppa points out, "*Lady Windermere's Fan* is notably lacking in poetic justice: not only does Lady Windermere escape the consequences of her mistake but so does Mrs. Erlynne" (121). Brown links this lack of poetic justice to Wilde's inability to theorize human evil: "Without a conception of evil," she writes, "Wilde could not bring himself to punish any of the characters in his comedies" (xix). To Wilde, sin is conceived of as a violation of social mores, which paradoxically causes it to become ethical. "By its curiosity," he writes in "The Critic as Artist," "Sin increases the experience of the race. Through its intensified assertion of individualism, it saves us from the monotony of type. In its rejection of the current notions about morality, it is one with the higher ethics" (*Intentions* 134). Wilde challenges narrow cultural views of morality, and his complex view of morality makes the standard melodramatic ending impossible for *Lady Windermere's Fan*. Coppa explains, "Part of what Wilde realized is that melodrama falls apart when the underlying certainties—that one can distinguish good from bad, reality from pretense, truth from fiction—stop being certain" (122).

Wilde was not simply playing with conventions in *Lady Windermere's Fan* as an aesthetic novelty. The ethical purpose of the play is to provide corrective social information that encourages metacognition, awareness of ones own cognitive processes, and more accurate, or at least cautious, information processing in the audience. As the characters realize their errors in meaning making, the audience realizes their own and are made to see the injustice that can result from false assumptions and gossip. In a speech given to the Royal General Theatrical Fund in 1892, Wilde stated, "'Those who have seen *Lady Windermere's Fan* will see that if there is one particular doctrine contained in it, it is that of sheer individualism. It is not for anyone to censure what anyone else does, and everyone should go his own way, to whatever place he chooses, in exactly the way he chooses'" (Ellmann, *Oscar* 368). Mrs. Erlynne is the victim of such censure, but the gossip about her is mostly false and the moral high ground on which Lady Windermere and others in her society stand ultimately proves shaky when they commit, or nearly commit, their own indiscretions. By the end of the play, the audience, like Lady Windermere, is forced to consider alternative schemas, prototypes, and information processing routines when those that they were using throughout most of the play are proven to be faulty.

Richard Lazarus explains that "appraisal consists of continuing evaluation of the significance of what is happening for one's personal well-being" (144). He also theorizes that "cognitive activity causally precedes an emotion in the flow of psychological events" (127)—that is, our emotional responses to a situation are based on a cognitive appraisal. Lazarus describes this as a human adaptive function where we evaluate objects and circumstances as either a threat or non-threat and respond with the appropriate emotion. While this system generally contributes to our survival, it is also prone to error. We make appraisals based on available information and then draw from our pre-formed schemas and prototypes to categorize such information. But these schemas and prototypes, these categories, are not always correct. In his contribution to the essay collection *Performance and Cognition*, Neal Swettenham explains,

> Categorization [...] is a way of reducing or "simplifying" the information being processed. It helps us to perceive objects, people, relationships, and so on, and to group them together quickly and efficiently. The advantages of this are obvious: speed of response, ease of processing, the convenience of shorthand. The disadvantages are also plain: subtle differences are elided, snap judgments are made, and modes of perception can become rigid and inflexible [209].

Humans make judgments of people and other things by putting them into categories that our minds have created from experience and memory. We use these categories to appraise situations and respond with the appropriate emotion and course of action. Lazarus writes that after an appraisal brings about an emotional response, "subsequent cognitive activity is also later affected by that emotion" (127). This system is circular: our initial appraisal leads to an emotion, which influences future appraisals. In Lady Windermere's case, an initial misappraisal leads to an inappropriate emotional response that clouds future appraisals and leads to a course of action—specifically, her nearly running off with Darlington—that would have had dire consequences.

One of the ways that we process information, in this case social information, is through pre-set schemas, organizing principles or general ways of seeing people and the world. We see flaws in Lady Windermere's general person-schemas early on in the play. In his book *Literature and Social Justice*, Mark Bracher lists several of these general person-schemas that carry negative social consequences. He writes, "the ultimate source of distorted, harmful assessments that people make about each other is not stereotypes per se, but certain faulty 'knowledge' or beliefs about 'human nature,' or persons in general" (7). Lady Windermere is guilty of using what Bracher calls a homogeneity schema. He explains,

> The *homogeneity* schema homogenizes self and other into all good or all bad, thus blocking awareness of one's own negative qualities as well as the positive qualities of others who may have evinced negative behaviors or character traits. The schema thus enables categorization of people as either good or bad, and the division of the moral landscape into "us" versus "them" [15].

We see this schema at work in Lady Windermere in her conversation with Darlington during the opening moments of the play where she insists on the strict division between right and wrong and allows for "no compromise" (1.81–82). Bracher writes that homogeneity, along with atomism or seeing human relations as competitive rather than cooperative, can "blind people to the profound sameness and interconnectedness they share with all other humans" (14). These faulty person schemas can have profound consequences for social justice on a wide scale, but can also lead to unjust appraisals on an individual level. By the end of the play, Lady Windermere learns that she is capable of the same faults that she projects onto Mrs. Erlynne and, thus, that neither of them is entirely good or bad. She also learns that Erlynne is not a competitor and a threat as initially perceived, but is willing to sacrifice herself to save Lady Windermere.

Appraisals are also made using prototypes, "our constructs of what we take to be the typical member of a particular category," which are primarily cultural (Bracher 16). Prototypes hold a powerful influence on our thinking even when they are based on limited information. Bracher explains, "When a prototype is activated, it usually preempts further information processing by providing us with a prefabricated assessment of the person along with an emotional response and an action tendency or script" (16). Like the rest of her society, Lady Windermere assumes that Erlynne fits the prototype of an "other woman," and that Lord Windermere fits the prototype of the adulterous husband. We see from Duchess Berwick and others in the play, like Dumby and Lady Plymdale, that these prototypes and this practice of adultery are common in late Victorian London high-society. In spite of the fact that Lady Windermere appears to have a stable marriage, it is easy for her to accept her husband in the role of adulterer because she already sees her society as corrupt, or through a schema of corruption, full of bad people who have no loyalty to each other. When confronting her husband, she asks, "Why should you be different from other men?" (1.471) Her trusted friend Berwick also does much to normalize adultery in their society and reinforces the schemas and prototypes that Lady Windermere uses. Berwick paints a picture for Lady Windermere of a society where "wicked women get our husbands away from us" (1.323–324) and "all men are monsters" (1.331). Of course, Berwick has her own motivations because she is a victim of adultery. Her emotional course of action is to cope by seeing it as inevitable, normal, and out of the hands of the females in their society. The naïve ingénue, Lady Windermere, is unable to read Berwick's motivations and, thus, adopts her faulty appraisal that Lord Windermere is having an affair with Erlynne.

During Act One of the play, the audience will tend to apply the same prototypes to Mrs. Erlynne and Lord Windermere as Lady Windermere does. Bruce McConachie discusses how prototypes influence the audience's appraisals of characters during a performance:

> All spectators carry social prototypes in their mind/brains when they enter the playhouse, and many of these figures have been prejudged along the continuum of sympathy and antipathy that type cast them. We watch plays after having already made up our minds [...] and can generally spot these prototypes immediately when they appear on stage [101].

From the opening scenes of the play where Lady Windermere is in her morning-room arranging roses in bowl, audiences recognize her as a female domestic moral exemplar, a Victorian Angel of the House, and she appears to see herself this way. Drawing from simulation theory, McConachie explains that "before spectators form a sympathetic response to actor/characters in most dramatic situations, they must ascribe beliefs, desires, intentions, and emotions to them" (66). While the audience may question Lady Windermere's rigid worldview, her beliefs fit ideals about the world that many value. She values her child, her marriage, and the institution of marriage in general, and we recognize that her admirable goal is to maintain an ideal family.

Peter Raby describes the play as beginning in innocence until Darlington makes an offer of friendship to Lady Windermere; this "disturbs the innocent ritual momentarily, and reveals the unquiet reality beneath the smooth social patina" (146). Immediately we feel that Lady Windermere is threatened by Darlington who the audience will recognize as fitting the Wildean cultural prototype of the fashionable pleasure seeker or the dandy. In the stage directions for Act One, audiences see a physical enactment of a subtle cat and mouse game taking place under the guise of a cup of tea: Darlington's handshake is refused under a weak pretense (1.10–12); Lady Windermere retreats to fortify herself behind the tea table and Darlington follows (1.30–33); when the conversation becomes too uncomfortable, Lady Windermere moves back to the table of roses on the other side of the room and asks Darlington to remain seated (1.121–123). Powell explains that Darlington belongs to the tradition of "old-fashioned domestic comedies in which a dandy or poet of 'honeyed words' and 'showy graces' nearly seduced the heroine from the strong, silent husband whom she must learn again to appreciate and love" (15). By presenting the potential for an adulterous affair, Darlington poses an immediate threat to Lady Windermere's goal of a perfect family life. When Mrs. Erlynne is later introduced in conversation as Lord Windermere's mistress, we appraise her, like Lady Windermere does, as posing an even more serious threat to the Windermere marriage.

All of these initial character appraisals that the audience will tend to share with Lady Windermere are shown to be faulty as the play progresses. We eventually come to better understand Darlington's motivations and, perhaps, appraise him more sympathetically. By the end of Acts Two and Three, we recognize that he may really love Lady Windermere and feels she is being treated badly by a husband who does not recognize her worth. While he does pose a serious threat to the Windermere marriage, Darlington is also the character in the play who points out the hypocrisy of their society and who first corrects Lady Windermere's homogeneity schema. He tells her, "It is absurd to divide people into good and bad," adding that instead "People are either charming or tedious" (1.117–119). Powell points out that part of the appeal of "dandiacal seducers" is that they "function as critics of society" (15). Amanda Anderson explains, "For Wilde, the dandy ideally represents the function of criticism in the modern era, which seeks to further self-consciousness by subverting custom, habit, and the oppressive social stability that they work to secure" (159). Darlington's conversational style of saying something serious and subversive, then undercutting it with a joke, provides a parallel to Wilde's style in the play. Raby writes, "The juxtaposition of the comic and the serious is one of Wilde's most successful dramatic techniques; once the absurd and the patently false have been established, the serious emotions and ideals which are explored have been given a context which prevents them from ever seeming too solemn" (147). Of course, while he serves as a voice for Wilde's opinions on morality and society, Darlington is also equally guilty of a misappraisal of the Windermeres' marriage—a misappraisal based purely on gossip.

Lord Windermere is initially seen as a perfect husband to his wife, but soon becomes the prototypical wealthy, adulterous male. He goes from being sympathetic to threatening only to become sympathetic again when the audience realizes the true nature of his relationship with Mrs. Erlynne. Even though he is being blackmailed by Erlynne, Lord Windermere is the one character who appraises her as a non-threat at the beginning of the play. He tells his wife, "as far as I have known Mrs. Erlynne, she has conducted herself well" (1.410–411). To him, she is a tragic figure who made some regrettable mistakes in the past. Ironically, in the end, after she is discovered in Darlington's rooms, he tells Lady Windermere, "I was mistaken in her. She is bad—as bad as a woman can be" (4.66–67). Feeling betrayed for sticking up for her early on, Lord Windermere is especially cruel in his attacks on Erlynne in Act Four. This happens at the same time that his wife is forced to revise her appraisal of Mrs. Erlynne to a more complex and positive one. Of course, Lord Windermere can never know the real reason why Erlynne was in Darlington's rooms—to rescue Lady Windermere—just as, we must assume, he will never tell Lady Windermere that Mrs. Erlynne is her mother. The secrets in the play go unrevealed to the characters who would be most affected by them. The lies told, or truths left untold, at the play's conclusion recall the "beautiful untrue things" that Wilde sees as the proper aim of art in "The Decay of Lying" (*Intentions* 56). Lord Windermere is allowed to maintain the image of an ideal wife, and Lady Windermere will presumably never question the nature of Lord Windermere and Mrs. Erlynne's relationship so that she can maintain the image of an ideal husband and a good, loving mother. As she tells Erlynne, "If I lost my ideals, I should lose everything" (4.310–311). In the end, the Windermeres must learn to trust each other and deal with uncertainty.

Mrs. Erlynne emerges in the play as the most significant faultily appraised character. Wilde's investment in Erlynne and her plight has been traced by Richard Ellman to his friendship with the real-life actress Lillie Langtry, with whom he had been close since the late 1870s. Langtry had been lovers with, among others, the Prince of Wales. She left London society for a spell around 1880 to give birth to an illegitimate child, only to return without her daughter in 1881 (*Oscar* 112–113). Wilde admired Langtry's courage and was sympathetic to her as a friend, just as his play is ultimately sympathetic to Erlynne. In a letter to an unidentified recipient, Wilde discusses his psychological interest in his character:

> The psychological idea that suggested to me the play is this. A woman who has had a child, but never known the passion of maternity (there are such women),

suddenly sees the child she has abandoned falling over a precipice. There wakes in her the maternal feeling—the most terrible of all emotions—a thing that weak animals and little birds possess. She rushes to rescue, sacrifices herself, does follies—and the next day she feels "This passion is too terrible. It wrecks my life. I don't want to know it again. It makes me suffer too much. Let me go away. I don't want to be a mother any more." And so the fourth act is to me the psychological act, the act that is newest, most true [*Letters* 331–332].

Powell traces Erlynne's origins to trends in nineteenth-century drama, which she ultimately subverts. He points out that the late nineteenth-century stage saw "an increasing number of plays depicting derelict mothers who abandon their husbands and children" (16). These "familiar figures" typically ended their stories with repentance and punishment. Powell explains,

> In one play after another, both French and English, they are seen deserting their families, following their lovers, but returning home full of repentance at last. Nothing, however, atones for their having transgressed the most basic precepts of a woman's duty. They may repent—and usually do—but justice demands they die, with or without medical cause, or enter a convent at least. The extremity of their case invited the kind of clear-cut and melodramatic division of right and wrong which was increasingly difficult in the modern world. By 1892—the year of *Lady Windermere's Fan*—the absconded mother was a stock character who could be relied upon for a tearful curtain and a nostalgic invocation of settled values and undisturbed norms of conduct [16].

Wilde sought to unsettle these values and disturb norms of conduct with Erlynne by working "through the dramatic formula, only to upset everything at the end by repudiating the categorical assumptions about right and wrong, sin and punishment, upon which this curious dramatic type was founded" (Powell 21). Wilde showed a certain pride in his literary creation, referring to her in a letter to George Alexander as "a character as yet untouched by literature" (*Letters* 309). In Erlynne we get a modern and complex female character who defies the dated and simplistic standards of melodrama.

Erlynne violates the audience's prototype of the repentant, absconded mother in the end, but what is perhaps more significant is the way she violates the prototype of the immoral, predatory other-woman that is applied to her throughout the play by both audience and by other characters in the play. In doing so, Erlynne forces Lady Windermere to revise not only her view of Mrs. Erlynne as an individual exemplar, but the homogeneity and atomism schemas through which Lady Windermere processes social information in general. The audience is forced to reassess their meaning making processes as well, especially since we learn more about Erlynne's actual motivations than Lady Windermere does. Erlynne is initially appraised as a threat to Lady Windermere's marriage, but only becomes a threat because of Lady Windermere's faulty appraisal and her subsequent rash, emotional decision to leave with Darlington. Erlynne begins to emerge as a sympathetic character during the revelation of her identity at the end of Act Two when the audience sees her take on a very different prototypical role—that of a mother. In her monologue she pleads with herself, "How can I save her? How can I save my child?" (2.494). Her transformation in the eyes of the audience comes when she proves willing to sacrifice her own goal of getting back into society in order to save Lady Windermere. Ultimately, she rejects the mother prototype, as well. Before leaving London, she tells Lord Windermere, "Only once in my life have I known a mother's feelings […]. They were terrible—they made me suffer—they made me suffer too much" (4.232–234). Melodrama cannot hold up with its black-and-white worldview, so we get no tearful reunion or poetic punishment that restores the family or social order. Instead, Erlynne serves as a corrective exemplar to Lady Windermere and to the audience when she contradicts the various prototypes that had been applied to her. Erlynne is not purely innocent—blackmailing your daughter's rich husband by threatening to disgrace her is fairly reprehensible—but she does prove to be heterogeneous and contradicts the homogeneity schema.

Lady Windermere and the audience are also forced to abandon any absolutist thinking when Lady Windermere commits her own indiscretion by nearly doing the very same thing that her mother had done many years before—leaving her husband for another man. Driven by unwavering principles and faulty information, she nearly becomes one of those consistent, "tedious people who carry out their principles to the bitter end of action" (*Intentions* 5). Kaplan discusses the visual parallels that George Alexander's dressmakers, Mesdames Savage and Purdue, created between Erlynne and Lady Windermere during the play's first run by making them wear "outfits of almost identical colour and cut" ("Wilde" 250). The social categorizations of these two characters ultimately prove to be unfounded as the parallels between them become evident. The play's subtitle, *A Play about a Good Woman*, and its original title, *A Good Woman*, both imply absolutism and homogeneity. But, of course, this must be taken ironically: there is no "good" woman, or person, because humans are all heterogeneous. Wilde writes that "To be good, according to the vulgar standard of goodness, is obviously quite easy. It merely requires a certain amount of sordid terror, a certain lack of imaginative thought, and a certain low passion for middle-class respectability" (*Intentions* 221). Lady Windermere is "good" by society's standards, but these standards are not only vulgar, but unstable and dubious. Wilde describes the prig as "a very interesting psychological study," but felt that "of all poses a moral pose is the most offensive" (*Intentions* 184). On the surface, Lady Windermere lives an ethical life; whereas Mrs. Erlynne lives, perhaps, the aesthetic life. However, it is Erlynne who shows herself capable of the kind of "love" and "sacrifice" that her daughter values so highly (1.90); and it is Lady Windermere who nearly becomes one of those women who, by her own standards, should "never be forgiven" (1.133–134). But Wilde does not cast any moral disparagement on Erlynne's past or Lady Windermere's near *faux pas*. His ethical stance is simply that we should be less rigid and absolute in our judgment of others, especially since our appraisals are so prone to error.

Wilde felt that "self-consciousness and the critical spirit are one" (*Intentions* 127). By engaging his characters and audiences in this critical spirit, and increasing their capacity for metacognition, Wilde sought to bridge the gap between the aesthetic and the ethical. A number of concepts from cognitive science provide us with helpful tools to better understand Wilde's moral strategies in *Lady Windermere's Fan* and to better understand how these strategies have affected audiences from the late nineteenth-century up to today. Wilde challenges the validity of general person-schemas of homogeneity and atomism. He shows through art that we should be careful in judging people because those who society perceives as good people can do reproachable things, and vice versa. Perceived enemies can turn out to be allies, and competitors can turn into helpers. The prototypes that we all use to categorize and judge people are convenient and serve an evolutionary purpose, but they are not necessarily accurate. Wilde shows that these misappraisals that audiences will recognize as so common in human beings, especially when compounded by emotional rashness, can lead to unjust actions and bad decisions with potentially serious, negative consequences for ourselves and others.

KUTZTOWN UNIVERSITY OF PENNSYLVANIA

WORK CITED

Anderson, Amanda. "'Manners Before Morals': Oscar Wilde and Epigrammatic Detachment." *The Powers of Distance: Cosmopolitanism and the Cultivation of Detachment.* Princeton: Princeton University Press, 2001. 147–176.

Bracher, Mark. *Literature and Social Justice: Protest Novels, Cognitive Politics, and Schema Criticism.* Austin: University of Texas Press, 2013.

Brown, Julia Prewitt. *Cosmopolitan Criticism: Oscar Wilde's Philosophy of Art.* Charlottesville: University of Virginia Press, 1997.

Cohn, Elisha. "'One Single Ivory Cell': Oscar Wilde and the Brain." *Journal of Victorian Culture* 17.2 (2012): 183–205.

Coppa, Francesca. "Teaching Melodrama, Modernity, and Postmodernity in *Lady Windermere's Fan.*" *Approaches to Teaching the Works of Oscar Wilde.* Ed. Phillip E. Smith II. New York: Modern Language Association, 2008. 117–125.

Ellman, Richard. Introduction. *The Artist as Critic: Critical Writings of Oscar Wilde.* Ed. Richard Ellman. Chicago: University of Chicago Press, 1982. xxvi–xxvii.

_____. *Oscar Wilde.* New York: Knopf, 1988.

Kaplan, Joel. "A Puppet's Power: George Alexander, Clement Scott, and the Replotting of *Lady Windermere's Fan*." *Theatre Notebook* 46.2 (1992): 59–72.

_____. "Wilde on the Stage." *The Cambridge Companion to Oscar Wilde*. Ed. Peter Raby. New York: Cambridge University Press, 1998. 249–275.

Lazarus, Richard. *Emotion and Adaptation*. New York: Oxford University Press, 1991.

Mackie, Gregory. "The Function of Decorum at the Present Time: Manners, Moral Language, and Modernity in 'an Oscar Wilde Play.'" *Modern Drama* 52.2 (2009): 145–167.

McConachie, Bruce. *Engaging Audiences: A Cognitive Approach to Spectating in the Theatre*. Series: Cognitive Studies in Literature and Performance. New York: Palgrave Macmillan, 2008.

Powell, Kerry. *Oscar Wilde and the Theatre of the 1890s*. New York: Cambridge University Press, 1990.

Raby, Peter. "Wilde's Comedies of Society." *The Cambridge Companion to Oscar Wilde*. Ed. Peter Raby. New York: Cambridge University Press, 1998. 143–160.

Swettenham, Neal. "Categories and Catcalls: Cognitive Dissonance in *The Playboy of the Western World*." Eds. Bruce McConachie and F. Elizabeth Hart. *Performance and Cognition: Theatre Studies and the Cognitive Turn*. New York: Routledge, 2006. 207–222.

Vermeule, Blakey. *Why Do We Care About Literary Characters?* Baltimore: Johns Hopkins University Press, 2010.

Wilde, Oscar. *Intentions and the Soul of Man*. Vol. 8. *The Collected Works of Oscar Wilde*. Ed. Robert Ross. London: Menthuen, 1908.

_____. *The Letters of Oscar Wilde*. Ed. Rupert Hart-Davis. New York: Harcourt, Brace & World, 1962.

_____. "Lady Windermere's Fan." *The Importance of Being Earnest and Other Plays*. Ed. Peter Raby. New York: Oxford World's Classics, 2008.

Primal, Pure or Something in Between? Aida Walker, Dance and Sexuality

Elizabeth M. Cizmar

Abstract

In a 1953 issue of Jet, *editors paid tribute to Aida Walker and published a photograph of the actress reminiscent of the Gibson Girl, instead of the arguably more memorable portrait as the first black Salome. The image of a black woman with a white buttoned-up blouse and a bouffant hairstyle proves that the New Negro Woman movement's efforts to thwart conceptions of the primitive black female left lasting impressions in the African American community. Walker's conflation of sexuality and acceptable norms of Victorian femininity as Salome resulted in mixed reviews due to public expectations of black female sexuality. This study situates Walker in her historical moment and considers the breadth of her portraiture including a country bumpkin, an orientalist, and a seductress. Walker constantly negotiated her position as a black performer to create agency by reversing notions of the sexual mulatto and at the pinnacle of her career, striving for acceptance by mainstream critics by performing the quintessential femme fatale.*

In a 1953 issue of the African American magazine *Jet*, editors commemorated Aida Walker, the popular turn of the century performer for her success and influence in the entertainment industry. The photograph next to her biography is her iconic portrait [see Figure 1] instead of the arguably more memorable image of Walker as the first black Salome [see Figure 2]. For a magazine to choose an image of a black woman with a white buttoned-up blouse and a bouffant hairstyle shows how the efforts of the New Negro women's movement to challenge stereotypes about black women left a profound impact on public perceptions forty years later. However, starkly contrasting photographs of Aida Walker in the Schomburg archives establish her modesty and sex appeal. These diverging images suggest that Walker's sexuality, whether subdued or expressed, serves a critical role in challenging stereotypes of black women during her lifetime and decades later.

In the archives, iconographic evidence reveals Walker's reconciliation of her own sexuality against both audience and critics' expectations and accepted norms of Victorian femininity. She balances the ideals of the New Negro women's movement within the context of "Salomania" to push boundaries and promote progress for black female performers. The most common image associated with Walker is indeed the Salome portrait because, as Daphne Brooks asserts, Walker created her own version of the dance in a charged cultural context (331). In addition, scholars such as David Krasner highlight her negotiation between achieving commercial success in a prejudiced industry and assuaging black middle class standards of propriety.[1] This study expands research to consider the breadth of Walker's portraiture that shows her in personas as diverse as a country bumpkin, an orientalist, and a seductress. As a woman, Walker stands out from her male co-stars, Williams and Walker, because of the way in which she made deliberate character choices that consistently questioned commonly held beliefs about female black sexuality. As the evidence shows, one cannot place Walker in a dichotomy of sexual versus asexual because the extant portraits show her moving regularly between polarities. At the pinnacle of her career, she performs the quintessential femme fatale, Salome, and strives for further acceptance from mainstream critics. Her Salome illustrates a conflation of sexuality and Victorian ideals that resulted in mixed reviews because Walker did not meet public expectations regarding primal black female sexuality.

Figure 1. Aida Overton Walker (n.d. Schomburg Center for Research in Black Culture, NYPL, New York).

This essay examines Walker's complexity by exploring her historical moment of the early twentieth century and particularly the New Negro women's movement. The influence of Victorian ideals manifest by the popular Gibson Girl cartoon is also critical for analyzing her performance choices. In African American studies there is a paucity of documentation in the archives because historically white performers are privileged over black performers. However, through access to iconographic evidence in the Schomburg collection, academics can deepen their understanding of performers and their impact on the American theatre. The range of Walker's photographs display her attempts to (1) achieve mainstream acceptance from critics and audiences, and (2) confront preconceived notions about black female sexuality. This trajectory exposes flawed misconceptions that oversimplify and distort the representation of black female performers in the past and present.

A suggestive photograph of Walker with a particular inscription is housed in the Schomburg Archives, and it validates Walker's provocative

Figure 2. Aida Overton Walker as Salomé, ca. 1911 (Schomburg Center for Research in Black Culture, NYPL, New York).

approach to presenting Salome's seductive nature [see Figure 3]. The print provides no contextual clues such as the date, photographer, or the purpose of the portrait. It is possible that the portrait is a publicity shot for Salome or a nonspecific portrait of the performer. However, one potentially telling clue is the inscription: "To Minnie with memories of other days. The same, AOW."[2] Walker's nostalgic tone implies that she wrote it after the Williams and Walker team disbanded. *Bandanna Land* proved to be the all-black company's last

Figure 3. Aida Walker (n.d. Schomburg Center for Research in Black Culture, NYPL, New York).

show, even though Walker continued to perform her dance of Salome as a solo act. It is difficult to ascertain when she wrote the inscription. In the 1910s Jim Crow legislation was in full effect, and segregation rules were strongly enforced throughout the post-reconstruction era. The note implies a longing for better days when Aida's fame was rising and the Williams and Walker team were wildly successful. As a solo female black performer, it stands to reason that facing discrimination alone would be far more difficult than in an already established, commercially successful Broadway company.

Comparing this unknown image with better known photographs of Walker as Salome and other well-known characters, the more familiar images iconographically integrate the tenets of Victorian femininity to a greater degree. However, in this image her hair is short, natural, and tussled. She gazes out the side of her titled head, flirting with the camera. Her costume exposes her body and accentuates her womanly shape. Her sinuous pose and sultry glance suggest the sensuality associated with the dance of Salome. When discussing Walker's Salome, one cannot deny the presence of sexuality. Even though Aida Walker's seductiveness is evident in her portrait, critics of her Salome performance were disappointed that she did not fulfill their expectations of the primal African savage. Walker's debated performance evoked mixed reviews because she did not fit into the primal or pure categorization.

The degree of sexuality expressed from performance to performance must have wavered due to the puritanical laws that varied from state to state and potentially influenced audience reception. These laws may lead critics to believe that Aida purifies her performance based on certain costume choices, but, due to the fleeting nature of theatre, the specific performance choices are unknown. Historians need to reflect on the legal context when discussing her costume and choreography choices and consider that those decisions were not necessarily of her volition. Due to the lack of documentation of African American performers at this time, a high degree of speculation is unavoidable. Nevertheless, scholars can do so in an informed way with supporting historical and iconographic evidence. When negotiating between seduction and propriety, inevitably at different performances across state lines, Aida's sexuality in performance varied, especially when performing as a solo dancer outside the context of a Broadway show.

In performance and especially early on in her career, Aida Walker's response to stereotypes on stage aligns with the efforts of the New Negro women's movement challenging perceptions of the lascivious nature of African American women. In her book *A Voice from the South* Anna Julia Cooper, a prominent African-American activist at the time, describes the standards black women must strive for to achieve equal footing in society. Alleged black impropriety derives from white Americans' prejudices during the peak of the slave trade in the eighteenth and nineteenth centuries. Cooper fights for racial equality and disputes perceptions of African Americans as three-fifths human. Her core approach lies in Judeo-Christian morality:

> By laying down for woman the same [Christian] code, the same standard of purity, as for man; by refusing to countenance the shameless and equally guilty monsters who were gloating over her fall—graciously stooping in all the majesty of his own spotlessness to wipe away filth and grime of her guilty past and bid her to go in peace and sin no more [57].

Cooper suggests that the tainted souls of black women needed salvation; this assertion seems to perpetuate the white hegemonic belief that blacks were animalistic and primitive. She contends that a moral code given by Christ gave ideals for humanity applicable to women as well as men (Cooper 60). Church doctrine certainly supports efforts to encourage proper behavior through baptism and purification. Moreover, the woman influences the man at birth and has the ability to shape man into the ideals of Christ to perpetuate a more civilized society. She believes that this purification of race and social mobilization begins with the woman in the home. The New Negro women's movement assumed Christian values in order not only to subvert commonly held beliefs about African Americans but also to create a community focusing on racial uplift.

Another significant leader in the New Negro woman's movement, Margaret Washington, wife of Booker T. Washington, argues that African Americans must adopt Victorian ideals in addition to Christian ideals in order to distance themselves from stereotypes dating back to slavery. She asserts that racial progress is directly tied to social propriety: "An emphasis on self-help, racial solidarity, temperance, thrift, chastity, social purity, patriarchal authority, and the accumulation of wealth" (Patterson 51). The movement's objective is to divorce the next wave of African Americans from the painful history of slavery and Jim Crow, focusing instead on the acquisition of bourgeois lifestyles of the early twentieth century. This New Negro woman fights stereotypes including mammies, topsies, coons, shiftless darkies, and lascivious mulattos to promote cleanliness and purity. The black bourgeois adopted the Victorian ideals of cleanliness, domesticity, morals, and manners as a reaction against stereotypes about African American women. Adopting Victorian ideals included adopting Victorian dress and hairstyles, which gave the message that a particular woman followed particular rules and social behaviors. Assuming such clothing and behavior was all in an effort to thwart the savage image.

During this historical moment, the New Negro woman emulated the popular Gibson Girl, in terms of her physical appearance and her socially progressive ways. Named after her creator Charles Dana Gibson, the Gibson Girl became popular in newspapers, advertisements, and fashion magazines and at the turn of the century became an icon for both black and white women. She wears buttoned-up blouses, long skirts, corseted waists, and bouffant hairstyles. As far as her moral character, she is affluent, politically progressive, and educated. In addition, the Gibson Girl rarely appears with a male companion which may symbolize women's fight for suffrage. Even though she fights for the right to vote, she maintains the lady-like behavior society expects from a woman; in the domestic sphere, she upholds the standards of cleanliness and Christianity while serving her husband dutifully. The Gibson Girl was both politically active and independent, two important values for the New Negro women's movement and certainly an appropriate model for a woman in the entertainment industry.

Aida Walker brought the New Negro woman's philosophy into the theatre and presented herself as an iteration of the Gibson Girl, both socially progressive and a model of propriety. In the early twentieth century the theatre was notorious for lewd conduct and immorality. In contrast, she promoted the theatre as a place of respectability, appropriate for young women seeking upward mobility. In her article, "Colored Men and Women on the Stage" (1906), she defends the stage and claims that in recent years the theatre had evolved into something more respectable (Walker "Colored American Magazine"). She urges young African American women to join the profession: "if she be a girl of good thoughts and habits, and she chooses the Stage for the love of the profession and professional work, then I should say to her, "Come for we need so many earnest workers in this field; and by hard work, I am sure the future will repay you and all of us." Not only does the stage provide an opportunity for young hard-working girls, but it also provides another employment option aside from white wealthy homes. Hence, a young lady can free herself from the domestic service industry while simultaneously promoting racial progress. Walker exemplifies the Gibson Girl in both visual representation and her well-crafted language.

Both *Colored American Magazine* in 1910 and *Jet* in 1952 chose this particular photo of Walker because she projects respectability and femininity [refer to Figure 1]. Like the Gibson Girl iconography, her smoothly ironed hair swoops up with a black velvet bow. Her crisp white blouse buttons up to her neck with lacy trim suggesting femininity and wealth. A serious and pensive expression with an upright posture indicates decorum and exemplifies the New Negro woman. It is unclear whether this photo was selected by editors or by the actress herself, but either way Aida appears as an exemplary Gibson Girl. The image was paired with the article in *Colored American Magazine* in an attempt to bring further respectability to both the stage and African American women.

The success of *In Dahomey* in London in 1903 supported her claim that the theatre promoted racial progress. She wrote "I am sure Williams and Walker's visit ... reflected credit on the race and left a lasting impression in the

Figure 4. Scene from *In Dahomey* (n.d. Schomburg Center for Research in Black Culture, NYPL, New York).

minds of proud and highly cultured Englishmen" (Walker "Colored American Magazine"). Reviews of the 1903 production described a sense of nostalgia the British felt while watching the performance in that "Bert Williams and George Walker reminded [*The Times*] critic of the know-about artists of the British vaudeville" (Green 25). Certainly the social reality of England versus the racially charged reality of America contributed to the warm reception of the Williams and Walker team, but Aida calls attention to "high culture" of the English, the epicenter of Victorian values in the nineteenth century. The British aristocracy set the example for good behavior, taste, and propriety. Furthermore, they invited African American actors of *In Dahomey* into familial salons for private performances; King Edward VII, by special command, welcomed the team to Buckingham Palace in June 1903 (Green 36). Aida thus leveraged the popularity of the comic team in London to legitimatize their presence in the United States while simultaneously promoting the New Negro woman's agenda.

Figure 5. Alexander Rogers (left), Aida Overton Walker and Bert Williams in a scene from an unidentified Williams & Walker musical comedy, 1900s (Schomburg Center for Research in Black Culture, NYPL, New York).

Despite the Williams and Walker team's gambling habits and indiscretions with women, they took pride in the way their company followed a strict moral code and performed recognizable types in good, clean musical comedy (Green 31). While their musical comedies certainly perpetuated problematic stereotypes, within their individual nuanced performances the actors clearly employed double consciousness. The most recognizable group image of *In Dahomey* represents all these types: Bert Williams as the happy darkey, George Walker as the dandy, Lottie Williams and Hattie MacIntosh as the mannered ladies and Aida Walker as the juvenile country bumpkin [see Figures 4 and 5]. *In Dahomey* was the first full-length musical comedy conceived and performed by an all–African-American team. This watershed production legitimized African Americans in the entertainment industry and provided the foundation for Walker to claim in *Colored American Magazine* that the stage was indeed a place where young black female performers could achieve financial success.

In *In Dahomey*, Walker played the part of a pre-pubescent child that suggested innocence at the same time as it promoted racial progress. Critics and audiences responded positively to the character, Rosetta Lightfoot, because she did not exude sexuality and therefore did not offend white puritanical values. At the same time, the character sends an inspirational message to young black women similar to that of her newspaper article. Walker's solo in the show, "I wants to be a actor lady" represents innocence, purity and hope:

> I wants to be a actor lady
> Playing you know
> Star in the Broadway,
> Spotlight for me, no back row shady
> I'm the real thing
> I dance and sing [Brooks 261].

The lyrics encourage young African American girls from modest means to pursue the Broadway stage. This suggestion relates to what Richard Newman identifies as a "secret message to those who have ears" (Newman 479).[3] The female character does not pose a threat, but rather she longs with youthful exuberance for a better life in show business. According to bell hooks, African American theatrical music tended to challenge the predominant thought that black folks were not fully human. In Walker's portrayal of Rosetta Lightfoot, she subverts the primitive notion of the black woman and represents ideals of purity. Early in her career, it stands to reason that she would play the role of an innocent, nonthreatening child to appeal to wholesome black and white audiences. Essentially, Walker redefines the Topsy stereotype through Rosetta Lightfoot's aspirations to leave her country bumpkin life and become a successful performer.

Walker's portrayal of the aspiring actress infuses the Topsy stereotype with the Gibson Girl. Her costume reflects country bumpkin innocence while her posture appears upright and dignified [refer to Figure 4] She wears a short, youthful dress with black tights and a large hat. Even as Rosetta Lightfoot, she subverts the primitive notion of the black woman and represents the ideals of purity. However, she complicates the image of the African American woman by removing sexuality completely. Early in her career, audiences accepted the palatable character because she is seemingly nonthreatening, but Walker encourages young African American women to pursue careers beyond the status quo.

In her next role in *Abyssinia* (1906), she challenges notions of exoticism by continuing to integrate the dignity of the New Negro woman into the minor character Miriam, the modest African fruit seller. Set in exotic West Africa, *Abyssinia* followed on the heels of *In Dahomey*'s successful run. Monica White Ndounou suggests that it reflected the "evolving consciousness of the duo" in which the characters employed the King's English and addressed confrontations within African America identity (Ndounou 69). The very employment of the King's English in this colonial parody shows the sophisticated capabilities of these performers.

Walker brought further sophistication to the role when in scene five she confronts the Shambul Bolasso, a captain in the army, to ask for Rastus's (Williams) and Jasamine's (Jenkins) pardon for committing a petty crime. She politely requests, "After much persuasion by women folks [...] I ventured to come here to ask you, if you wouldn't be lenient and possibly to use your influence [...] to have them returned to their friends" (Shipp, "Abyssinia"). Miriam's articulate dialogue contrasts to the stereotypical dialectic more commonly employed during this period in African American drama. Furthermore, the dialogue is significant in revealing the influence of women in terms of Cooper's assertion of the power of black women. The diction and elocution echoes the idea of ladylike behavior in the New Negro

Figure 6. Aida Overton Walker, ca. 1910s (Schomburg Center for Research in Black Culture, NYPL, New York).

women's movement and also illustrates the significant role women can play in political matters at this time.

The photograph in Figure 5 showcases Aida Walker, Bert Williams, and Alexander Rogers and further supports Walker integrating propriety in her performance. When comparing the photograph with the script, one discovers that the photo is indeed a publicity shot and not a scene from the play. In the script, Miriam appears solely in Scene Five, and Miss Primly (Lottie Williams) accompanies her without Rastus (Bert Williams). The choice to include Walker in the photograph with Bert Williams and Alexander Rogers perhaps demonstrates the appeal and public attraction to the actress. The scene shows her leaning back in a moment of surprise or fear contrasting to the stable male dignitary, played by Rogers, standing beside her.[4] Williams pleads on one knee in his blackface mask, which indicates a low character status. In her Gibson Girl bouffant, she wears an Orientalist matronly dress with an apron that suggests domesticity. The hairstyle and beaded headband matches up with another image of Walker in the Schomburg Archives dated circa 1910s [see Figure 6]. Like many archival photos, this individual portrait lacks information such as location, photographer, purpose, but the connection to *Abyssinia* seems plausible. Her proper posture projects confidence, her chest exposes more skin, and her hair swooped up appears more natural than the Gibson Girl photograph. In both images, Walker embodies modest femininity in her Orientalist costumes in which she brings a sense of purity to the preconceived notions of primal, savage Africans.

The most exotic character for a black female performer to perform on a commercial stage in the 1910s is the seductress Salome during the craze known as "Salomania." One year prior to Salome's popularity, Strauss's opera introduced the character to the commercial stage on 22 January 1907, but it did not return for an encore performance the following night (Hamberlin 634). Initially, Americans felt uncomfortable with an opera that focused on incest, murder, and female sexuality on the mainstream stage.[5] However, over the next year Salome's dance seduced the public in various theatres and vaudeville houses that combined both high and low art. Bianca Forelich, the ballerina from the Metropolitan Opera production, joined the high and low in the Salome craze when she took the "Dance of the Seven Veils" to Lincoln square Theatre, a popular vaudeville house. The puritanical reaction of the Metropolitan Opera patrons propelled Salome's popularity as the quintessential rebel.

By 1908 at least twenty-four dancers performed Salome in New York City and among them were Gertrude Hoffman and Maud Allan, followed by Aida Walker in 1908–9.[6] The photographs of these actresses remained consistent in costume and pose [see Figures 7 and 8]: breastplates with circles of

Figure 7. Maud Allan as Salomé, 1908 (Dance Collection, Toronto).

Figure 8. Gertrude Hoffman as Salomé, 1908 (Jerome Robbins Dance Division, NYPL, New York).

jewels, chains of pearls and more jewels draped over the hips and breasts; an ankle-length transparent skirt revealing bare legs and feet.[7] Allan's and Hoffman's facial expressions depict ecstasy, and their sinuously posed figures expose their scantily dressed bodies. The connection between African Americans and Salome's promiscuity relates to the hegemonic beliefs that black women were innately oversexed creatures. In this historical moment then, there is a clear tension between Salome's immodest wardrobe and the mannerisms that New Negro woman personified in 1909. As David Krasner observes, Walker "challenged the accepted notion that only white women could perform the classics," but as a working actress-dancer during Salomania, a successful performance would advance her career and celebrity (Krasner 64). As one of her last roles on the commercial stage, her experience prepared her to take on this challenging role, and the established legitimacy of the Williams and Walker team allowed her the opportunity to perform a risqué character. Walker joined the Salome craze and attracted audiences to the next Williams and Walker show, *Bandanna Land.*

When the Williams and Walker team premiered, they faced a legacy of the hegemonic conception of the African Americans as the savage other. The white perception of the black body as primitive imposes superiority on African Americans and furthermore evolved into a fascination with the Negroes' supposedly innate rhythm. One black art enthusiast of the time period, Albert C. Barnes, reflected this attitude by proposing black art as legitimate and "sound" because it was created in a primitive context that a white man's education could never harness (Krasner 64). Essentially, white patrons of black art did not view primitivism as a negative quality, although their beliefs reveal racist attitudes. The reduction of black culture in this way resulted in "a double bind: relegated to the lowest rung of the evolutionary ladder, yet looked to as a source of visceral originality as well" (Krasner 59). The myths associated with the lascivious Negro woman and the visceral nature of Black culture attracted white audiences to Walker's performances. In the late nineteenth and early twentieth centuries, the idea of primitivism offered whites the opportunity to let go of their puritanical values through music, theatre and dance spectacles. For the African American artistic community, the skewed but popular ideas about black art afforded them an entry to mainstream culture where they depicted exaggerated representations and took advantage of paying white folks.

For black women, it was difficult to find performance opportunities that went beyond the limitations of stereotyping because black and white audiences expected to see the manifestation of the oversexed octoroon, which is also related to the notion of the savage other. Therefore, many of Aida's critics expressed disappointment regarding her interpretation of Salome. Expectations were undoubtedly higher because of performers such as Maud Allen and Gertrude Hoffman who titillated audiences. With a black performer, a supposed oversexed creature, audiences expected to be aroused. Conversely, New Negro women who wore their crisp white-laced shirts for Sunday church presumably opposed a black female dancer playing the role of an exotic seductress. Walker, however, did not fall into the primal or the pure dichotomy.

As Salome, Aida Walker confronted both the New Negro woman's expectations of propriety and white critics' anticipation of lasciviousness. She combined the philosophy of the New Negro women's movement and the exotic other to mixed reviews. Walker, the first commercially recognized black Salome, worked against public expectations to watch the lascivious mulatto stereotype on display. For example, a popular song, "I'm going to get myself a Black Salome" in 1908 includes the lyrics: "I'm going to get myself black Salome, / A hootchie-kootchie dancer from Dahomey, / All that she'll wear is a yard of lace / And some mosquito netting on her face" (Hamberlin 658). The song's lyrics allude to a black woman with minimal and transparent clothing from Dahomey, the name of the commercially successful Williams and Walker show. Hence, Aida directly challenges the lyrics of the role through her nuanced performance. Her performance choices include omitting the final kiss on the decapitated head of John the Baptist and dressing in suggestive (but not entirely revealing) clothing. However, she does not solely sanitize the role or redefine the black female body. Rather, she brings a sense of her own sensuality and the philosophy of the New Negro women's movement to promote racial progress and further her career.

In order to properly assess Walker's performance in her historical moment, a thorough analysis of iconographic evidence paired with performance reviews provides the keenest insight into Walker's representations of black female sexuality. David Krasner describes the Salome image [refer to Figure 2] as "light, airy and energetic. Her hands are expressive and her body appears to be fluid in motion [...]. Her costume was [...] a chemise that flowed—but it also covered much of her body, unlike that of other Salomes" (68). While all these attributes are true, one must take into account the nuances. Her three quarters stance with hands clasped and her posture and facial expression project dignity and respectability. Her hair is less refined than early images, which traditionally in portraiture suggests madness or, in this case, sexuality. Finally, in comparison to her contemporary Salomes, her costume is modest, but still suggestive, exposing her chest and her chemise contouring the shape of her body.[8] Furthermore, in this description Krasner suggests Walker sanitizes her sexuality. In performance while Walker certainly integrated the propriety of the New Negro woman, a *Vanity Fair* review complicates this understanding. The article describes her performance expressing "pantherine movements" and performing "all the languorous grace which is traditionally bound up in Oriental dancing" (69). Looking at further iconographic evidence in the archives reveals another dimension to Aida. This review recalls the seductive side of Aida reflected in the unknown portrait [refer to Figure 3] as opposed to preconceived notions about Aida's demure portrayal of the femme fatale.

The theories that surround Aida Walker and her intentions remain largely speculative due to the limitation of research with regard to African American theatre history, including lack of documentation, inaccurate or missing dates, and so forth. However, through access to photographic evidence in the archives and her article in *Colored Men and Women on the Stage*, respectively, we see her making distinct character choices and positioning the theatre as a place for racial progress. Moreover, the breadth of images provides an opportunity to historically situate her and examine the polarities she constantly negotiates from the primitive, the virtuous, and everything in between. Other areas of study to consider include Aida's early career and relationship with Sissieretta Jones, a more extensive analysis of portraits, Aida's drag performance of her ailing husband's role in *Bandanna Land*, and finally Bert Williams' parody of *Salome*, immediately following her performance.[9] A thorough examination of Walker's iconography is relevant today to further understand the complexity of the artist in the context of the Williams and Walker team as well as her short career as a solo performer. A myopic focus on one performance or photograph limits her legacy. As bell hooks points out, the same issues of black female sexuality still persist in the entertainment industry today when considering performers such as Tina Turner, Beyoncé, and Iman. The trajectory of Aida's career with Williams and Walker reveals a constant balancing of oppositions in a prejudiced industry. Other roles need consideration to prove that her negotiations of sexuality, purity, and exoticism in a white-dominated industry do not strictly fit into the primal versus pure dichotomy.

TUFTS UNIVERSITY

NOTES

1. For a more comprehensive review of Williams and Walker's commercialism and broad appeal, see David Krasner's essay "The Real Thing" in W. Fitzhugh Brundage's *Beyond Blackface: African Americans and the Creation of American Popular Culture, 1890–1930* (Chapel Hill: University of North Carolina Press, 2011).

2. The recipient, Minnie, is unknown.

3. In Newman's "The Brightest Star" he discusses the social protest messages embedded in Walker's songs including "I Want to be the Leading Lady" (1903), which appears to be an iteration of "I wants to be a actor lady."

4. Alexander Rogers was also a co-writer of *Abyssinia* along with Jesse A. Shipp.

5. Salome was performed at the World's Fair prior to 1907 in the form of belly dancing, or "the dance that women turn away from."

6. Walker premiered the Dance of the Seven Veils in *Bandanna Land* and continued to perform in solo productions after the closing of the production including a revival by William Hammerstein in 1912. For more detailed production history, refer to Richard Newman's "The Brightest Star."

7. The inspiration according to Hamberlin derives from the nineteenth century paintings by Gustave Moreau and other French exoticists as opposed to Middle Eastern dancers.

8. The well-known Aida Walker cartoon of Salome depicted the stereotype of the tribal, primitive savage.

9. In the scene following Aida's dance, Williams parodied the Dance of the Seven Veils, substituting John the Baptist's head with a watermelon.

WORKS CITED

Belcher, Fannin S. "The Negro Theater: A Glance Backward." *Phylon (1940–1956)* 11.1 (1950): 126–132.

Brooks, Daphne A. "Divas and Diasporic Consciousness: Song, Dance, and New Negro Womanhood in the Veil." *Bodies in Dissent: Spectacular Performances of Race and Freedom, 1850–1910.* Ed. Ken Wissoker. Durham: Duke University Press, 2006. 281–342.

Cooper, Anna Julia. "A Voice from the South." *The Voice of Anna Julia Cooper.* Eds. Charles Lemert and Esme Bhan. Lanham, MD: Rowman and Littlefield, 1998.

Dunbar, Paul Laurence, and Jesse A. Shipp. "In Dahomey." *Black Theatre USA: The Early Period 1847–1938.* Eds. James V. Hatch and Ted Shine. New York: Free Press, 1996. 64–83.

Gibson, Charles Dana. *The Gibson Book Volume II: A Collection of Published Works Artist Charles Dana Gibson 1867–1944.* New York: Charles Scribner's Sons and R.H. Russel, 1906.

Green, Jeffrey P. "'In Dahomey' in London 1903." *The Black Perspective in Music* 11.1 (1983): 22–40.

Hamberlin, Larry. "Visions of Salome: The Femme Fatale in American Popular Songs before 1920." *Journal of the American Musicological Society* 59.3 (2006): 631–696.

hooks, bell. "Selling Hot Pussy: Representations of Black Female Sexuality in the Cultural Marketplace." *Black Looks: Race and Representation.* Eds. Lawrence Grossberg, Cary Nelson, and Paula Treichler. Boston: South End Press, 1992. 61–77.

Krasner, David. "Exoticism, Dance and Racial Myths: Modern Dance and the Class Divide in the Choreography of Aida Overton Walker and Ethel Waters." *A Beautiful Pageant: African American Theatre, Drama, and Performance in the Harlem Renaissance, 1910–1927.* Eds. Harry J. Elam and David Krasner. New York: Palgrave Macmillan, 2002. 55–80.

_____. "Parody and Double Consciousness in the Language of Early Black Musical Theatre." *African American Review* 29.2 (1995): 317–323.

Newman, Richard. "'The Brightest Star': Aida Overton Walker in the Age of Ragtime and Cakewalk." *Prospects: An Annual of American Culture Studies* 18 (1993): 465–481.

Ndounou, Monica White. "Early Black Americans on Broadway." *The Cambridge Companion to African American Theatre.* Ed. Harvey Young. Cambridge: Cambridge University Press, 2013. 59–84.

Patterson, Martha A. "Margaret Murray Washington, Pauline Hopkings, and the New Negro Woman." *Beyond the Gibson Girl.* Ed. Laurie Matheson. Urbana: University of Illinois Press, 2005. 50–78.

_____. "Selling the American New Woman as Gibson Girl." *Beyond the Gibson Girl.* Ed. Laurie Matheson. Urbana: University of Illinois Press, 2005. 27–49.

Reff, Theodore. *Art in Context, Manet: Olympia.* New York: Viking Press, 1977.

Shipp, Jesse, and Alex Rogers. *Abyssinia.* Chicago: Alexander Street Press, 2012.

Sotiropoulos, Karen. "Morals, Manners, and Stage Life." *Staging Race: Black Performers in Turn of the Century America.* Eds. David Lobenstine and Joyce Seltzer. Cambridge: Harvard University Press, 2006. 163–196.

"Yesterday in Negro History." *Jet.* 11 October 1953.

Walker, Aida Overton. "Colored Men and Women on the Stage." *Colored American Magazine.* 1905. Web. 17 Apr 2013.

Mediating East-West Binarisms: A Study of Al-Hakim's Hybrid Plays

AHMED MOHAMMED GHALEB

Abstract

This essay aims at creating a space of mutual understanding between the East and the West by bringing the two polar opposites as close as possible to each other. I explore the plays of Tawfiq al-Hakim, Egypt's famous playwright. His plays are construed within "a liminal space" that is thoroughly "hybrid" or what Homi Bhabha terms "the third space." These hybrid texts are made of multiple writings drawn from Eastern (Arabic-Islamic) and Western cultures, entering into mutual relations of dialogue and understanding. The essay examines al-Hakim's hybrid plays at three different levels: Textual (or intertextual), stylistic, and linguistic. Textual hybridity is the appropriation of a text or theme from the Western tradition and reshaping it into the Arabic-Islamic context. Stylistic hybridity involves employment of an Arabic or Islamic text or theme in a Western form or style. Linguistic hybridity shows al-Hakim's talent for "third language": A combination of the standard Arabic and Egyptian dialects.

Tawfiq al-Hakim (1898–1987) is recognized as Egypt's best-known playwright. He has occupied a central place in the Arab literary scene since the 1930s. He is known primarily as the writer who introduced theatre to modern Arabic writing. He has produced some seventy plays, and one of Cairo's theatres has been named after him. Though he had gone to Paris in 1925 to complete a doctorate in law, al-Hakim chose instead to steep himself in Western culture. Imbibing a sense of the role and power of drama in its Western form, he determined to replicate it in the context of Arabic-Islamic society. The three years he spent in Paris as an impressionable young man in his twenties were crucial in forming his consciousness as a young artist. The encounter with Western culture led to a process of unending probing of the Self and the Other in his professional writings beginning in the 1930s. With his natural artistic talent and hybrid techniques to mix the Eastern (Arabic-Islamic) literary tradition and heritage with the Western dramatic tradition, al-Hakim gave to the Arabic theatre the foundations of respectability and seriousness it most needed.

Tawfiq al-Hakim's plays are characterized as hybrid texts: they are construed within "a liminal space" (Bhabha 5) or what Homi Bhabha terms the "Third Space" (54). This is a space located between East and West, Self and Other, past and present, as well as tradition and modernity (Amine 145). This essay attempts to explore and evaluate the hybridity of al-Hakim's plays and the ways in which al-Hakim interweaves the Eastern (Arabic-Islamic) tradition with the Western tradition(s). Aware of the fact that drama as a genre is new to the Arabic tradition, and also aware of its significance and impact on the lives of the masses as a tool of change and amelioration, al-Hakim has successfully manipulated such aspects of hybridity to bring about improvement in Egyptian drama specifically and Arabic drama generally. He dexterously welds Western forms with Arabic-Islamic issues in order to orient his views, criticism, and ideas. He also lends an invaluable hand to developing the much needed dramatic genre in Arabic literature.

Al-Hakim's hybridity can be examined at three different levels: textual (or intertextual),[1] stylistic, and linguistic. Textual hybridity is the appropriation of a text or theme from the Western tradition, reshaping it into the Arabic-Islamic context, such as *Al-Malik Odib* (*Oedipus the King*, 1949), *Praxa aw Mushkilat al-Hukm* (*Praxa or the Problem of the Government*, 1939) and *Pygmalion* (1942). Textual hybridity is also related to intertextuality and how a text can lead or refer to other texts. Like T.S. Eliot, al-Hakim thinks that the past and the present are inseparable. He adopts the literary works of past writers to reflect upon Arabic and Egyptian contemporary life. Stylistic hybridity involves the employment of an Arabic or Islamic text or theme in a Western form or style as in *Ahl al-Kahf* (*The Sleepers in the Cave*, 1933), *Ughniyyat al-Mawt* (*Song of Death*, 1956), *al-Sultan al-Ha'ir* (*The Sultan's Dilemma*, 1960), and *Bank al-Qalaq* (*Bank of Anxiety*, 1967). Linguistic hybridity reflects al-Hakim's artistic and linguistic talent in employing "third language": a combination of the standard Arabic and Egyptian dialects. *Al-Sqfqah* (*The Deal*, 1956) and *al-Wartah* (*The Dead Trouble*, 1966) are interesting examples of this "third language." This essay examines a play as an example of each category.

Textual (or Intertextual) Hybridity

Textual (or intertextual) hybridity is explored in *al-Malik Odib* (*Oedipus the King*, 1949) in which al-Hakim presents a new interpretation of the Western model. In the introduction to his version of *Oedipus Rex*, al-Hakim explains that he rewrote the Greek play in order to bring it into line with Islamic thinking and to explore his metaphysical theme of "truth" versus "reality" (42–52). The play follows Sophocles's *Oedipus Rex* except in these points: first, Oedipus has never been destined to kill his father and marry his mother; second, Tiresias is coincidentally responsible for the downfall of Oedipus; third, Oedipus asks his wife-mother to remain in wedlock with him even after he has known the terrible facts about his parenthood; fourth, there is no Sphinx. Tiresias made up the story of the Sphinx in order to frighten the Thebans. Oedipus killed a lion but he tells the Thebans that he killed the Sphinx.

According to al-Hakim, man is not predestined to suffer. That Oedipus should be punished for a crime he never planned to commit but was predetermined to commit seems inhuman and foreign to Islamic thinking (al-Shetaiwi 108). To humanize the struggle in the play, al-Hakim gets rid of the element of divine intervention (the Delphic oracle) in Oedipus's fate, and replaces it with the struggle between Oedipus and other human beings. Removing the "un-Islamic" element from the play does not, however, mean that Arab playwrights cannot stage plays that are incompatible with Islam. In fact, what al-Hakim means by bringing the Greek myth in line with Islamic thinking is that removal of divine intervention helps him better portray Oedipus, Creon, Tiresias, and the High Priest as human beings involved in political strife (108).

According to al-Hakim, Sophocles's play suggests that Oedipus is not to blame for his crimes. He has to struggle against a fate which had already predestined him to kill his father and marry his mother. However, al-Hakim wants to portray Oedipus as free and God as innocent of determining the course of Oedipus's life. That is according to Islamic philosophy: man is free and should be well aware of his actions. God does not trap man into committing a crime or a sin for His pleasure (108). Al-Hakim's Oedipus killed his father coincidently, and not as a result of a divine oracle. As a result, there is no struggle between Oedipus and the divine fate.

Moreover, al-Hakim's play seems to suggest that it is man who tends to hurt his fellow men for one reason or another. That is why in his play Tiresias is responsible for the tragedy of Oedipus. He exploits the Thebans' veneration for him to make them believe that he receives the oracle from God. Oedipus says: "Tiresias, this clever blind man told you—by himself and not by the revelation of God—to make that hero a king" (Act I).[2] He fabricates the story of the oracle in order to make Laius get rid of his son because he wants to finish off Laius's dynasty in Thebes. Therefore, he uses his power and prestige as a religious seer to inform Laius that the gods warned him against a forthcoming son who would kill him and marry Jocasta. To avert such disaster, Laius orders his shepherd to expose Oedipus on the mountains. In this way, al-Hakim's evil-minded Tiresias assumes the role of fate to meddle with the destiny of human beings.

The play depicts Oedipus as an ambitious man who wants to be a king by any means. Therefore, he collaborated with the evil-minded Tiresias. This is contradictory to the Greek myth which depicts Oedipus as a demigod who rescues the Thebans from the Sphinx. When Sophocles's play opens we see the Thebans imploring Oedipus to help them get rid of the plague. In al-Hakim's play Oedipus allows himself to be regarded as a hero for a deed he never actually did. In order to become a king and marry the widowed queen, he agrees to share Tiresias's deception of the Thebans.

Furthermore, in the Greek play Oedipus has never been in doubt of his greatness until he is aware of the truth. His pride appears when he insists on finding the killers of Laius and insults Tiresias. Al-Hakim strips Oedipus of all his majestic characteristics and presents him as a man torn between his love for his family and his search for truth (al-Shetaiwi 110). After seventeen years of ruling Thebes, Oedipus regrets that he lied to the Thebans and to his family about the story of the Sphinx. He feels pain whenever his children boast of his heroic fight with the Sphinx. He threatens Tiresias to reveal the truth to his people: "I am not a hero [...] and I did not kill the Sphinx; you believed it because of your naïve imagination [...] But I killed a lion" (Act I). Oedipus succumbs to Tiresias because he wants to keep his family happy.

The play suggests that Oedipus agreed to collaborate with Tiresias and live in deception despite his love for truth.[3] As a young man full of fire and ambition, his collaboration with Tiresias in order to achieve his personal ambition to become a king might once have been understandable. But why does he agree to continue living in deception for seventeen years? Though Oedipus is aware of his hypocrisy and deception to his people and family, he accepts his situation because he does not want to break the happiness of his family, If the truth is exposed that he is not a hero after all, his family will be greatly disappointed and may become resentful of his actions. Al-Hakim focuses on Oedipus as a family man who loves his wife and children in order to explain his behavior and to justify the ending of the play (al-Shetaiwi 111).

Some Arab critics note that the end of the play fails to comply with Islamic thinking. For instance, Hasan Muhsin argues that the ending of the play is incompatible with Islamic philosophy (181–185). He adds that the audience would treat Oedipus with disgust rather than sympathize with him. Al-

Hakim divests the Greek play of its mythological background but fails to make the ending acceptable to Islamic and Arabic tradition when he makes Oedipus insist on remaining in wedlock with his mother (185–190). After knowing that he is guilty of incest and patricide, Oedipus is supposed to break off his incestuous relationship with his mother or to harm himself as Sophocles's Oedipus does.

However, critics who claim that *al-Malik Odib* does not follow Islamic ideology and Arabic tradition see in the play a religious treatise, which is not the intention of the author (Al-Shetaiwi 111). When al-Hakim states that he wants to make the play agree with the Islamic thinking, he means that Oedipus should become a simple man, not a mythical hero as in the Greek play. Besides, Oedipus is free to choose and determine his fate. That man is free is the very essence of Islam. For example, Oedipus's insists on remaining married to his mother at the very end of the play. He tells his mother-wife: "I will stay with you and struggle against thunder [...] the twist of fate [...] and the curses of human beings" (Act III). Al-Hakim could have ended the play the way Sophocles did and saved himself the trouble of being misunderstood. But he ends the way he does intentionally because he sees in the Greek myth a conflict between "truth" and "reality." The "truth" of Oedipus is the fact that he killed his father and married his mother. The "reality" of Oedipus is living happily with his mother-wife and children (al-Shetaiwi 112).

The idea that truth may be destructive is manifested in Sophocles's play. Oedipus, who thinks of himself as a man of truth, realizes too late that he is the man being hunted. At first he refuses to accept this truth, and accuses Tiresias and Creon of conspiracy against him. As a proud king he never imagines that he could be a killer. Oedipus finds out that truth, if known, may become harmful. Al-Hakim also maintains the same theme. Al-Hakim's Oedipus says: "I have seen the truth [...] how ugly is the truth [...] it is a curse!" (Act II). As Starkey indicates, "al-Hakim seems to imply that looking for the truth is not only a waste of time but is actually positively dangerous" ("Philosophical" 144). To accept "truth," al-Hakim's Oedipus has to destroy "reality," his happiness, and his family (Al-Shetaiwi 114).

By divesting the Greek myth of divine intervention, the Sphinx, and the superhuman nature of Oedipus, al-Hakim re-creates an Arabic-Islamic play (115). He depicts a man torn between "truth" and "reality": the truth that he did not kill the Sphinx because it never existed, and the reality that he does not want to destroy the ideals of his family; the truth that he has coincidently killed his father and married his mother, and the reality that he is having a happy marriage. The truth that he should break the wedlock of incest and follow the dictates of "reasonable thinking," and the reality that he can exercise free will by remaining married to his mother. By revealing the tension between

Oedipus's attempt to maintain a happy family and his implacable pursuit of truth, al-Hakim raises a fundamental question: why should one pursue truth if it can be so destructive? Is it worth pursuing truth at any cost? While departing from the purpose and techniques of the original play, al-Hakim has managed to hybridize the play to suit the Arabic, Islamic milieu in his own way, stressing man's freedom of choice and the value of truth in relation to reality.

By writing intertextual hybrid plays such as *al-Malik Odib*, al-Hakim establishes "counter-narratives" and "counter contexts" which refute "the misguided belief that colonised people do/did not have a history [or drama] of their own" (Gilbert and Tompkins 110). In their *Post-colonial Drama: Theory, Practice, Politics*, Gilbert and Tompkins argue,

> Many plays [of colonized people] stage aspects of the pre-contact past in order to re-establish traditions, to lay claim to a heritage or territory, and to recuperate various forms of cultural expression [...] By establishing counter-narratives and counter contexts which refute, or at least decentre, orthodox versions of history, marginalised cultures insist on a more equitable and representative starting point from which to negotiate a post-colonial identity [111].

Stylistic Hybridity

Stylistic hybridity involves the employment of an Arabic or Islamic text or theme in a Western form or style. Though the plots of many of his plays are derived from Eastern culture (Arabic or Islamic), al-Hakim employs several Western styles and techniques ranging from naturalistic and realistic, to the romantic, the symbolic, and the surrealistic. The Shavian concept of a utilitarian drama of socially relevant ideas applies to many of his plays. Some of these plays even assume the Shavian formula of exposition, problem, and discussion. This is evident in the elaborate discussions of conflicts between man and time in *The Sleepers in the Cave*, the abuse of power in *The Sultan's Dilemma*, and the tradition of family or tribal revenge in *Song of Death*.

Ughniyyat al-Mawt (*Song of Death*, 1960) is a one-act tragedy, which dramatizes a serious Egyptian and Arabic issue: the perpetuation of blood revenge. This endless cycle of revenge controls and threatens the lives of the peasants in the rural areas of Upper Egypt. The play's setting is therefore representative of a southern village where poverty and ignorance prevail. The villagers in these areas are often blindly driven by what Andrew Parkin describes as "ancient codes of honour and revenge" (qtd in A. Said 76). The play calls for repudiating such traditional habits in favor of healthier modern concepts (76). To stress this sharp contrast between tradition and modernity, al-Hakim sets the village and the villagers against Cairo and its "educated" inhabitants.

He therefore constructs his play on a repeated pattern of dualities, which reinforce the conflict between tradition and modernity. All dramatic elements of the play, its structure, theme, character portrayal and setting, emphasize this conflict (76).

The play's action takes place in an unidentified village in southern Egypt. Alwan, the only son of a murdered man in a village in Upper Egypt, is secretly taken to Cairo by the widow, Asakir. She plans to have him apprenticed to a butcher so that he can remain there until he is old enough to come back quietly to the village to avenge his father's death, making full use of the skill he will have learnt in handling a knife. In the meantime, in order to mislead her enemies, she makes up the story that he has died in an accident in his childhood. But in Cairo the youth gets the chance of education at the theological University of Al-Azhar. As a result, he is filled with a passionate desire to improve the appalling conditions of life in his native village. When he returns to the village, his mother anxiously expects him to kill his father's murderer at once. But to her bewilderment, he talks to her instead about his program of reform and his intention to bring light and life into the village. He even suggests that the business of punishing the murderer had better be left in the hands of the police. She is horrified to hear him utter such words, and in shame and indignation disowns and curses him and even orders him to clear out of her home. When communication between them proves impossible, Alwan, now utterly defeated yet still retaining his dignified calm character, decides to take the next train back to Cairo. The mother has managed to get her nephew, Sumeida, to kill him before he boards the train in order to "wipe out" the shame and dishonor his continued life would otherwise bring to the family.

This play is a well-constructed, one-act naturalistic play. It is divided into four French scenes grouped in pairs, each dealing with different tensions (A. Said 77–78). The first tension arises in the opening moments and climaxes at the end of the second scene. The second tension arises by the middle of the third scene and snaps at the final moment of the play. Both tensions are connected, however, with the play's issue of revenge. Al-Hakim employs the naturalistic fourth wall; action is confined to a small room in the house of the play's heroine, Asakir. The opening scene between Asakir and her sister-in-law, Mabrouka, serves as exposition, providing background for the play's theme and characterization. Conforming to the play's pattern of dualities, al-Hakim restricts his cast to four, with only two characters in each scene. The play's four characters are: the heroine, Asakir, her son, Alwan, a theology student at Al-Azhar University, his aunt, Mabrouka, and her son, Sumeida, Alwan's cousin.

The play's climactic tension is initiated by Asakir and Mabrouka training their ears to listen for "significant" sounds. The play opens and closes with the sound of the train whistle, followed by Sumeida's singing. The first song is heard in the first scene, whereas the second is anxiously awaited for nearly the whole of the last scene. In fact, Asakir's psychological struggle in the fourth scene is positioned in contrast with the first scene (A. Said 78–79). While the first scene indicates the great hopes she places in Alwan's arrival, the fourth scene emphasizes her growing fears mixed with a faint hope for her son's escape. But whereas her hopes are renewed at the end of the first scene, her hopes are dashed when she hears Sumeida's song announcing his death. According to Badawi, this parallelism gives the play a neat circular shape, and the contrast between beginning and end has a powerful effect (55). Moreover, Sumeida's singing the same song helps to unify the play. The train's whistle heard from the station has the same connotations of Sumeida's song off-stage. Thus, al-Hakim employs off-stage sounds to symbolize states of life and death. Sounds off-stage in the first scene indicate the arrival of Alwan from Cairo and hence the revival of Asakir's hopes for a new life. The same sound in the last scene implies the death of her son as well as of her hopes: Asakir's last "fainted suppressed cry" then, contrasts sharply with her cry of joy on hearing the song in the first scene: "Today I'll rend the garment of shame and put on the robes of self respect" (81). In the final scene, Asakir appears as both victim and victimizer. It is the only scene in which she is endowed with a sympathetic humane touch, and her struggle becomes the main emphasis.

The play's settings are also indicative of the play's duality (A. Said 78–79). The fourth wall principle gives off-stage domains important roles in the development of the play's tensions. The room in Asakir's house in which all action takes place is symbolic of the hardness of the world of the village. It is in this room that decisions and plans to carry out murders are made. Cairo, on the other hand, is the opposite extreme. It stands for enlightenment reinforced by the education of its institutions, represented in the play by Al-Azhar University. This obvious contrast between the village and Cairo is implied in Mabrouka's statement: "How far our village is from Cairo! Can the voice of blood reach to the capital?" (80) The train station in itself has a dual nature: in the first scene it symbolizes birth and renewal of hope, while in the final scene it signifies death and the end of that hope.

Furthermore, Al-Hakim employs some other elements such as imagery, tragic irony, and premonition that play a major role in maintaining the unity of the play. Clothing images occur frequently, at Alwan's arrival Asakir cries jubilantly: "Has he come? Has Alwan come? Today I'll rend the garment of shame and put on the robes of self-respect" (81). After his departure she says to Sumeida, "Would that he were dead—we could have lived with our excuse and we would not have had to clothe ourselves in shame" (89). Alwan's religious dress is a mark of distinction distinguishing him from the rest of the peasants, stressing his different scheme of values. When she visited him in Cairo, Asakir found Alwan looking awe-inspiring in his religious garment. At one point she suspects Mabrouka of jealousy because, unlike Alwan, her son Sumeida wears the clothes of a common peasant. Looking at his own dress, Alwan asks his mother, "Am I to do this deed in these clothes?" She replies, "Take off those clothes of yours, I have an aba[4] of your father's. I've kept it for you" (85). The two women are dressed in black to emphasize their state of mourning. Instances of premonition, irony and tragic irony, sometimes arising from characters talking at cross-purposes, abound in the play. Mabrouka finds a bad omen in the fact that as a boy Alwan ran away from the butcher's shop. Alwan has come back to the village to bring life into it but ends up meeting his death. The knife with which her husband was murdered and which Asakir has jealously guarded is in fact used in the killing of her son. When asked by Mabrouka where Alwan has gone, after his departure Asakir says with grim irony: "Gone to whence he came" (92). This means he has gone back to the dust from which he came, while Mabrouka innocently understands that he has gone back to Cairo (A. Said 78–79).

In *Song of Death*, al-Hakim deliberately avoids using the humor characteristic of most of his plays in order to stress the gravity of the issue. Badawi supports this view and hints that using humor would have been unsuitable to "the intensity and the height of emotional pitch which characterise it from beginning to end" (56). The play's tragic tone and imagery are therefore intended to make the viewer confront the seriousness of the issue without relief. The play's structure and mood, Badawi argues, give it some affinity to the plays of Synge and Lorca. Al-Hakim's play, he indicates, has

> [...] the tragic intensity of J. M. Synge's *Riders to the Sea*, with which it has other features in common, such as its timelessness, its primitive atmosphere, its force of elemental passion and its depiction of the utter powerlessness of the individual in relation to a deeply entrenched age-old way of life—features which are reminiscent of the work of Lorca [53].

Perhaps the most striking feature of *Song of Death* is the masterly economy with which it is written. Every detail is functional (Badawi 56). Even the calf and the kid are not there just to create the appropriate Egyptian village atmosphere: Asakir has kept them in order to slaughter them when the time comes for the proper funeral rites for her dead husband to be performed, after his murder has been avenged. The dialogues are rich in references to various aspects of Egyptian village life, which not only strengthen the impression of a village, but also constitute a means of further characterization, giving more substance to the peasant characters and rendering them more vivid and convincing. In the first couple pages we are either shown or told about the peasant hut, the women squatting on the floor next to their animals, the water-wheel well where Alwan was allegedly drowned as a child, the village market where gossip and rumors are heard, the milking of shriveled-up cows, the bags in which ground corn is carried, farm dogs, shepherds, and owls in ruined buildings. In general, *Song of Death* is a highly esteemed hybrid play. In his article "Tawfiq al-Hakim: Leading Playwright of the Arab World," Paul Starkey claims that it is "the most successful" of the plays of the *Theatre of Society* (qtd in A. Said 87).

Linguistic Hybridity

By 1900 and throughout the first two decades of the twentieth century, Classical Arabic, or "fusha," was the standard medium of theatrical expression. Although the twenties and the thirties teemed with theatrical activities conducted in the vernacular, especially in melodrama, serious romantic dramas (mostly translations and adaptations) were mainly in Classical Arabic. The vernacular sentimental satires of Najib al-Rihani, Awad argues, were the most influential on the new dramatists (including Tawfiq al-Hakim) in the period before and after the 1952 revolution. Al-Rihani made use of the vernacular "in comedy and in tragi-comedy a living reality at least in Egypt, if not in the Arab world" (Awad 184).

However, when al-Hakim first used the vernacular in his celebrated novel *Awdat al-Ruh* (*The Return of the Spirit*, 1933) and in some of his plays such as *Kull Shay' fi Mahallih* (*Not a Thing Out of Place*, 1966), he was met with harsh criticism. Prominent Arab writer Taha Hussein led the critical charge against al-Hakim, condemning him as "a corruptor of the sacred tongue" (qtd in S. Said 14). These attacks caused al-Hakim to avoid the vernacular for a while and to use instead what W. M. Hutchins called a "hybrid language," a middle language between the classical and the vernacular. Hutchins comments on al-Hakim's linguistic hybridity:

> Al-Hakim has not only written works of diverse inspiration with diverse subjects but has written in different types of Arabic as well. He has written in literary Arabic which is not often spoken and in urban and rural spoken dialect which is not often written. In Incrimination, he has experimented with a language hybrid which he hopes will eventually bridge the gap between the different levels of Arabic [qtd in A. Said 29].

This compromise earned al-Hakim a membership in the Arabic Academy of Languages.

In the play *al-Safqah* (*The Deal*, 1959) with its themes of land ownership and the exploitation of the poor peasant farmers, al-Hakim couches the dialogue in something he termed "a third language," one that could be read as a text in the standard written language of literature, but that could also be performed onstage in a way which, while not exactly the idiom of Egyptian Arabic, was certainly comprehensible to a larger population than the literate elite of the city. The use of such "hybrid language" enabled al-Hakim to solve the diglottic problem in the field of drama (Somekh 74). In his postscript to the play, al-Hakim indicates that the type of language he devised is comprehensible both in terms of standard or classical and of spoken Arabic (al-Safqah 159–162). By producing such a text, the playwright is released from the dilemma over which of the two linguistic levels to use in his dialogue.

This device makes it possible to write plays which, when read in print, can be understood in accordance with the norms of Classical Arabic, but when staged, is automatically adaptable to the level of the local dialect. For example, the following written sentence can operate on two linguistic levels: اسمحوا لي بكلمة صغيرة can be read in standard terms as *Ismahu li bikalimatin saghiratin* [Allow me to say something]; it can also be realized in terms of Egyptian [Cairene] Arabic as *Ismahuli bikilma sughayyara* [Allow me to say something] (al-Safqah 41). Al-Hakim's "new hybrid language," then, is not only an experiment at producing a standard text which is reminiscent of the spoken idiom. It is also an attempt to create a bivalent text which exploits the inherent ambiguity of non-voweled Arabic script (Somekh 75). In fact, in his postscript to al-Safqah al-Hakim did not use the term "third language," but that term gradually came to denote the textual type inaugurated in al-Safqah.[5]

Al-Hakim also attempted to write bivalent plays in *al-Wartah* (*The Dead Trouble*, 1966) and *Bank al-Qalaq* (*Bank of Anxiety*, 1967). This time, however, he employed a number of forms and functionals which are exclusively dialectal. For instance, in *Bank of Anxiety* al-Hakim uses Egyptian dialectal phrases such as "ليه يا بني ليه"[6] (35), "لكن ايه"[7] (191), and "البوليس تاني؟"[8] (237). Similarly, in *al-Wartah* we find Egyptian forms such as *illi* [who or which] and *di* [this]. In the postscript to *al-Wartah* he contends that using such functionals is not really violating the norms of Classical Arabic because *illi*, for instance, is nothing but a short form of *alladhi* [the standard form of "who or which"] (al-Hakim, *al-Wartah* 189–199). The same applies in al-Hakim's view of words such as *aywa* [yes] and *ma'rafshi* [I don't know]. Roger Allen describes al-Hakim's innovation as a qualified success:

> Al-Hakim's search for a middle ground in this and other plays [...] did not satisfy the proponents of either side in the continuing dispute over the appropriate language for Arabic drama, but its acknowledgement of the existence of a myriad different levels of language between the literary and colloquial poles was at the very least a successful attempt at compromise [339].

Nevertheless, al-Hakim himself seems to have abandoned the idea of producing plays with bivalent texts. Most of the plays he wrote in the 1960s and 1970s are either in simplified standard Arabic or in straightforward spoken Arabic (Somekh 75).

Evaluating al-Hakim's Hybridity

Many plots and themes of al-Hakim's plays are derived from Greek or Eastern myths. Al-Hakim seems to suggest that texts of the past "can be appropriated, translated, rehistoricized and read anew" (Bhabha 55). For al-Hakim, past and present are inseparable; he employs the wisdom of the past in order to reflect upon the present life.[9] In harmony with the view proposed later by Homi Bhabha, al-Hakim seems to suggest that the author should not only "recall" the past, but rather "renew" it by "refiguring it as contingent 'in-between' space, that innovates and interrupts the performance of the present" (10). What makes al-Hakim distinct from other Arab dramatists and writers is that for him the past is not "'nostalgia' but a 'continuum' that links to the present and becomes a part of the necessity of living" (10).

Al-Hakim's hybrid plays indicate his power of creativity and innovation which "open up equal spaces of mixing that neither assimilate everything into one global pot, nor deny the right of special recognition to indigenous people and tradition"(Kuortti and Nyman 68). Moreover, al-Hakim's hybridity entails "a gentle modification of his perceptual apparatus to accommodate foreign concepts; and as a result the reader arrives at a new way of perceiving which is necessarily different from, yet accepting of, both cultures s/he encounters or inhabits"(68). In fact, al-Hakim's hybridity seems to be a result of his ceaseless experimentation[10] with the genre of drama in Arabic and with the linguistic capacities of Arabic in order to create a national and Arabic drama. As a dramatist, al-Hakim experimented with all possible forms and styles while projecting the various social and political issues of the day. In his book *al-Masrah al-Munuwwa* (Theatre of Variety), al-Hakim explains the reasons for his experimentation with various dramatic themes and techniques. He argues that his efforts were motivated by his awareness of the "frightful gap" that separates Arabic literature from the world's literature due to the lack of an Arabic dramatic heritage (303). He states,

> For this reason [...] I have looked to every age. I have created plays that draw inspiration from the Greek theatre [...] plays inspired by the Quran [...] [others] inspired by *The Thousand and One Nights* [...] plays inspired by our contemporary society [...] and then plays inspired by different sensations and settings [...] the voyage has toured different styles [...] has also been through assorted varieties [...]. I have tried to take in thirty years a trip on which the dramatic literature of other languages has spent about in two thousand years [303–304].

In this sense al-Hakim's experimental hybridity seems to be aesthetic [intentional] in Bakhtinian terms, which is described as "shock, change, challenge, revitalize or disrupt through deliberate intended fusions" and in so doing "create an ironic double consciousness" (qtd in Kuortti and Nyman 6–7). Al-Hakim's hybridity shows how elements from diverse, seemingly contradictory cultures can, without losing their uniqueness, combine to form a third space of identity (222).

More importantly, al-Hakim's hybrid plays which are constructed in the "liminal" and "third space" not only undermine the polarizations of East and West and Self and Other, but also attempt to bring these polar opposites as close as possible to each other. Like Edward Said and Homi Bhabha, al-Hakim seems to suggest that "cultures are not really pure but rather mixed and hybrid. They are not discrete phenomena, but being always in contact with one another" (E. Said 15). Moreover, they "actually assume more foreign elements, alterities, differences, than they consciously exclude" (15). In addition, al-Hakim's hybrid plays create new cultural meaning by means of rearticulating and translating elements that are neither Eastern [Arabic-Islamic] nor Western, "but something else besides which contest the terms and territories of both" (Bhabha 41). Al-Hakim is the dramatic genius among Arab writers who has benefited most from the potentialities of Western theatre as well as Eastern (Arabic-Islamic) tradition and heritage, producing a new form of dramatic writing in the process.

Al-Hakim's hybridity is an attempt to bridge the gulf between East and West, Self and Other, past and present, and tradition and modernity. The hybridized nature of his plays reflects dialogic exchange that negotiates the contact zone and constructs bridges across the gulf.

Unlike colonial texts that often focus on binary dynamics of resistance or absorption, al-Hakim's plays indicate a dialogic nexus of exchange between polarities and offer a multicultural vision. These plays weave together Eastern (Arabic-Islamic) tradition and Western literary tradition into transcultural texts. They reflect "dialogic strategies against colonial dialectics, and craft a hybrid borderland of resistance and freedom where possible worlds and multiple voices co-exist" (139).

UNIVERSITY OF IBB, YEMEN

NOTES

1. For more information on "intertextual" or "intertextuality" see Graham Allen's *Intertextuality*, 11–35.
2. Unless otherwise noted, all translations are my own.
3. In fact, he left Corinth in search of his identity.
4. Aba, in Arabic, is a cloak.

5. The term "third language" is used in the postscript to al-Hakim's play *al-Ta'am li–Kul Fam* (Food for Everyone, 1963), although the author seems to refer in that case to the simplified type of standard rather than to the strictly bivalent type.

6. Pronounced "laih ya bni laih" and literally translated as "Why, son? Why?"

7. Pronounced "lakin aih" and literally translated as "But what?"

8. Pronounced "el-bolees? tani?" and literally translated as "The police? Again?"

9. Cf. T. S. Eliot's celebrated essay "Tradition and the Individual Talent" 260–268.

10. Having written over seventy plays, al-Hakim has contributed a significant body of plays to modern Arabic drama. He experimented with different kinds of forms and themes. His major plays are classified chronologically and thematically into different categories: plays of his early experimentation with drama, theatre of variety that deals with comedy of manners and themes from society, theatre of the mind or intellectual theatre which deals with abstract ideas, theatre of society that deals with plays on social and political issues, plays dealing with issues related to the 1952 Revolution in Egypt and theatre of the absurd.

WORKS CITED

Al-Hakim, Twafiq. *Al-Malik Odib [Oedipus the King]*. Cairo: Maktabat Misr, 1949.

_____. *Al-Masrah al-Munuwwa [Theater of Variety]*. Cairo: Maktabat al-Adab, 1956.

_____. *Al-Safqa [The Deal]*. Cairo: Maktabat al-Adab, 1956.

_____. *Bank al-Qalaq [Bank of Anxiety]*. Cairo: Dar Misr Letteba'ah, 1967.

_____. *Song of Death. Fate of a Cockroach. Four Plays of Freedom*. Trans. Denys Johnson-Davies. London: Heinemann, 1973.

Allen, Graham. *Intertextuality*. London: Routledge, 2000.

Allen, Roger. *The Arabic Literary Heritage*. Cambridge: Cambridge University Press, 1998.

Al-Shetaiwi, Mahmoud F. "The Impact of Western Drama Upon Modern Egyptian Drama." Ph.D. Diss. University of Illions, 1983.

Amine, Khalid. "Theatre in the Arab World: A Difficult Birth." *Theater Research International* 31.2 (2006): 145–162.

Awad, Louis. "The Problems of the Egyptian Theatre." *Studies in Modern Arabic Literature*. Ed. R. C. Ostle. Warminster: Aris & Phillips, 1975. 179–193.

Badawi, M. M. *Modern Arabic Drama in Egypt*. Cambridge: Cambridge University Press, 1987.

Bhabha, H. K. *The Location of Culture*. London: Routledge, 1994.

Eliot, T. S. "Tradition and the Individual Talent." *Toward the Open Field: Poets on Art of Poetry 1800–1950*. Ed. Melissa Kwasny. Middletown: Wesleyan University Press, 2004. 260–268.

Gilbert, Helen, and Joanne Tompkins. *Post-Colonial Drama: Theory, Practice, Politics*. London: Routledge, 1996.

Kuortti, Joel, and Jopi Nyman. *Reconstructing Hybridities. Post-Colonial Studies in Transition*. Amsterdam: Rodopi, 2007.

Muhsin, Hasan. *al-Mu'athirat al-Gharbiyah fi al-Masrah al-Misri al-Hadith [The Western Influences upon Modern Egyptian Theater]*. Cairo: Dar al-Nahda al-Arabiyah, 1969.

Said, Aleya Salam. "Analysis of Form and Style in the Plays of Tawfiq al-Hakim." Ph.D. Diss. University of Georgia, 1990.

Said, Edward. *Culture and Imperialism*. New York: Knopf, 1994.

Somekh, S. "The Concept of 'Third Language' and Its Impact on Modern Arabic Poetry."
    Journal of Arabic Literature 12.1 (1981): 74–86.
Starkey, Paul. "Philosophical Themes in Tawfiq al-Hakim's Drama." *Journal of Arabic
    Literature* 8 (1977): 136–152.
_____. "Tawfiq Al-Hakim (1898–1987): Leading Playwright of the Arab World." *Theater
    Three: A Journal of Theater and Drama of the Arab World* 6 (1989): 21–30.

Fragments Shored: Some Remarks on T. S. Eliot's Drama and the Uses of Hugh Grant's Vacancy

DOUG PHILLIPS

Abstract

"The central insight of modern art," observes Alain de Botton, is that "by distorting what we take to be the real appearance of something [...] we can often get closest to its true reality." What truth there is, in other words, must be told aslant. Likewise, says Žižek (and Shakespeare before him), we must look awry in order to see what's really there. In my attempt to get at what's "really there"—or rather, what else is there—in T. S. Eliot's drama and dramatic theory, I proceed in this essay by way of distortion and looking awry, never more so, I suppose, than when I'm looking at Hugh Grant. Through the use of fragmentation, collage, quotation, allusion, pastiche, asides, free-association, footnotes, sideway-glances, potshards, and lots of broken glass, I hope to get a better look at what Eliot, in his 1951 essay Poetry and Drama, calls the "fringe of indefinite extent," the realm "beyond the nameable, classifiable emotions and motives of our conscious life" which, he claims, verse drama can most adequately detect.

"I am quite content to go down to posterity as a scissors and paste man for that seems to me a harsh but not unjust description."

—James Joyce, *Selected Letters*

1. I live with Strindberg.

2. If I told you my own story you would weep, so I won't, and will defer instead to T. S. Eliot, but not without first hurting you with Hugh Grant, whom we'll get to in a moment when I'm finished with Wilde.

3. An expert in all things conjugal but his own wife, Oscar Wilde said of marriage, and its one charm, "that it makes a life of deception absolutely necessary for both parties" (*Picture* 5). On one level, this may be read as a free pass for a fling, a happy reprieve from the dishwater and the measured drapes of marital bliss. On a deeper level, it has nothing at all to do with adultery and everything to do with the indispensable *fantasies* that uphold a marriage, without which a relationship risks a lasting silence of the Beckettian kind, where all that is escapes language. Strindberg ripens the point in his play *The Ghost Sonata*, informing us that the silence of the long-married is what results when all deception has died out:

> Student: Tell me—why do your parents sit so silently in there, never saying a word?
> Daughter: They have nothing to say to each other, for neither will believe what the other says. My father once said: "What is the point of our talking? We cannot deceive each other" [1964: 469].

With no more lies to tell, the couple in question may still take their meals together, but they will be as tight-lipped as the time before, entombed and emptied of words—the unwelcomed effect of transparency.

4. "This love is silent," writes T. S. Eliot in his 1958 and last play, *The Elder Statesman*. It's a "love that's lived in / But not looked at" (88).

5. If a finer point is called for here, and I suspect that it is, then let's turn our attention briefly to Hugh Grant. The film is *Notting Hill* and the scene concerns a divorce, his own. Asked why his marriage failed, Grant's character (William Thacker) replies: "She saw through me." The sense here is not that he's a fraud, whose foul rag and bone shop of the heart[1] his wife happened upon and was revolted by; rather, *who he is*, is quite literally a *zero*. A vacancy. Constitutive of our subjectivity, says Lacan, is not a *thing*, but a *void*, for which there is no language to encapsulate or render. This he calls the capital-R *Real*.[2] In other words, the self is sort of like Oakland: there is no *there* there.[3]

6. In his 1935 play *Murder in the Cathedral*, T. S. Eliot observes, "Man's life is a cheat and a disappointment" (41). He adds:

> All things are *unreal*,
> *Unreal* or disappointing [...]
> All things become less *real*, man passes
> From unreality to unreality [...]
> Passing from deception to deception [...] [italics mine, 41].

Later in the play Eliot famously states: "Human kind cannot bear very much reality" (69). Is Eliot's *reality*, however, the same as Lacan's *Real*? Is he, like Lacan (and like Grant's character's ex-wife), referring to the void—to the

Real—behind the mask, behind the *unreal*? Might we say that "human kind cannot bear very much *Real*" and mean the same thing?

7. Try as we might (and as others might) to get hold of who we are and what we are about and why we want what it is we *think* that we want, there is a dimension to our being—Lacan's notion of the *Real*—that eludes our grasp, that cannot be named or circumscribed; and what cannot be named is often terrifyingly *Real*.[4] To paraphrase Wilde, Caliban's rage at seeing himself in a mirror is more than a hatred for realism. It is a hatred for the Lacanian *Real*, which, like Philip Larkin's high windows, "shows nothing, and is nowhere, and is endless."[5] And so we elect—on most days, anyway—for the *unreal* instead.

8. "What is the *reality* of experience between two *unreal* people?" (italics mine, 47), asks Peter in Eliot's 1949 play *The Cocktail Party*.

9. Of course I don't live with the *real* Strindberg. Rather, I live with a Strindberg *enthusiast*.

10. What would be the consequences, I wonder, of a love both *lived in* and *looked at*? I mean *really* looked at? Would we, like the listener in Wallace Stevens's poem—and like the ex-wife in *Notting Hill*—behold the "nothing that is not there, and the nothing that is"?[6] In which case, would this love be silent still? In his 1934 play *The Rock*, Eliot writes of the "endless cycle of idea and action" which "Brings knowledge of motion, but not of stillness; / Knowledge of speech, but not of silence" (96).

11. In relation to our study of Flaubert's *Madame Bovary*, a professor of mine—the eminent John Dowell[7]—explained in brief the self-deception and disillusionment inherent to every wedding and its aftermath. "All marriage ceremonies conclude the same way," the old codger told the class. "The groom walks down the aisle believing she will *never* change; the bride walks down the aisle believing he *will* change. And they are both wrong." After the son-of-a-bitch had had his say, we were all, I confess, less dewy-eyed. The belief at work in Professor Dowell's anecdote[8] refers precisely to those *fantasies* that undergird a marriage, the *unreal* of Eliot's aforementioned *Cathedral*. However, what Dowell didn't mention, and what Eliot seems to neglect, is that these fantasies serve as a kind of prophylactic against what Beckett calls the *mess*,[9] the amorphous and *unnamable Real*, the void around which we place our rings, and over which we exchange our vows. If as Beckett says "we cannot know and we cannot be known" (*Proust* 49), then we fill this void with fantasies about ourselves and others—with what Ibsen in *The Wild Duck* calls the "vital lie" (203). In lieu of such a necessary lie, suggest Ibsen and Beckett and Strindberg, there must be a necessary silence.

12. To hear Larkin tell it,

> Talking in bed ought to be easiest [...]
> An emblem of two people being honest.
> Yet more and more time passes silently [...].[10]

13. Of his dreamy photographs and squeegee-scraped paintings, the artist Gerhard Richter, borrowing from John Cage, said: "I have nothing to say and am saying it" (qtd in Storr 36). Richter's art—like Beckett's work, like Larkin's poem, like Eliot's love—envisions the *Real* in its silence.

14. If, as Lacan says, the self is a void, then the way in which we fill that void—the story we tell ourselves in order to fashion a "self"—is through deception. For Wilde, this is never truer than in matters of romantic love: "When one is in love, one always begins by deceiving one's self, and one always ends by deceiving others. That is what the world calls a romance" (1998: 58–9). Whatever sense we have of a "self" is only and always a *mask*, behind which is the always unknowable *Real*. Is it any wonder then Prufrock can't bring himself to *presume*? Strangers all, we must pretend otherwise, which makes our everyday reality *unreal*.

15. *A cheat and a disappointment.*

16. "Man is least himself when he talks in his own person. Give him a mask, and he will tell you the truth," said Wilde (*Critic* 118).

17. "The first time I met you I thought you were a bit blank," a woman tells Will Freeman (Hugh Grant) in the film *About a Boy*. "I am a blank," replies Will. "I'm really nothing."

18. In what is perhaps his best known essay, "Tradition and the Individual Talent," Eliot prescribes the *extinguishing of personality*; and in his equally well known *Love Song*, the speaker of that poem, Prufrock, is a bundle of unrealized desires, who flits between every tense but the present, while steeling himself to partake in the grand charade by which, he says, "we prepare to meet the faces that we meet." Count him then among the *human kind* who, says Eliot, cannot bear too much reality. Or is that *really* the case after all? According to Žižek, "the emotions I perform through the mask (the false persona) that I adopt can in a strange way be more authentic and truthful than what I assume that I feel in myself" (32). In other words, the role I play as boss at work or as husband in my marriage[11] or as "Dragon-Slayer" online[12] may be the obverse of a mask after all. It may be me at my most *authentic*—a glimpse of the terrifying *Real*, in fact—which my so-called real (i.e., *unreal*) self at home or among friends cannot possibly bear.

19. The Strindberg enthusiast with whom I live sometimes quotes Strindberg *accusingly*: "In silence you can't hide anything […] as you can in words" (1983: 286).

20. In a piece called "The Marriage Paradox," Clancy Martin writes, "The benevolent power of self-deception is, in fact, what makes long, happy marriages—and all successful relationships—possible." He then asks: "Do we really want to know the *truth* about our lovers? We don't even know that about ourselves—it's simply too elusive, too protean, too complex—and we don't

want to know it, we don't need to know it" (Martin). The truth to which Martin refers is another way of talking about the Lacanian *Real*. By definition it's what *escapes* definition: it's "too elusive, too protean, too complex." And so we don't want to know because it's simply too much to bear, though Lacan urges we *should*. And for good reason. To encounter the *Real* is one such way—perhaps the *only* way—of figuring out what we really want, what we really *desire*.

21. "There are moments," writes Wilde in his play *Lady Windermere's Fan*, "when one has to choose between living one's own life, fully, entirely, completely—or dragging out some false, shallow, degrading existence that the world in its hypocrisy demands" (26).

22. In Eliot's play *The Cocktail Party*, Julia says of Edward and his estranged wife Lavinia that "when they are stripped naked to their souls, / And can choose, whether to put on proper costumes / Or huddle quickly into new disguises / They have, for the first time, somewhere to start from" (147). Lord Claverton, in Eliot's play *The Elder Statesman*, echoes the point:

> I've spent my life in trying to forget myself,
> In trying to identify myself with the part
> I had chosen to play. And the longer we pretend
> The harder it becomes to drop the pretense,
> Walk off the stage, change into our own clothes
> And speak as ourselves [102].

Our "own clothes"—our "proper costume"—are but metaphors for Lacan's *Real*, as is a soul *stripped naked*. The "pretense"—the "new disguise"—is another way of talking about the *unreal*.

23. "I would say this is something approaching the naked truth, isn't it?" (64), asks Lenny in Pinter's *The Homecoming*.

24. *This love is silent.*

25. A psychiatrist in *The Cocktail Party* explains the void at the heart of it all, the unbearable *Real* or *reality* behind our everyday deceptions—behind the face we prepare to meet the faces that we meet:

> Ah, but we die to each other daily.
> What we know of other people
> Is only our *memory* of the moments
> During which we knew them. And they have changed since then.
> To pretend that they and we are the same
> Is a useful and convenient social convention
> Which must sometimes be broken. We must also remember
> That at every meeting we are meeting a stranger [71–72].

Put this way the *Real* may be indeed unbearable, but it's also desirable, because with the rupture of "useful and convenient social conventions" comes a chance to see things anew, and to experience a new way of being. If only temporarily, it's a way out from the oppressive dream of the other, whether the other be a stranger on the street, the person with whom you sleep, or Lacan's *Big Other*: the complex network of language and customs and laws into which you are named and sorted, then nudged this way and that by desires not quite your own. Whatever the case, the memories and self-deceptions and dreams which others have of and for us get in the way of our true desire.

26. After having "discovered" Hugh Grant, the stage director Richard Digby Day promptly cast him in a London production of Wilde's *Lady Windermere's Fan*.[13]

27. *I have nothing to say and am saying it.*

28. "Perhaps my life has only been a dream / Dreamt through me by the minds of others" (97), says Harry in Eliot's 1939 play *The Family Reunion*. This is a problem, not only for Harry, but also for the characters in *The Cocktail Party*—and for you and me too. It may even be a question of ethics. As Lacan tells us, "the only thing of which one can be guilty is having given ground relative to one's desire" (321).

29. The psychiatrist in *The Cocktail Party* tells Edward, "You've lost touch with the person / You thought you were." Edward then asks, "To what does this lead?" The psychiatrist replies, "To finding out who you really are [...] What you really feel, what you really are among other people" (30–31).

30. In Ford Madox Ford's 1915 novel *The Good Soldier*, the narrator John Dowell[14] confesses: "Conventions and traditions, I suppose, work blindly but surely for the preservation of the normal type; for the extinction of proud, resolute, and unusual individuals" (334–335).

31. Set in a London flat in the 1940s, *The Cocktail Party* concerns a husband (Edward) and wife (Lavinia), their respective young lovers (Celia and Peter), a psychiatrist (Unidentified Guest/Reilly), and two officious friends (Julia and Alex) who—comically on point—frequently interrupt the action. By the end, all of the characters but one is saved.

32. Or is it that only one of the characters finds salvation, while the rest return docilely to their traps? Which is to say all the "normal types" in the play are, in Ford's words, *preserved,* while a certain proud and resolute individual—Celia—is saved through her *extinction*.[15]

33. "You never heard such silence," I tell the Strindberg enthusiast.[16] Personally, I always preferred Pinter.

34. Of theoreticians and their labyrinths Gilles Deleuze may be less of a Daedalus than Jacques Lacan, but he's every bit the wit. "If you're trapped in the dream of the other," warns Deleuze, "you're fucked."[17] Were psychoanalysis not inherently suspicious of such easy reductions, this would make a nice little epigraph for the entire profession, I think. It would also make a nice through-

line for *The Cocktail Party*, first produced in 1949 after Hollywood's decade-long smorgasbord of psychoanalytic screenplays—from *Now Voyager* to *Spellbound* to the *Secret Beyond the Door*—and just before the late stretch in the 1950s known as the "Golden Age of Psychiatry."[18] From the beginning, Eliot's work showed more than a passing familiarity with the psychiatric currents wafting outside his London door, and his oddling Prufrock, penned early on, is to this day every psychiatrist's paragon for neurosis. *The Cocktail Party*, however, deals with psychoanalytic concerns *directly*, not least of which the hypothetical posed by Deleuze. In a version less *French* and more expansive, Deleuze writes,

> People's dreams are always all-consuming and threaten to devour us. What other people dream is very dangerous. Dreams are a terrifying will to power. Each of us is the victim of other people's dreams [...]. Beware of the dreams of others, because if you are caught in their dreams, you are done for [Deleuze 318].

In *The Cocktail Party*, the problem for the principal players—the particular way in which each, as it were, is *fucked*—is that they too are trapped in the dream of the other.

35. Celia, for example, says of her affair with Edward:

> Perhaps the dream was better. It seemed the real reality,
> And if this is reality, it is very like a dream.
> Perhaps it was I who betrayed my own dream
> All the while: and to find I wanted
> This world as well as that [...] [62].

36. Whatever Noel Coward–like associations you may have about a play called *The Cocktail Party*, I would ask that you now sock them away, for good. Nothing kills a martini buzz quite like a crucifixion, and only T. S. Eliot—that mood-darkener, that *rotter*—could conceive of it. Yes, the play ends with notice that one of the characters has been crucified while off doing good deeds in a distant land. Like the cross itself, the crucifixion in *The Cocktail Party* may be read in various ways, one of which is that she—Celia—who gets crucified got caught in the dream of the other.

37. The Strindberg enthusiast with whom I live loves *A Dream Play* above all.

38. Eliot himself was well-acquainted with what it was like to be trapped in the dream of the other, in particular the roving, ferret-like dreams[19] of his first wife, Vivienne, whose late marital hallucinations of whether her husband had been beheaded must have been no small source of consternation for him, enough in fact to put him under, which it sort of did. The buried life, as one of his biographers has noted, is the over-arching theme of Eliot's work.[20] He wrote about it at every turn, along with its chief consequence: the loss of the

coordinates of one's desire. "That is the worst moment," says a character in *The Cocktail Party*,

> When you feel you have lost
> The desire for all that was most desirable,
> And before you are contented with what you can desire;
> Before you know what is left to be desired;
> And you go on wishing that you could desire
> What desire has left behind [65].

39. "This is the saddest story I have ever heard" (7), so begins John Dowell in Ford's *The Good Soldier*.

40. In *The Cocktail Party*, Edward, whose wife has run out on him, is counseled by her psychiatrist. Sounding every bit the voice of a poem by Philip Larkin, the psychiatrist sketches for Edward a potential "new way of being," a life out from underneath the dream of the other, where the truth of his desire— the *Real*—isn't compromised:

> It will come to you slowly:
> When you wake in the morning, when you go to bed at night,
> That you are beginning to enjoy your independence;
> Finding your life becoming cosier and cosier
> Without the consistent critic, the patient misunderstander
> Arranging life a little better than you like it [...]
> And, turning the past over and over,
> You'll wonder only that you endured it for so long [28].

41. "He's a much better-looking version of Philip Larkin," the film director Marc Lawrence said of Hugh Grant.[21]

42. Like any good philosopher-cum-poet-cum-playwright-cum-essayist-cum Nobel Prize Winner, Eliot thought the *Real* important enough to at least take a peek, and so he devised a strategy for doing so, via verse drama. While he laid the groundwork in his early essay "The Possibility of a Poetic Drama" (1921), Eliot would wait some thirty years to really flesh things out in an essay called, simply, "Poetry and Drama." Perhaps he needed first to put into practice what he could only theorize early on, and so in the intervening years wrote five of his seven plays, all in verse.[22] Whatever the case, "Poetry and Drama" appeared just after *The Cocktail Party* in 1951, the very year that Lacan would begin holding his now famous seminars, all of them in some way concerned with the *Real*, and the truth of our desire.

43. "To find a form that accommodates the mess, that is the task of the artist now," says Beckett.[23]

44. Note: These are answers to questions posed to T. S. Eliot in his 1959 *Paris Review* interview.

Q:

A: I think *The Family Reunion* is still the best of my plays in the way of poetry, although it's not very well constructed.

Q:

A: It sometimes happens, disconcertingly, at any rate with a practitioner like myself, that it isn't always the things constructed most according to plan that are the most successful.

Q:

A: I am no longer very much interested in my own theories about poetic drama, especially those put forward before 1934.

Q:

A: You've raised a very good point there. I think you're right, it does make it more difficult.

Q:

A: There may be honest poets who do feel sure. I don't.

45. In a recently discovered essay on George Chapman, Eliot compares the Elizabethan translator of Homer to Dostoevsky, in whose works, Eliot argues, "there are everywhere two planes of reality, and that the scene before our eyes is only the screen and veil of another action which is taking place behind it" (2013: 63). Eliot also writes,

> The characters themselves are partially aware of this division, aware of the grotesque futility of their visible lives, and seem always to be listening for other voices and to be conducting a conversation with a specter. Hence their distraction, their inability to attend to the business at hand in a practical way [61].

46. Other voices. A specter. The void. The unreal. The *Real*.

47. *I have nothing to say and am saying it.*

48. If psychoanalysis proposes that we are strangers to ourselves, then theatre proposes to make us better acquainted. Like Lacan, Eliot is interested in the unconscious, in the estranged side of ourselves, and refers to it directly or indirectly, more than a half-dozen times in his essay "Poetry and Drama." He also has an interest in desire, and what becomes of us, when, in the words of Lacan, we give ground relative to it—our desire, that is. For Eliot, the result is simple: a "sordid, dreary daily world" (141). In making his case for the value of verse drama, Eliot first counters the perception that poetry in drama is little more than a form of prettifying, ribbons of decorative rhyme to please theatregoers who have an ear for that sort of thing. If anything, he argues, "the verse rhythm should have its effect upon the hearers, without their being conscious of it" (134), the cumulative effect of which checks and accelerates the "pulse of our emotion without our knowing it" (136), as well as "intensifies the drama" (137).

49. More is at stake with verse drama, however, than a means toward heightened sensitivities. For Eliot, it's nothing less than the "illumination and

transfiguration" of the aforementioned "sordid, dreary daily world." Anticipating Beckett, as well as Lacan's notion of the *Real*, Eliot writes of the *unnamable*, of the *fringe of indefinite extent*, of those emotions and motives that escape our conscious life, as well as elude prose drama's ability to adequately express them. "It seems to me," he writes,

> that beyond the *nameable*, classifiable emotions and motives of our conscious life [...] the part of life which prose drama is wholly adequate to express [...] there is a *fringe of indefinite extent*, of feeling which we can only detect, so to speak, out of the corner of the eye and can never completely focus [...]. This peculiar range of sensibility can be expressed by dramatic poetry [verse drama], at its moment of greatest intensity [145, italics mine].

Not only is Eliot's definition of the "fringe of indefinite extent" totally evocative of Lacan's notion of the Real (as something that is unnamable, unclassifiable), but his solution for experiencing it is precisely that of Žižek. In order to detect the *Real*, we must look out of the corners of our eyes; this "peculiar range of sensibility can be expressed by dramatic poetry" (Eliot 145). Žižek refers to this exact method of discernment as "looking awry," a phrase he borrows from—what else?—a passage of dramatic poetry.[24]

50. There's a "T. S. Eliot Compatibility" website in which celebrities and notable public figures are indexed according to their physical, emotional, and intellectual biorhythmic cycles in relation to those of T. S. Eliot. Overall, Hugh Grant is 35 percent compatible. In contrast, Tom Cruise is only 27 percent compatible, while Natalie Portman is 89 percent compatible.[25] To grasp the *Real* of this website, its *fringe of indefinite extent*, one must indeed squint.

51. The Strindberg enthusiast with whom I live has a cat, whose silence far exceeds my own.

52. Whoever thinks dramatic poetry is for the birds—aloft, flighty, a flock of high ideals overhead, and only ever *overheard*—Eliot thinks otherwise, arguing in his 1934 lecture "After Strange Gods" that the world of "actuality"—of *reality*—belongs decidedly to verse.[26] In the same year, in a collection of essays called "The Use of Poetry and the Use of Criticism," Eliot concluded with remarks on what the *actual* is, and what poetry may do for us in relation to it:

> It [poetry] may make us from time to time a little more aware of the deeper, *unnamed* feelings [actuality] which form the substratum of our being, to which we rarely penetrate; for our lives are mostly a constant evasion of ourselves, and an evasion of the visible and sensible world [149].

Here, as everywhere for Eliot, the buried life—self-evasion along with those deeper, unnamed feelings—is vital. Were it not for the vulgarity of the image, which no doubt would have furrowed Eliot's brow even more than his umbrella,[27] we might say of him, as Saul Bellow says of a character in his novella *The Actual*,[28] that "he wore a condom over his heart" (14).

53. From the eponymous Madame Bovary, Eliot derived the term *Bovarysme*: "the human will to see things as they are not" (*Selected Essays* 130–31).

54. **1951**: The year of Eliot's and Lacan's respective theorizing on the *fringe of indefinite extent*—on the *Real*—is also the year of Beckett's *Molloy*: "a mist [...] rises in me every day and veils the world from me and veils me from myself" (37–38), says Molloy. "Yes, there were times when I forgot not only who I was, but that I was, forgot to be" (65). "A man like me cannot forget, in his evasions, what it is he evades" (167). For Eliot, there's an antidote to all this handwringing, expressed by the father in his last play *The Elder Statesman*: "I've been freed from the self that pretends to be someone; and in becoming no one, I begin to live" (129). Two pages over, his daughter affirms, "In becoming no one, he has become himself" (131). This, I submit, is Lacanian psychoanalysis *in sum*, were such a thing possible. This, I submit, is William Thacker (*Notting Hill*). This is Will Freeman (*About a Boy*). This is Eliot. This is *me*. This is *you*.

55. **1951**:

- The year in which *The Catcher in the Rye*—a novel about desire, identity, and the *Real*—is published.
- The year in which *All About Eve*—a film about desire, identity, and the *Real*—wins the Academy Award for Best Picture.
- The year in which the film adaptation of *A Streetcar Named Desire*—a play about desire, identity, and the *Real*—premieres.

56. Whenever I learn of a friend's woeful marriage, whether on the rocks or already in ruin, I am reminded of Alfred Schweigen, the narrator of John Updike's "The Music School." Toward the end of that fugue-like story, he observes, "My friends are like me. We are all pilgrims, faltering toward divorce" (340). Schweigen's marriage—like Edward's in *The Cocktail Party*—is listing to one side, in danger of sinking, but that's not what's behind his epiphany, not entirely anyway. It derives instead from a number of *events*, unrelated except for the fact that the lives involved are "transfigured by a strange irruption" (337), after which nothing for them will ever again be the same. Such irruptions are breaks or ruptures in the fabric of our everyday deceptions, those "useful and convenient social convention[s]" which, Eliot says, we pretend exist, but "which must sometimes be broken." Such a break is referred to in Theory-speak as the capital-E Event,[29] though we might as easily call it the capital-D Divorce. And for Lacan, it's the *Real*. Pilgrims all, we're ever faltering toward the big Event, toward the *Real*, toward the radical break whereby busi-

ness can't go on as usual, but few of us, it seems, have nerve enough to see it through. It's a reality human kind can't bear very much of.

   57. T.S Eliot: Merton College, Oxford, 1914.

      Philip Larkin: New College, Oxford, 1940.

      Hugh Grant: St. Johns College, Oxford, 1979.

   58. In Neil Labute's play *The Mercy Seat* the immediate trauma of 9/11 has ripped open an opportunity for a man to fulfill his desire, which is to leave his wife and children and run away with his mistress. However, the moment he comes too close to encountering the *Real*—the *truth* of his desire—the man quite predictably loses his will, and by the curtain's close has failed to *act*. In order to awaken from the *Real* of his desire and return to the dream of his ordinary life (where his mistress is kept at a proper distance), the man need only answer his phone, on the end of which, we presume, is his wife. The real infidelity here, we might say, is to the *Event*, to the *Real*. As Eliot says, "Only those who will risk going too far can possibly find out how far one can go."[30]

   59. "Till human voices wake us, and we drown," concludes Prufrock.

   60. "A delusion is something we must return from" (134), says the psychiatrist in *The Cocktail Party*.

   61. "I was nothing until you started dicking around with me. I admit it. No-thing" (81), Adam tells Evelyn in Labute's play *The Shape of Things*.

   62. **1951:**

- The year of Graham Greene's novel *The End of the Affair*: "What happens if you drop all the things that make you I?" (125).

   63. Oscar Wilde: Magdalen College, Oxford, 1874.

   64. For Edward and *his* wife in *The Cocktail Party*, their moment of a radical break comes and goes, and with it the opportunity to trade the deceptions of their dream life for the truth of their desire. Such truth is never without cost, however. In fact, Lacan has a word for desire once it's fulfilled: *nightmare*.

   65. At the close of the film *Four Weddings and a Funeral*, Hugh Grant's character, Charles, proposes to his love interest, in the rain: "Do you think— after we've dried off, after we've spent lots more time together—you might agree *not* to marry me? And do you think not being married to me might maybe be something you could consider doing for the rest of your life?"

   65.5. "Nothing will come of nothing," warns Lear.

   66. In every marriage there is a fault-line between deception and transparency. Both are vital to marital maintenance, but an excess of either can potentially cause a break, an eruption, in the form of a traumatic wound (the *Real*; the *Event*), from which one of two things is most assured. The wound will either fester into the silence of the maritally dead or, as Eliot suggests in his play *The Cocktail Party*, it will open the way to a higher plane, to enlight-

enment, to *salvation*. We're all familiar of course with the pain that follows hard upon the undeceived, of *having been found out* or, as the case may be, having *found out*. If though you somehow remain unacquainted with that exquisite experience, then consider John Dowell of Ford's *The Good Solider*, whose discovery of his wife's nine-year infidelity is simply too much for him to bear. For the sake of self-preservation, he can't acknowledge what's happened, convinces himself otherwise, and learns to live out his years behind the fantasy of his own self-deception. For Dowell, the trauma of transparency, of *too much* truth, can torpedo a life as easily as too little of it.

67. "If people were really honest the world would come to an end" (464), the Strindberg enthusiast tells me, quoting Strindberg.

68. "If a right to the secret is not maintained, we are in a totalitarian space" (59), says Derrida.

69. "*What* in us really wants "truth"? [...] *Why not rather* untruth? And uncertainty? Even ignorance?" (9), asks Nietzsche.

70.   Ford Madox Ford.

      Ford Mad-Ox-Ford.

      Ford Mad Oxford.

      For Ford, the only Oxford was in his name.

71. "When people were married there was an end to loving" (307), says John Dowell.

72. "No human relations are adequate to human desire" (*Selected Prose* 235), says Eliot.

73. *This love is silent.*

74. And so the couple in *The Cocktail Party* retreats and the play concludes with the two of them newly reconciled, safely ensconced back inside the dreams they have of each other. Their fantasies re-tooled for another go, they seem all too privy to the disturbing flipside of Deleuze's proposition: If you're NOT trapped in the dream of the other—if you're NOT trapped in their deceptions and self-deceptions—you're also *fucked*.

75. As Philip Larkin says, it's *useful to get that learnt*.[31]

UNIVERSITY OF ST. THOMAS

ACKNOWLEDGMENTS

The author wishes to express his deepest gratitude to Amy and Mr. Dowell, muse and dear friend.

NOTES

1. The image belongs to Yeats, from his poem "The Circus Animals' Desertion."

2. For those unacquainted with Lacan's work or who may be in need of a refresher, then Žižek's *How to Read Lacan* is a good place to begin.

3. The quip about Oakland is of course Gertrude Stein's.

4. In this sense, Lacan's notion of the Real brings to mind the unnamed terror of Edna and Harry in Edward Albee's 1966 play, *A Delicate Balance.*

5. See the closing line of Larkin's poem "High Windows."

6. See the closing line of Stevens's poem "The Snow Man."

7. Professor John Dowell should not be confused with the John Dowell of Ford Madox Ford's novel *The Good Soldier,* whom Professor Dowell once described as "the most clueless character in all of Western literature."

8. The anecdote, it must be admitted, smells not quite of Wilde but of Shaw. Or maybe Meredith. In any case, Dowell didn't claim to be the originator.

9. See Tom Driver, "Interview with Samuel Beckett" in *Samuel Beckett: The Critical Heritage,* 218–219.

10. From Philip Larkin's poem "Talking in Bed."

11. This for the sake of argument. I'm not married.

12. Again for the sake of argument. To date, I've no online moniker.

13. See Richard Digby Day's interview: http://www.tft.ucla.edu/2014/03/all-the-worlds-a-stage/.

14. No relation to my professor, I assure you.

15. Crucifixion, to be exact.

16. See Harold Pinter's *The Homecoming,* 8.

17. Deleuze is reported to have said this in a lecture, refined in his essay "What Is a Creative Act?"

18. See Krin Gabbard's book *Psychiatry and the Cinema.*

19. Virginia Woolf famously referred to Vivienne as a "bag of ferrets" worn around Eliot's neck.

20. See Craig Raine's excellent *T. S. Eliot* (Oxford University Press's *Lives and Legacies* series)

21. See Holly Millea's piece "Hugh Grant: About a Man" in *Elle,* 15 December 2009. http://www.elle.com/pop-culture/celebrities/hugh-grant-interview.

22. In "Poetry and Drama," Eliot writes, "the self-education of a poet trying to write for the theatre seems to require a long period of disciplining his poetry" (144).

23. See note 9.

24. Žižek derives his metaphor from Shakespeare's *Richard II.* For a detailed analysis, see Zizek's *Looking Awry: An Introduction to Jacques Lacan through Popular Culture.*

25. I'm not making this up: http://www.facade.com/biorhythm/relationship/?Celeb=T_S_Eliot&Celeb2=Hugh_Grant.

26. Eliot writes, "I should say that in one's prose reflections one may be legitimately occupied with ideals, whereas in the writing of verse one can only deal with actuality" (qtd in Blackmur 121).

27. According to Eliot's 1965 obit in the *New York Times,* "Eliot's dress was a model of the London man of business. He wore a bowler and often carried a tightly rolled umbrella."

28. While I don't know if Eliot's notion of actuality is what inspired the title of Saul Bellow's late novella *The Actual* (1997), there are plenty of echoes inside to suggest as much, beginning with a character who has a fondness for all things T. S. Eliot, and whose quite-literal buried life (he was mistakenly buried next to his ex-mother-in-law who, in life, despised him), along with the figurative one of his best friend (the novella's narrator), is the book's basic architecture.

29. See Alain Badiou's *Ethics: An Essay on the Understanding of Evil.* Trans. Peter Hallward. New York: Verso, 2001.

30. See Eliot's Preface to *Transit of Venus.*

31. See Larkin's poem "Wild Oats."

WORKS CITED

About a Boy. Dir. Chris Weitz and Paul Weitz. Universal Pictures, 2002. Film.

Beckett, Samuel. *Molloy.* New York: Grove Press, 1955.

_____. *Proust.* New York: Grove Press, 1957.

Bellow, Saul. *The Actual.* New York: Viking, 1997.

Blackmur, R. P. "T. S. Eliot: from 'Ash Wednesday' to 'Murder in the Cathedral.'" *Form and Value in Modern Poetry.* New York: Doubleday, 1957.

Deleuze, Gilles. "What is a Creative Act?" *Two Regimes of Madness: Texts and Interviews 1975–1995.* New York: Semiotext(e), 2007.

Derrida, Jacques, and Maurizio Ferraris. *A Taste for the Secret.* Trans. Giacomo Donis. Cambridge: Polity, 2001.

Eliot, T. S. "Baudelaire." *Selected Prose of T. S. Eliot.* New York: Farrar, 1975.

_____. *The Cocktail Party.* New York: Harcourt, 1950.

_____. *The Complete Poems and Plays 1909–1950.* New York: Harcourt, 1952.

_____. *The Elder Statesman.* New York: Farrar, 1959.

_____. *The Family Reunion.* London: Faber, 1939.

_____. *Interview: T. S. Eliot. Writers at Work: The Paris Review Interviews.* Second Series. New York: Viking Press, 1963. 89–110.

_____. *Murder in the Cathedral.* New York: Harcourt, 1935.

_____. "A Neglected Aspect of Chapman." *New York Review of Books.* Vol. LX, Number 17. 7 November 2013.

_____. "Poetry and Drama." *The Selected Prose of T. S. Eliot.* New York: Harcourt, 1975.

_____. "The Possibility of a Poetic Drama." *The Sacred Wood and Major Early Essays.* New York: Dover, 1998.

_____. *Selected Essays, 1917–1932.* London: Faber, 1932.

_____. *The Use of Poetry and the Use of Criticism.* Cambridge: Harvard University Press, 1964.

Ford, Ford Madox. *The Good Soldier.* Los Angeles: Green Integer, 2004.

Four Weddings and a Funeral. Dir. Mike Newell. MGM, 1994. Film.

Greene, Graham. *The End of the Affair.* New York: Viking, 1951.

Ibsen, Henrik. *The Wild Duck. Four Major Plays: Volume I.* Trans. Rolf Fjelde. New York: Penguin, 1992.

Labute, Neil. *The Mercy Seat.* London: Faber, 2003.

_____. *The Shape of Things.* New York: Broadway Play Publishing, 2011.

Lacan, Jacques. *The Ethics of Psychoanalysis, 1959–1960.* New York: Norton, 1992.

Martin, Clancy. "The Marriage Paradox." *The Chronicle of Higher Education.* 24 Feb. 2014.

Nietzsche, Friedrich. *Beyond Good and Evil.* Trans. Walter Kaufmann. New York: Random House, 1989.

Notting Hill. Dir. Roger Mitchell. Universal, 1999. Film.

Pinter, Harold. *The Homecoming.* New York: Grove Press, 1965.

Storr, Robert. *Gerhard Richter: Forty Years of Painting.* New York: MoMA, 2002.

Strindberg, August. *The Ghost Sonata. The Plays of Strindberg. Volume I.* Trans. Michael Meyer. New York: Modern Library, 1964.

_____. *The Ghost Sonata. Strindberg: Five Plays.* Trans. Harry G. Carlson. Berkeley: University of California Press, 1983.

Updike, John. "The Music School." *Forty Stories.* New York: Penguin, 1987.

Wilde, Oscar. *The Critic as Artist.* Kobenhavn: Green Integer, 1997.

_____. *Lady Windermere's Fan. Five Plays by Oscar Wilde.* New York: Bantam, 1969.

_____. *The Picture of Dorian Gray.* New York: Modern Library, 1998.

Žižek, Slavoj. *How to Read Lacan.* New York: Norton, 2007.

Cabaret and the Avant-Garde

BRIGITTE BOGAR *and*
CHRISTOPHER INNES

Abstract

This study demonstrates that from the very beginning of the Avant-Garde movement these artists, known generally for their aesthetic challenges, sought to link their work with the most populist types of performance: Cabaret and fairground. It explores the reasons this choice was made: The avoidance of censorship; the advantage of challenging bourgeois standards from a working-class and "anti-art" perspective; and the political subtext. The argument also links the historical and contemporary variants of the Avant-Garde. The discussion focuses on two contemporary directors usually considered very dissimilar from the Avant-Garde style of the early twentieth century, selecting productions in which each has taken a play by Brecht and remounted it in a postmodern style of pastiche, which equally uses cabaret and clown-show images.

Theoretically the historical Avant-Garde from the early nineteenth century is generally held to be very different from the contemporary postmodern trends to abstraction, digital experiment, and post-dramatic theatre that define today's equivalent movement. However, in practice there are distinct connections, particularly in the area of adaptation, which in borrowing texts or techniques from the historical Avant-Garde colors the contemporary Avant-Garde, creating equivalents. At the same time, the distinctions are still significant. Where the historical movement was politically committed and ideologically extreme, the contemporary tends to more general and oblique social commentary; and even though in their own time both the historical and the new Avant-Garde break stylistic limits to challenge bourgeois or standard aesthetic categories, the effect from today's perspective looks very different since many of the historical Avant-Garde—for instance, the Expressionist dramatist Frank Wedekind, or the originator of Epic Theatre, Bertolt Brecht, as well as 1930s British equivalents such as Auden or Eliot—are today seen as classics. So their art is, at least officially, what the contemporary Avant-Garde attempts to demolish. Yet because one of the defining characteristics of today's art is its use of pastiche, contemporary theatre tends to revisit and revise works from the historical Avant-Garde. In addition, it turns out that not only historical but also contemporary Avant-Garde artists have adopted the same populist and down-market forms of entertainment as their dominant styles—something that few critics have recognized, and that has hardly been explored in any detail.[1]

We will demonstrate these connections through two selected contemporary productions, each of which focuses on Brecht, although we could easily have dealt with other examples (for instance, the way Vegard Vinge and Ida Müller treat Ibsen) as well as exploring the centrality of links between the Avant-Garde and Cabaret, Fairground performance, and Circus. The Avant-Garde is generally considered stylistically challenging and difficult. Yet from the beginning almost all Avant-Garde artists resorted to the most popular performance types to develop their revolutionary styles of expression. So for example, both Dada and Brecht based their work on Cabaret; a painter like Chagall focused on Circus; while Kander & Ebb adapted Isherwood's 1930s Berlin novel into musical theatre, giving it an iconic title: *Cabaret*. Cabaret in its nightclub form may be considered little more than sexual titillation, yet even this type of Cabaret is intrinsically political, which is why it was adopted by the most extreme of the historical Avant-Garde. We intend to show how these popular arts have been used as source and iconography, and to demonstrate how they have become an integral part of the contemporary Avant-Garde.

From the very beginning of the AvantGarde, artists who were the founders of the movement adopted the most populist and unartistic forms as the medium for expressing both their radical politics and their revolutionary aesthetics. Cabaret, Clowns, and Circus are truly popular arts: down-market; sand and sawdust; fairground songs and crude red noses; sexuality and alcohol; the widest appeal for the lowest common denominator. Such features are memorably represented in the Marlene Dietrich film *Der Blaue Engel*. The original poster for the 1930 film emphasizes this through contrasting the bourgeois professor in his upper-class box with a dirtily-dressed working-class audience standing on the nightclub floor. The audience smirks at the figure of Marlene Dietrich dancing on stage and looking up seductively, while the Professor's expression seems aloof and sneering [see Figure 1].

Throughout the whole Avant-Garde movement artists embraced Cabaret with a passion. Why? Partly at least they did it because adopting the most

Figure 1. *The Blue Angel*, 1930 film poster.

popular, down-market, and anti-intellectual art form was a slap-in-the-face to bourgeois artistic pretensions; and partly because the so-called "light-enter-tainment" disguised the social criticism of the songs and skits from repressive authorities. As Peter Jelavich has argued in his Berlin Cabaret history, Cabaret has always been openly political and impolite, provoking the audience to spon-taneous reactions and favoring brief interludes and revue-style episodes (Jelavich 15, 43). All of these qualities were celebrated by Dada and by the futurists, and indeed even paralleled in the Harlem style of Cabaret in New York. Tracing the history of the Cabaret School from the 1920s to the end of the century in *The Scene of Harlem Cabaret: Race, Sexuality, Performance*, Shane Vogel shows almost exactly the same radicalisms and Marxist leanings, though here taking more openly racial and sexual aspects (black nationalism, gay gender) than the Cabaret traditions of Berlin or London from the 1890s onwards. Vogel identifies an equal break with normative ideologies and middle-class respectability by the artists who worked there. So there is a sense of uni-versality—chronologically, inter-continentally, and politically—about the adoption of Cabaret as a preferred form of artistic expression.

Following this line to emphasize the popular, the very first Avant-Garde artist, Alfred Jarry, borrowed from Grand Guignol puppetry, as in the grotesque figures reflected in a sketch for his 1896 *Ubu Roi*. Notably, from 1881 through the 1890s, the French Avant-Garde made their home in what became the iconic French nightclub, the Chat Noir. The Chat Noir artists labeled themselves a "*Salon des Arts incoherents*" fuelled by absinthe, where the spectators were almost always other artists, so that throughout its existence it was a hive of Avant-Garde activity. Indeed, Eric Satie, the cabaret pianist for the Chat Noir widely appreciated as the progenitor of contemporary artis-tic movements such as minimalism and repetitive music (and even as a pre-cursor to the Theatre of the Absurd), also embraced popular forms. One of the Satie compositions that survive from this period is music to *Jack-in-the-Box* (which Satie, tellingly, called a "clownerie"), a pantomime by Jules Depaquit, the cartoonist who illustrated a satirical journal *Le Rire (Laughter)*. Of course, the aim was not simply to amuse, but in the French Avant-Garde cliché to "*epâter les bourgeoisie.*"

There's a splendid illustration of this in the advertisement for one of the German cabaret dancers of the period, Gert Valeska. Advertising her "Dialogue and Dance" performance at the Berlin Blüthnersaal, the poster emphasizes the word "Grotesque"—"Gesprochene und getantzte GROTESKEN." A Berlin newspaper cartoon that graphically demonstrates the bourgeois audi-ence's response to Valeska's performances illustrates her as dancing with sex-ually splayed legs, a serving-woman's under-dress hitched up to show the tops of her stockings, and a distorted facial expression. Meanwhile, all the males

Figure 2. Gert Valeksa poster, 1925.

in the cartoon are peering through binoculars, leering and smiling, though their women companions appear distressed and alienated [see Figure 2].

If in Germany Cabaret automatically became politicized, it was largely because of the strict censorship imposed. The Kaiser had declared: "Art is an arm of government" (cit. Jelavich 24). As a result, in order to attack or even simply criticize the economic or socially hierarchical system, writers were forced to find ways that didn't count as art. German artists adopted Cabaret and clownery specifically because, as "popular" and "unartistic" nightclub entertainment, these forms allowed freedom for satire and trenchant social commentary.

This becomes clear with the very first Cabaret troupe that opened in Munich in 1901: the *Elf Scharfrichter* (Eleven Executioners). The imagery of the posters advertising their skits is just as iconic as the Chat Noir: a militaristic marching challenge to the status quo (represented in one image by the bourgeois audience, faces blue with fear) who clearly feel threatened from the axes carried by the masked singing dancers [see Figure 3]. Photos of the group show the accuracy of the posters. Burly men with leather half-masks brandish real swords or axes. The masks are not only mimicking executioner's headgear but are also there to preserve anonymity. Nightclub sexuality was included, of course, as one of their many posters shows, with a stern black-gowned lady facing the audience while behind her are eleven white plates with the black heads of demons displayed. In another poster a lissome young woman embraces an almost naked executioner with a huge axe, a red mask, and a G-string. Her facial expression and eyes clearly indicate that she is suggesting people in the audience for him to behead, graphically illustrating the dangerous sexuality of a femme fatale. In general the posters are deliberately perverse and satiric, with overtones of a sadistic love for violence and revenge on middle-class morals. The posters announce daily performances, indicating their popularity.

Indeed, the politics were particularly effective because the Eleven Executioners attracted Avant-Garde German artists. For instance, the most provocative early expressionist German playwright of the era, Frank Wedekind, became the Eleven Executioners' lead singer [see Figure 4]. Other performers assumed sinister stage-names for disguise, like "Dionysus Death" or "Bloody Clown." However, Wedekind's scandalous reputation, and his prison sentence for insulting the Kaiser, made such a persona unnecessary for him. Not surprisingly the German authorities closed down the Munich Cabaret in 1903, forcing the Eleven Executioners' move to Vienna.

One might note that as a youth Wedekind had worked backstage for circuses in Paris; and Bertolt Brecht, who became the leading figure for the Avant-Garde in Germany after the First World War, followed explicitly in Wedekind's footsteps. Not as a playwright—but as a cabaret artist. As a young man, in

Figure 3. The Eleven Executioners poster, 1901.

1922 Brecht performed at Trudy Hesterberg's "Wild Stage Cabaret" in Berlin, singing his "Legend of the Dead Soldier," which caused outrage and got him pelted from the stage. The song was so politically powerful at the time that Georg Grosz published a cartoon illustrating the most grotesque moment in this powerful political satire. A soldier is killed at the front in the First World War and buried. The Kaiser regrets this, and a medical commission is sent to dig up the body. A doctor examines him, declares he's fit and has only lost his nerve— the scene that Grosz's cartoon illustrates—so they fill up his corpse with schnapps, drape naked ladies around him and parade him through the city.[2] As he's been taught, he swings his legs from his ass in the standard goose step. They march him back to the front where he is killed again. It was

Figure 4. Cartoon, Wedekind with guitar, 1913.

hardly surprising if in 1921 that song caused a riot. Brecht delivered it in Wedekind's distinctive singing style that he had praised in an obituary after Wedekind's early death in 1918, describing the sound as "a brittle voice, monotonous and quite untrained." However, it became characteristic of the performance style that Brecht demanded from the singers in all his plays and which he developed with Kurt Weill. As the cover of the original score for *Die Driegroschenoper* declares, this was indeed "Music for All."

Cabaret had its effect on the English Avant-Garde, too, with high modernist poets of the 1920s and 30s like W. H. Auden and T. S. Eliot turning to theatre to reach a working-class public. Perhaps for the obvious reason that music is an emotional intensifier, both wrote poetic pieces with music which were produced by Rupert Doone's Group Theatre. The most influential piece by far is the 1934 play by Eliot, *Sweeney Agonistes,* which was performed by the Group Theatre together with Auden's *Dance of Death.* Fragmentary and episodic, with jazz representing the spiritual wasteland of modern life, *Sweeney Agonistes* is a disjointed, experimental musical performance piece that had a great impact at the time. Indeed, it specifically influenced Brecht, who was present at its London production. It even inspired a contemporary Avant-Garde painter, Roger Bacon, to produce a "Sweeney Agonistes Triptych" that shows a graphic mix of sex and murder in naked bodies on a carousel stage. Cabaret was a standard form for the poetic 1930s Avant-Garde in Britain. For instance, Auden wrote "Stop All the Clocks"—later revised into "Funeral Blues" with music by Benjamin Britten—as a cabaret song for Heidi Anderson, who studied in Berlin and became lead singer for the Group Theatre. Britten also wrote music for numerous other cabaret pieces, such as "Tell Me the Truth about Love."

Britten's deceptively simple tunes in these songs cover and contrast with the despair and emptiness of modem life depicted in the words. Exactly the same tone can be found in Kurt Weill's music for Brecht's plays: despair mixed with dreams and longing, though with a slightly harsher twist. This is particularly clear in a song such as "Surabaya Johnny" from *Happy End,* which is typical of Brecht's style: abrasive, mixing the political and the personal, and devastatingly emotional. This musical tone disguises the political messages in the verses in the same way that other presentations had at Zurich in 1916, where the Dada movement formed around the Cabaret Voltaire. Jelavich speaks of a "cabaretic modernism" (8)—and the Cabaret Voltaire is a prime example of this—sound poems, simultaneity, and an attack on all accepted artistic principles. In addition the Dada performers wore formalist, geometrical costumes; and from this there is a direct line to Avant-Garde surrealist abstraction, such as Oscar Schlemmer's well-known Bauhaus "Triadische Ballet." There is a striking similarity in the way the human figure is abstracted and mechanized. But while Dada is generally (and mistakenly) seen as primarily an anti-aesthetic movement, in fact this was combined with a strongly political edge. This tendency could be clearly seen in the first Belin Dada exhibit (1921), mounted in a public urinal, where spectators were offered an axe to hack at a wooden block labeled "The State" while a young girl in white communion-dress recited Marxist slogans and sexual obscenities. The Dada attack on art was also an attack on social morality, and their aim was to provoke their bourgeois audiences.

Dadaists represented the Avant-Garde in its purest form in their total rejection of all social and artistic traditions. But their artistic principles were an expression of their politics. As one of Tristan Tzara's manifestoes declares, logic and morality are the foundations of social slavery; psychology, philosophy, and all systems of thought only serve to authenticate bourgeois dominance. As Fascism took over Germany, the Dadaists' integration of popular Cabaret and Avant-Garde abstraction became the only remaining form for political protest. Their work was of course front and center at the infamous Nazi exhibition of Degenerate Art in 1937—all of the paintings and sculptures being burnt at the closing of the exhibition—but even so, the Dadaists remained a primary force of Avant-Garde protest. Later the same year, 1937, Filippo Marinetti had the temerity to invite his erstwhile Dadaist colleagues to a Berlin state dinner in his honor. Marinetti was once a leader of both the Dada and Futurist movements; in the 1930s he became Mussolini's Minister for Culture and was then on an official visit to Germany. All Hitler's Nazi ministers were present at the head table of Marinetti's state dinner. László Moholy-Nagy (a photographer and light engineer who had been one of the professors at the Bauhaus School) as well as the "*Merz*" artist Kurt Schwitters (whose highly individual art movement, based on collage, took its name from the middle syllable of "*Kommerzial*") were seated at a table together with the heads of the Hitler Youth, the Folk Culture Organization, and the "Strength Through Joy" Movement. Moholy-Nagy's wife, Sybil, described the event in a letter, providing significant insight into the political dimensions of Avant-Garde art as well as its complete rejection of bourgeois aesthetics:

The more Schwitters drank, the more fondly he regarded his neighbor. [...]

"You think I'm a Dadaist, don't you," he suddenly started again. "That's where you're wrong, brother. I'm *MERZ*." He thumped his wrinkled dress shirt near his heart. "I'm Ayran—the great Aryan *MERZ*. I can think Ayran, paint Ayran, spit Aryan." [...] "You will not prohibit me from *MERZing* my *MERZ* art?"

The word "prohibit" had finally penetrated the foggy brain of the "Strength Though Joy" man.

"Prohibited is prohibited [*Verboten ist verboten*]," he said with great firmness and a heavy tongue. "And when the Führer says '*Ja*' he says '*Ja*' and when the Führer says '*Nein*' he says '*Nein*.' *Heil Hitler*!"

[In response] Marinetti had risen from his chair. He swayed considerably and his face was purple.

"My friends," he said in French. "After the many excellent speeches tonight"— the silent officials winced—[...] "I shall recite my poem 'The Raid on Adrianople.'"

"*Adrianople est cerné de toutes parts SSSSrrr zitzitzitzit PAAAAAAAgh Rrrrrrrrr*" roared Marinetti.

"*Ouah ouah ouah, departs des trains suicides, ouah ouah ouah.*"

The audience gasped [...].

"*Tchip tchip tchip—féééééééééééééééééééééééééééééééélez*!"

He grabbed a wineglass and smashed it to the floor.

"*Piiiiiiiiiiiiiiiiiing, sssssssrrrrrrrrrrrrrrrrrrr zitzitzit toum toum Patrouille tapie—*"
Marinetti threw himself over the table.
"*Vanitéeeeee, viande congeléeeeee vieleuse de La Madone*"
expiring almost as a whisper from his lips. Slowly he slid to the floor, his
clenched fingers pulling the tablecloth downward, wine, food, plates, and silver-
ware pouring into the laps of the notables.
   Schwitters had jumped up at the first sound of the poem [...]
   "Oh Anna Blume," he whispered, and suddenly breaking out into a roar that
drowned the din of protesting voices and scraping chair legs, he thundered:
   "*Oh, Anna Blume*
   Du bist von hinter wie von vorne
   A-N-N-A."[3]

The Moholy-Nagys had already booked train-tickets to England, and this was
to be their last night in Berlin. In fear of official response they went directly
from the dinner to the train station, while Schwitters was to flee to Norway
the same year, then after the outbreak of war also to England. The event is
pure Dada: Schwitters with his apparently abstract challenge to Aryan morality
("Anna" was a well-known poem Schwitters had written in 1919), aligned with
Marinetti's Futurist sound poem as a calculated—if disguised as a drunken
and therefore involuntary—insult to the Nazi hierarchy, intensified by of
Marinetti's choice of the French language. As here, given the extreme censorship by the Nazi government, any political protest against the Fascist regimes
had to be abstracted and disguised, which meant resorting (as the AvantGarde
had under the Kaiser at the beginning of the century) to forms like Cabaret.
   Even in occupied countries like Denmark, this was the case. A typical
example is the song, "Chained Up," from a cabaret show titled *Dyveke* (named
after the mistress of a thirteenth century Danish King Christian II). Verse
three runs like this:

> They tie us mouth and hand, but you cannot bind the spirit
> And no one is trapped when thought is free.
> We have an inner fortress, strong in its own worth,
> As long as we fight for what we believe in.
> Those who keep an upright soul can never be a slave.
> No one can govern you, since you decide for yourself.
> So we promise with hand and mouth, in the dark before dawn
> That the dream of freedom will never end.[4]

Performed in 1940, just after the Nazi invasion of Denmark, it has a clear message for the Danish resistance, even under the Cabaret lightness with the tango
rhythm and the ostensibly long-ago historical subject.
   The composer, Poul Henningsen, had to escape to Sweden in 1943 due
to his strong anti–German attitude. *Dyveke* went on a tour throughout Denmark for the next year and a half and was, strikingly, performed around 400

times during the Nazi Occupation. The verse above explicitly refers to the occupation, but was written in a way to avoid censorship. The tango music composed for these words is quite unusual for a "National Anthem." The audience at the opening performance became dead silent during the last verse. When the last line was spoken, all stood up and left the theatre in silence. Even today the text of the third verse can bring tears to a Danish eye, since the song and the circumstances surrounding it are still well-known. Originally the song had four not three verses with a refrain "This is true in love and war: all promises are fraudulent and nobody can trust the words of a human." This refrain and the original third verse were deleted by the German censors; and since Poul Henningsen made no attempt to reinstate the deleted text after the end of the war, it is generally argued that he wrote this verse to distract the attention of the censors from the rest of the song.

The links between the Avant-Garde approach in the first half of the twentieth century and the contemporary, postmodern Avant-Garde are particularly clear in the way both adopt similar brands of popular culture, in particular Cabaret, even if, following the postmodernist principles of irony and adaptation, the images are more self-conscious and indeed parodic. A couple of strikingly relevant examples have been selected for illustration. Significantly, both examples are based on early plays by Bertolt Brecht, *Drums in the Night* and *The Threepenny Opera*.

Brecht included his Cabaret song "Legend of the Dead Soldier" in his early expressionist play *Drums in the Night* (written in 1919–20, first performed in 1922). In 2011 Aleksandar Lukac directed a contemporary adaptation for a Serbian theatre company, which was specifically intended as a response to the Serbian conflict. It won the top prize in 2011 at Serbia's Festival of Festivals. Most modern productions of *Drums* insert Cabaret songs for which Brecht wrote the lyrics, but Lukac decided instead to use original Cabaret music from the 1920s that might have influenced the Berlin playwright. As he said in his Director's Notes:

> This production is an attempt to capture that youthful energy that led Brecht not only into unexplored theatrical territories but also into the realm of truth about human beings that no regime would like to see on stage.
> I have allowed myself the audacity of adding, or quoting, a few long forgotten cabaret acts that were contemporary to the play in an attempt to follow the theory of Epic Theater—adding an art history context to the play that is already rich with socio-political content. A number of Dadaist, Futurist, Surrealist and other Avant-Garde skits are included to challenge or invite the actors to play with the young Brecht's aesthetic.[5]

The performance was not only Cabaret-like, but the costumes came directly from Oscar Schlemmer's Bauhaus ballet, transferred from almost a full century

Figure 5. Aleksander Lukacs's production of *Drums in the Night* at Šabac Theater in Serbia in September 2010. From left, Vladimir Milojevic, Deana Kostic, Ljubiša Barovic, Sladjana Pajčic, Duško Stevanovic, Ivana Jokic and Dragana Radojevic (courtesy Aleksander Lukacs).

ago to the contemporary Avant-Garde and the contemporary politics of the Serbian civil war. Of course, the elements from the 1920s have a Doppler effect, both in and out of context—contemporary to Brecht, but antique to the contemporary political message—which contains an element of pastiche as well as metatheatricality (in the obviously artificial costumes and performative Cabaret elements) that make this production postmodern.

Another production that expands on this approach, although predating it by several decades, is Roberto Ciulli's 1987 staging of Brecht's famous *The Threepenny Opera* (first performance, 1928). What needs to be remembered is that Brecht's career didn't just start in Cabaret, but in fairground performance, which can be seen in a well-known picture from the 1919 *Oktoberfest* in Augsburg [see Figure 6]. The same image forms the cover-picture to John Fuegi's 1987 "Directors in Perspective" study of Brecht. This shows him performing (on clarinet) with a famous comedian Karl Liebknecht (on tuba) in the traditional fairground *"Bänkelgesang*," a horror-story with strongly political overtones, or "*Moritat*." The photo includes a picture titled "Mister Wau Wau" depicting a circus strongman being run over by a car filled with sinister, cheering, goggled, wealthy citizens. This fairground Cabaret already featured the major techniques that were to mark Brecht's epic style: third-person acting (the compere in top hat is actually a woman), a montage of short scenes, and the use of a half-curtain. Indeed, the *Moritat* becomes the theme song for Brecht's most directly Cabaret-like early piece, *Die Driegroschenoper,* for which typical Cabaret costumes were originally designed. The *Moritat* form is also directly copied in the opening song of *The Threepenny Opera*, "Mackie Messer" ("Mack the Knife"), as well as in the fantasy social revenge song of "Pirate Jenny."

The Threepenny Opera is one of Roberto Ciulli's most iconic productions. Ciulli, the Italian director who founded the Theater an der Ruhr in central Germany in 1981 and still runs it, is truly postmodern. What he performs in Mülheim or directs across Asia (in his international "Silk Road" project) are mainly adaptations of classics, whether European or Eastern, rather than original plays. As Linda Hutcheon has asserted, adaptation is the sign and definition of the postmodern, particularly in the elements of (1) parody, (2) pastiche of previous work or other art forms, and (3) self-referentiality. The latter element, in terms of drama and performance, includes the play-within-the play,

Figure 6. Bänkelgesang with Brecht (on clarinet), Augsburg 1919.

metatheatre, and other overtly revealing production techniques usually hidden beneath the artistic surface.

Ciulli' s version of *The Threepenny Opera* was a literal deconstruction of Brecht, underscoring its theatricality by setting the whole action directly in a

Figure 7. Roberto Ciulli as Brothel Madame and two unidentified performers in *Three-penny Opera*, 1990 (photograph by A. Köhring).

Cabaret, instead of in early-nineteenth-century England on the eve of Queen Victoria's coronation. Ciulli presents Brecht's scenes as a series of variety acts: skits separated from each other by songs and farcical clown acts. It was also set in a very modern Italian mafia context, with Ciulli himself acting several smaller roles including a clown-like jailer (with the red nose that is one of the recurrent costume pieces in Theater an der Ruhr productions) and the brothel madame. The makeup in this production was exaggerated so that the one female prostitute had lipstick defining inch-thick lips and mascara giving the impression of two black eyes: a parody of the sexual suggestiveness of standard feminine makeup that questioned gender stereotypes. The same is true of the scene where prostitutes surround and attempt to seduce Mackie. They are clearly males wearing cliché female dresses, while the fortune-teller is a woman dressed as a man. In this adaptation gender-bending transforms Brecht's capitalist underworld of murderers ("Mack the Knife"), brothels ("The Song of Sexual Dependency"), and antisocial dreams ("Pirate Jenny") into a fantasy of sexual politics.

The influence of cabaret on the Avant-Garde is clearly demonstrated in the two productions discussed here. In different ways this popular working-class form, still very current if not quite so political as in the early twentieth century, has been picked up by contemporary AvantGarde artists, particularly in terms of stage productions. Even in contemporary theatre there is a strong sense of the down-market, gritty, and sordid space of the Cabaret—not just the glamorous and sexy image of a Marlene Dietrich film or the politically extreme performance of the Eleven Executioners—but still a graphic rejection of standard aesthetic principles. However, both the examples selected highlight how very direct the link to the earlier Avant-Garde from a hundred years ago actually is. They also demonstrate the major postmodern elements. The stylistic elements may be almost exactly the same from the opening of the twentieth century to today. However, the way these elements and Cabaret references become exaggerated and presented out of context, or indeed represented as things with historical reference, automatically introduces a quality of pastiche as well as emphasizing the performative artifice of the stagings of each director, automatically giving their productions a metatheatrical emphasis and explicitly associating their productions with the postmodern movement.

YORK UNIVERSITY, TORONTO

NOTES

1. One exception is Oliver Double and Michael Weston's "Brecht and Cabaret" in *The Cambridge Companion to Bertolt Brecht* (Cambridge & New York: Cambridge University Press, 2006), 40–63.

2. See "The Faith Healers" by Georg Grosz at http://www.tribemagazine.org/gazette/category/george-grosz.

3. Sibyl Moholy-Nagy, cit. Richard Huelsenbeck (ed.). *The Dada Painters and Poets: An Anthology* (New York: George Wittenorn, 1951) (*Documents of Modern Art, Vol. 8*), xxiii–xxiv.

4. *Dyveke* score. Trans. Brigitte Bogar. Reprinted by permission of Edition Wilhelm Hansen AS, Copenhagen. Originally this was the fourth verse of the song, but German censors cut a verse, so it now appears as the third verse.

5. Published in the Belgrade program, this translation from Serbian was provided by and reprinted with the permission of its author, Aleksandar Lukacs.

WORKS CITED

Fuegi, John. *Bertolt Brecht: Chaos, According to Plan.* Cambridge: Cambridge University Press, 1987

Henningsen, Poul, and Kjeld Abell. *Dyveke.* Revykomodie i to akter. Copenhagen: Gylendal, 1967.

Huelsenbeck, Richard, ed. *The Dada Painters and Poets: An Anthology.* New York: George Wittenorn, 1951.

Hutcheon, Linda. *A Poetics of Postmodernism: History, Theory, Fiction.* London: Routledge, 1988.

Jelavich, Peter. *Berlin Cabaret.* Cambridge: Harvard University Press, 1993.

Vogel, Shane. *The Scene of Harlem Cabaret: Race, Sexuality, Performance.* Chicago: University of Chicago Press, 2009.

Fifty Years of Ariane Mnouchkine and the Théâtre du Soleil: The Director as Dramaturge, Theater Historian and Public Intellectual

ALLEN J. KUHARSKI

Abstract

This essay frames a critical summary of the fifty-year professional history of contemporary French director Ariane Mnouchkine and her company, the Théâtre du Soleil, with the author's twenty-year-long teaching of a seminar on theater history at Swarthmore College with Mnouchkine's work as the theme. Mnouchkine's theatrical career provides a vehicle for five areas of critical inquiry: Company- or ensemble-based theater-making; the theory and practice of contemporary directing; diverse practices of production dramaturgy; the project of theater history as archive, critical practice, and artistic resource; and the role of the theater artist as public intellectual. The essay presents Mnouchkine and her company as exemplars of "experimental theater" understood as "research and development in the pursuit of best new standard practices" as well as addressing the apparent contradictions of such a mission for a unique theatrical auteur. Transmission of the results of such performance research is addressed through comparative discussion of Mnouchkine's relevance and influence to contemporary American theater practice.

Ariane Mnouchkine, America and the Academy

The fiftieth anniversary of the founding of the Théâtre du Soleil in France by director Ariane Mnouchkine and her early collaborators roughly coincides with the twentieth year of an experiment in teaching theater history to undergraduates at Swarthmore College that I began in 1995. The seminar has enjoyed a long and vigorous life, its syllabus evolving in tandem from afar with the ongoing work of the company, with the first week traditionally devoted to the Théâtre du Soleil's most recent production. The seminar's premise is to examine critically a major theater company as a case study, reflecting our department's larger curricular emphasis on company-based work as an alternative to the "independent contractor" model that is considered normative in American professional theater and conservatory training. While the seminar is cross-listed with French and Gender & Sexuality Studies (the successor to Women's Studies at Swarthmore), its emphasis is broadly comparative, and weekly discussions are consistently framed by questions raised for contemporary American theater practice by comparison and contrast with that of the Théâtre du Soleil.

Another rationale for the seminar is to provide a critical focus on the professional biography of a director as an extension of the directing curriculum that I have also taught alongside the seminar since 1991. No one would be surprised by a seminar devoted to playwrights such as Shakespeare, Brecht, or Beckett, but playwrights are not the only artists that matter in the history of the theater, especially theater as it has evolved over the last fifty years, where the work of *auteur* directors and companies such as Mnouchkine and the Théâtre du Soleil have largely defined new movements in the field. For a theater student, the in-depth study of an artist such as Mnouchkine has the same potential value as a seminar on Tolstoy or Dostoyevsky for a student of Russian, Proust for a student of French, Faulkner or Toni Morrison for American literature, Picasso or Andy Warhol for a student of art, or Balanchine or Pina Bausch for dance. As with Morrison, it important that Mnouchkine is a mature living artist, still making work.

My own expertise on Mnouchkine and the Théâtre du Soleil is largely the product of this teaching, which I was able to jumpstart thanks to the work of my colleague Helen E. Richardson, who wrote a groundbreaking dissertation on the work of Mnouchkine while we were graduate students in theater at Berkeley in the 1980s.[1] My working knowledge of French, admiration for the company's work when I saw the group live in performance in Montreal and New York, and broader interest in directing theory and practice were my points of entry into the subject. While I have published on a wide variety of other notable contemporary directors, this is my first writing on Mnouchkine. My interest in Mnouchkine and the Théâtre du Soleil, like my more immediate work with contemporary Polish theater and with the American director Joseph Chaikin, was in the service of an ongoing critical interrogation of the assumptions and standard practices of theater in the United States, and the goal of preparing students to become effective reformers of the contemporary American theater. I have often been misunderstood by colleagues in Poland and elsewhere as a promoter of Polish theater: my work there in directing workshops and in the Mnouchkine seminar has always been in the service of creating a different American theater for my students than was available to me entering the field. I have never considered life as an expatriate a meaningful artistic or professional option, for all that I have learned and admired abroad.

Approximately 100 theater students from Swarthmore, Haverford, and Bryn Mawr Colleges have completed the seminar over the years, and approximately 40 percent of those have used the seminar as part of Swarthmore's honors program, which culminates with written and oral examinations given by external examiners at the end of the senior year. Those examiners have included Judith G. Miller, author of *Ariane Mnouchkine* (Routledge, 2007) and the leading American authority on the director and her company.

Mnouchkine and the Théâtre du Soleil: 1964–2014

Ariane Mnouchkine (b. 1939) founded the Théâtre du Soleil ("the theater of the sun") in Paris in 1964 with a group of other recent French university graduates, all roughly of the same age. Many of the original group, all non-actors, remained part of the company for decades afterwards. Today Mnouchkine is the only remaining member of the founding group. The company has had several overlapping waves of actors since 1964, with some actors involved for twenty or more years. The Théâtre du Soleil can be described as Francophone and French by address, history, avowed citizenship, and government support, yet in practice it is today diversely international and polyglot in membership. Mnouchkine herself is French by citizenship and language, but not by family origin. Her father was the noted French film producer Alexandre Mnouchkine, who emigrated from Russia as a young man, and her mother was an English actress. The Théâtre du Soleil's long-time playwright Hélène Cixous is similarly a child of displaced Jewish parents from Morocco and Czechoslovakia who met in Algeria before the family became political refugees in France.

Mnouchkine and the Théâtre du Soleil emerged in the 1960s as a part of a wave of such *auteur* directors and companies around the world, with significant parallels to the work of Peter Brook in Great Britain, Jerzy Grotowski in Poland, and Joseph Chaikin's The Open Theatre and the San Francisco Mime Troupe in the United States, among others. An impulse behind this movement in European and American theater was perhaps best articulated by

Jerzy Grotowski's dramaturge Ludwik Flaszen in 1967 in an essay titled "After the Avant-Garde." He argued that if the philosophical, political, and theatrical givens of Samuel Beckett's theater were fully embraced, there would be no reason to do any other theater going forward—that the perfection of Beckett's thought and theatrical vision was itself an artistic and philosophical endgame. Flaszen's argument included the Absurdist movement as a whole. In Flaszen's words:

> These [playwrights] deconstructed the theatre's traditional image; they showed the possibilities of a new sensitivity; they pushed language's disintegration to its very limit, after which came only stillness and silence. Within this field, Beckett's works are truly great: he has the courage to take things to the edge. His ideal would be an empty unlit stage with no sound reaching the audience. [...] However, the 1950s creative wave of destruction is over. Wonderful avant-garde playwrights are alive and well and they may still surprise us with their future pieces, yet there is no doubt that the body of their work is finished. Therefore the most important question to be asked should be: what next? [...] Language and text—as the bearers of discursive content—have reached the limits of their function. The avant-garde has proved this fact in the theater, but only in the realm of language and text. To be consistent, we must go further: to create theatre we must step beyond literature; theater starts where the word ends. The realization that theatrical language should be autonomous, built of its own substance rather than the language of words, was a radical step already attempted by Artaud in his dreams [115, 117].

Mnouchkine's early teacher and mentor Jacques Lecoq created a post-dramatic pedagogy and aesthetic of naïveté (the clown) as a knowing response to both Europe's history with fascism through World War II and the postwar theater of anomie represented by the existentialists and absurdists such as Beckett and Ionesco. While these historical and political concerns were never explicit in Lecoq's pedagogy, his early career was deeply intertwined with that of Italian playwright, actor, and designer Dario Fo, where active social and political engagement was always foregrounded.[2] In American theater, Joseph Chaikin spent much of his career moving between embracing and rejecting Beckett on these terms: the theatrical expression of his rejection of Beckett was the combination of ensemble-based devised theater with his own philosophical explorations and off-stage activism, creating a theatrical hybrid of the theories of Artaud and Brecht with his own version of collective creation.

The work of Mnouchkine could be broadly defined in the same terms. The combination of political engagement, theatrical exuberance, and philosophical seeking among these theater artists can be understood as an international generational search for an alternative to the dramaturgy of Beckett, the other Absurdists, and the existentialist playwrights that preceded them. That existentialism and absurdism were movements and terms that first crystalized in Polish and French drama makes Mnouchkine's response of particular significance in France at the time. I would argue that her youthful move away from the existentialist/absurdist drama so predominant in France in the 1960s was not only part of the larger emergence of such *auteur* directors and companies, but also provides a defining point of departure for her specific understanding of the role of the theater artist as a public intellectual. Mnouchkine's theater has been described as "a theater of celebration," which I think succinctly captures her quite complex artistic polemic with the French and European theater of her youth. At the core of Mnouchkine's "theater of the sun," her pursuit of theatrical *jouissance* is a tacit polemic with the drama, theater, and philosophical givens of Beckettian anomie.

Today the international prestige of the Théâtre du Soleil has made it the de facto national theater of France. In Mnouchkine's vision from early on, she if anything intended it to be the antithesis of France's official national theater, La Comédie Française (the same could also be said of the work of Samuel Beckett). The company is certainly the most significant theatrical venture in France of the last half of the twentieth century. One need look no further than Mnouchkine's landmark production of *Tartuffe* in 1997, set in a contemporary North African Muslim household threatened by religious fundamentalism, to measure her accomplishment: it stands as certainly the most notable French production of the play since World War II. The process of rehearsing *Tartuffe* was documented by Mnouchkine in the film *Au soleil même la nuit* (1997), providing a late twentieth-century counterpart to Vasily Toporkov's classic account in *Stanislavsky in Rehearsal* of the Russian director's historic final workshops devoted to Molière's play at the Moscow Art Theatre just before his death in 1938.[3]

After fifty years, the reputation, originality, and influence of Mnouchkine and the Théâtre du Soleil can be compared historically to that of Constantine Stanislavsky and the Moscow Art Theater, Bertolt Brecht and the Berliner Ensemble, or Jerzy Grotowski and the Polish Laboratory Theatre. In terms of total years of activity, Mnouchkine and her company surpass all of these. In comparison, the Moscow Art Theater under Stanislavsky's leadership lasted 43 years, with Stanislavsky hardly at Mnouchkine's current level of productivity at the end. The institutional life of Jacques Lecoq's influential school in Paris is just as long, but Lecoq himself passed away in 1999. For absolute longevity, possibly the only longer-lived company would be The Living Theatre under Judith Malina in New York, but that group's artistic trajectory over time is ultimately distinct from that of the Théâtre du Soleil (though The Living Theatre's historic production of Kenneth Brown's *The Brig* in the 1960s profoundly influenced Mnouchkine's subsequent production of Arnold Wesker's *The Kitchen*). The ongoing work of Mnouchkine, now in her 70s, remains risky, accomplished, and unpredictable, with a major new production of Shakespeare's *Macbeth* opening in April 2014 at the Théâtre du Soleil's long-time home at the Cartoucherie (a former armaments factory) in Vincennes, in the outer suburbs of Paris.

The trajectory of Mnouchkine and the Théâtre du Soleil over the last fifty years is one of the ultimate illustrations of "experimental theater" in practice. My preferred definition of experimental theater is that of *sustained research and development in the pursuit of new standards of performance practice and excellence*—or perhaps more succinctly (in the language of the corporate world), *best new standard practices.* This frees such work from assumptions that it is the pursuit of esoteric, elitist, or superficially novel ends; of the avant-garde understood as essentially a self-limiting niche activity, a narrow high-end theatrical market resembling at times the limitations, excesses, and ephemerality of high fashion. It is helpful to remember on this score that Stanislavsky's approach to acting began in Russia as an avant-garde and radically revisionist project, as was also the case when his theories and practices were later transplanted to the United States in the 1920s and '30s. Stanislavsky was also one of the original *auteur* directors in modern theater, which is a key dimension to his work that was never successfully transmitted to his followers in the United States. The various phases in the history of the Théâtre du Soleil can perhaps be best understood as a series of sustained investigations of ensemble-based collaboration, the in-depth exploration of acting practice, and every possible permutation of work with performance text (with the possible exception of silent pantomime). Paradoxically, the company's work with classic texts by Shakespeare or Aeschylus is best understood itself as such an exploratory process of research and development usually done in anticipation of unprecedented original new works. At times, Mnouchkine assumes the role of an unapologetic member of a theatrical *arrière-garde* or even that of a *passéist.* But this is always the means to another yet undiscovered theatrical end.

Using this definition of experimental theater reveals a consistent inner contradiction in regard to Mnouchkine's commitment to such sustained research and development. As "basic research" into new possibilities for contemporary theater practice, it has proven undeniably original and generative. The absolute originality of Mnouchkine's work as a director with her company, however, is also one of the ultimate examples of "auteurism" in contemporary theater. Mnouchkine and the other great *auteur* directors of her generation and after have in myriad ways created *new works that are un-reproducible beyond the company of origin.* Since the 1960s, Mnouchkine and other such directors have in effect created a canon of un-reproducible classic *productions* in lieu of the modernist theater's creation of a canon of highly reproducible classic *play texts*. Most strikingly, this was no less true of Mnouchkine's initial collaborations with Hélène Cixous as playwright for the company, which began as an extraordinarily lavish investment in the nurturing of precisely such new dramatic texts. Thus, the combination of revelatory discoveries and artistic excellence made by Mnouchkine's commitment to such basic performance research are rarely able directly to become the basis of anything like a *new standard practice*. Her profound originality as an artist confounds the possibility of the work of the Théâtre du Soleil carrying on in a recognizable way after her departure. The same could be said for Tadeusz Kantor in Poland and many other such theatrical innovators.

What we are left with then is the unique and immense legacy of a visionary theater director over a fifty-year career. Another of Mnouchkine's many contradictions is that she has never sought to foreground her work as a director within the ensemble, and plays down the significance of directing practice in favor of the work of actors and playwrights. Yet it is her consistently catalyzing directorial presence that defines this history. It must be noted that this directorial presence is also combined with the ambition and determination required to found and lead a large and complex theatrical institution for the past fifty years.

And last, but not least, she has done so as a woman and a lesbian.

The Director as Dramaturge

Over time, Mnouchkine's work with text with the Théâtre du Soleil has incorporated virtually every category of dramaturgical practice, that is, of collaborative work with texts and writers in creating theatrical performance. In spite of her rejection of the theater of playwrights such as Beckett or Ionesco, Mnouchkine has been on an exhaustive career-long quest for an appropriate poetics of theatrical text and language no less than her similar searches for new categories of acting and relating with audiences. These varied practices over time cover essentially every known category of dramaturgical practice in live theater (the one possible exception would be the work of dance dramaturges with choreographers such as William Forsythe). As such, when I introduce my seminar with Mnouchkine and her company as the focus, I point out that this range of practices with texts, writers, and a theatrical ensemble makes our subject as much *production dramaturgy* as an introduction and investigation of *theater history*. These practices have included:

Work with existing classic texts by major playwrights, both living and dead; both writing in French and a variety of other languages. These playwrights include Maxim Gorky, Arnold Wesker, Shakespeare, Aeschylus, Euripides, and

Molière. Mnouchkine's 2014 production of *Macbeth* marks her third pass at staging Shakespeare (her first was *A Midsummer Night's Dream* in 1968; her second was her Shakespeare cycle in the early 1980s). This will be her first production of one Shakespeare's tragedies, though she has long flirted with the idea of staging *King Lear.* This kind of dramaturgy could be described as virtual collaboration with dead or otherwise absent playwrights.

The creation of new translations of classic plays suitable for contemporary stage performance in French. This has consisted of new acting versions of Shakespeare's *Twelfth Night, Richard II, Henry IV, Part I,* and *Macbeth,* as well as the first two parts of Aeschylus's *Oresteia* (the third part was translated by Cixous). These translations have been published, and Mnouchkine's translations of Shakespeare are highly regarded by critics as contemporary acting versions of these plays. Such translation is the most intimate form of dramaturgical collaboration with a dead or otherwise absent playwright writing in a foreign language. Actors in collaboration with a translator are also arguably the most valuable (and expensive) editors and consultants for a performance text in a target language.

The stage adaptation of non-dramatic works. For Mnouchkine, this has included dramatizations of novels by Théophile Gautier, Klaus Mann, and Jules Verne. It is perhaps significant that such adaptations bookend her work over the last five decades: among her earliest productions was an adaptation of Gautier's 1863 novel *Captain Fracasse,* and her most recent completed work was based on Verne's posthumous political allegory *The Survivors of the Jonathan* (completed in 2010 and now available on DVD).

Ariane Mnouchkine herself as a playwright. The one instance in which Mnouchkine has taken playwriting credit herself was for her dramatization of Klaus Mann's 1936 novel *Mephisto,* produced by the Théâtre du Soleil in 1979. She also took credit for the screenplay of her 1977 film *Molière.* The script for *Mephisto* has been published, including an English translation by British playwright Timberlake Wertenbaker, and the text is an exception among those generated by the Théâtre du Soleil in actually having a history of theatrical production by other companies, particularly in Germany. In 1989, Mnouchkine also shared screenwriting credit with Hélène Cixous for a television film called *La nuit miraculeuse* (*The Miraculous Night*), which was commissioned for the bicentennial of the start of the French Revolution.

The collaboration of Mnouchkine and the Théâtre du Soleil with a living playwright, Hélène Cixous, on the development of a series of original plays. These have included *The Terrible but Unfinished Story of Norodom Sihanouk, King of Cambodia* (1985), *L'Indiade, or the India of Their Dreams* (1987), *The Perjured City* (1994), and *The Flood Drummers* (1999). In the parlance of contemporary American theater, this could described as "new play development by a company with a resident playwright." If Cixous here functions as the house playwright, then Mnouchkine in effect works as both director and developmental dramaturge.

The creation of ensemble-generated devised works, or "collective creations." Alongside Jacques Lecoq's school in Paris or Joseph Chaikin and The Open Theater in the U.S., Mnouchkine and the Théâtre du Soleil were groundbreaking practitioners of this "anti-literary" or "post-dramatic" approach to generating new work in their historic pair of productions in the early 1970s inspired by the French Revolution, *1789* and *1793*, which were book-ended by two ambitious productions inspired by *commedia dell'arte* and clowning, *Les Clowns* (1969) and *L'age d'or* (1975). These productions are all notable for the absence of any credited playwright or production dramaturge, and for the latter two the absence of any published script, even as a document of the performances. In the case of *L'age d'or*, the Théâtre du Soleil published a case book of documents and statements by various members of the ensemble in lieu of a performance script (the materials were significantly published with the subtitle "Première ebauche," or "first draft," announcing their understanding of the piece as a perpetual work-in-progress).[4] While the scripts for *1789* and *1793* have been published (and the text for *1789* even translated and published in English), in the position of "author" on the printed page and in bibliographies, library catalogues, etc., is emphatically "Le Théâtre du Soleil."[5]

1789 and *1793* were performed over several years for audiences that numbered in the hundreds of thousands, and *1789* was eventually documented on film by Mnouchkine herself. For the Théâtre du Soleil's Shakespeare cycle in the 1980s and for *Les Atrides*, their version of *The Oresteia* in the 1990s, attendance numbers again approached those of *1789* (well over 200,000 each).[5] With the reach of works such as *1789*, *Molière*, the Shakespeare cycle, and *Les Atrides*, Mnouchkine's experimental explorations have consistently reached a version of what Helen Richardson has aptly called the Théâtre du Soleil's "quest for popular theater in the twentieth century."

This radical de-emphasis on the presence of a playwright or dramaturge in practice surpassed Chaikin's work in the United States at the same time: while playwrights such as Jean-Claude van Itallie, Megan Terry, or Susan Yankowitz eventually stopped working as such on his productions, what emerged instead in the person of Mira Rafalowicz was a new kind of production dramaturge for the creation of ensemble-generated devised work.[6] Mnouchkine and the Théâtre du Soleil to this day return at times to making original works either without credited playwright or dramaturge or in collaboration "in harmony" with Cixous, with the writer here functioning arguably more as a resident developmental dramaturge than as a house playwright.

Such original, ensemble-generated, devised work, or collective creation, is today a category of standard practice in contemporary theater around the world, with the Théâtre du Soleil as both one of the historic pioneers of the practice and Mnouchkine as possibly the longest-living committed creator of such company-based *auteur* productions.

The Director as Theater Historian and Public Intellectual

A few words about the teaching of theater history in general, and about my seminar at Swarthmore in particular. For theater faculty and students alike, theater history is the unloved Cinderella of theater studies. My undergraduate professor for a required theater history class at UW-Madison (today a distinguished senior colleague in performance studies), announced the first day of class that he would never teach the subject if the department hadn't forced him to do so. Most theater students similarly would gladly forgo taking theater history if it were not required, and as a required field of study it has the unsavory flavor of a tuition bill or parking ticket that one simply has to pay. Essentially all of our students in theater departments come to us because of their interest in performance, and most that go on in the field after graduation do so as working artists rather than academics. While at Swarthmore we also send a significant minority of our students on to doctoral programs in anticipation of academic careers, the challenge is to introduce these students to theater history in a way that they leave the required class understanding why and how to do more in the field—including perhaps eventually practicing and teaching theater history themselves.

On a more fundamental level is what I describe as *theater history as an impossible project*. In graduate school at Berkeley, my professor Travis Bogard argued that he never understood the point of pursuing theater history since how could one write meaningfully and critically about a performance one has not personally *seen*. I had two contradictory responses to this: first, as a practicing theater person, I agreed immediately. How *dare* someone try to write something about *my show*, much less have an opinion of it, if they did not see it in performance? I only later understood, however, that Bogard had conflated the work of theater history with that of performance criticism.

As someone on the rebound from the declaration of martial law in Poland, however, I was also acutely aware that oppressive governments like the Jaruzelski regime very much wished for our knowledge of theater history to be selective and incomplete, especially when theater assumes a leadership role in resistance to such regimes—when theater artists assume one of their most significant roles as public intellectuals. In the case of Poland under martial law, the Polish actors union led a highly effective boycott of state-sponsored theater and television in protest against the regime, a form of political intervention publicly supported by Ariane Mnouchkine and her company at the time.[7] Not to insist on the project of theater history in the face of such political and historical forces seemed a surrender to those forces.

The theater person in me then also spoke up and pointed out that in practice no one is able to attend all the live performances that deserve our attention in the world today, much less in the past, least of all working theater people, who if successful are too busy making and performing their own work to see the work of others taking place around them (much less at a distance). So the *necessary impossibility* of theater history is to insist that we can make some sense of the theatrical past (which begins with yesterday's performance) with incomplete, imperfect, and wildly variable material evidence. Working with these materials is the nitty-gritty of theater historiography, as is creating and maintaining the performance archives of the future. The inevitable gaps in these theatrical archives, the result of neglect and chronic lack of resources as well as of the violence of history and political oppression, are best filled by the creative work of later artists wanting to invoke, claim, and complete this history. Today I understand that the work of theater history *begins* where the possibility of performance criticism *ends*: its purpose is to somehow access the performance that could not be seen.

The *Swarthmore College Bulletin 2014–15* lists over thirty different courses and seminars in highly diverse aspects of art history,[8] but our Theater Department for decades has strained to sustain this *one* offering to cover *all* of theater history (alongside three other courses in performance theory and dramaturgy). This situation is hardly unusual in theater departments around the country. And the reality is that there are vast gaps waiting to be filled in theater history scholarship. These gaps include significant ones in the area of translations of plays (both classic and contemporary works) written in languages other than English, including major languages such as German, French, or Japanese. Glaring examples include the work of contemporary playwrights such as Dea Loher in Germany or Toshiki Okada in Japan, or of modern classics such as Paul Claudel in French, or several of the Polish classic plays staged by Grotowski. I have had to hire a talented former student of French who took my seminar (now a doctoral student in dramaturgy at Yale) to translate two major scripts generated by the Théâtre du Soleil for our use in the seminar: *1793* and Cixous's *L'Indiade*, which have never appeared in print in English. Should we find this astonishing or not? These specific gaps are generally not being filled, nor do I see any sign they will be filled, by the often brilliant work being done by our colleagues in Performance Studies. The problem of massive gaps in our historical and cross-cultural understanding of theater history is compounded by comparable gaps in the archiving and documentation of contemporary theater for the future in ways starkly illustrated by the relative resources currently dedicated in the academy to art history or music history compared to theater history. Those thirty courses in art history at Swarthmore reflect an historical investment in tenure-line positions and the scholarship and curatorship they generate.

My seminar on Mnouchkine and the Théâtre du Soleil is one solution to these issues that I have been working on since 1995. The premise of the seminar is the history of Mnouchkine's company as a case study of a major artist and organization in the field from start to finish. The methodology of the teaching is that theater history is not only the domain of academic specialists, too often the graying Fausts of the tenured faculty (among whom I include myself these days), but also of working artists such as Mnouchkine: that theater history provides a set of tools and "stock" materials essential to the creative working lives of actors, directors, designers, and playwrights. The key to a typical unit in the seminar is the combination of historical and dramaturgical source materials with Mnouchkine's contemporary engagement with those materials: the various forms of influence and exchange between artists of different historical periods and cultures. Sometimes these relations are polemical: for example, how Mnouchkine's treatment of the French Revolution pointedly *differs* from other theatrical treatments of the history by Georg Büchner in *Danton's Death* or Peter Weiss in *Marat/Sade*. I also include Polish director Andrzej Wajda's 1982 film *Danton*, released at the height of the actors boycott in Poland, which is in turn based on the 1931 play *The Danton Affair* by Polish playwright Stanisława Przybyszewska.

The unique opportunity offered by such a comprehensive survey of the Théâtre du Soleil in particular is that the company's history over time encompasses most of the elements of a conventional undergraduate theater history survey: Greek tragedy; Shakespeare and Elizabethan/Jacobean theater and drama; *commedia dell'arte*; Molière and seventeenth-century French theater; Romanticism; the rise of social and psychological realism in Russia and Great Britain; Stanislavsky and Bulgakov in the context of Stalinist Russia; interwar German cabaret and political theater (and indirectly Brecht); a variety of classical Asian traditions, including Kabuki, Bunraku, Kathakali, and Korean court drumming; Lecoq, physically based acting, and collective creation; feminist and queer theater; and versions of verbatim and documentary theater addressing contemporary global social issues. Such a syllabus is inevitably a broadly comparative one, and includes not just the plays staged by Mnouchkine, but also key works for defining certain periods, genres, and subjects.

As a socially-conscious theater artist, Mnouchkine has turned repeatedly to the genre of the history play, both as received from earlier playwrights such as Shakespeare, and as a vehicle for major original works such as *Sihanouk* and *L'Indiade*. While she emphatically argues that all theater is *metaphor*, she also famously insisted that her productions of *Richard II* and *Henry IV, Part I*, were based on how Shakespeare was *not* our contemporary.

Among the most interesting facts that emerge from the history of the Théâtre du Soleil over time is that Mnouchkine and her collaborators not only mine social history and theater history as a source for their ongoing work, but that *theater history* per se repeatedly becomes the significant subject of the company's work. Her theme repeatedly becomes that of the theater artist in society, the responsibility and the challenges to theater artists individually and collectively to function as public intellectuals: theater history as social history, social history understood through the lens of theater history. Mnouchkine's interest in social history almost always somehow treats the role of theater artists in their time, most significantly in works from the 1970s such as her film *Molière* and her stage adaptation of Klaus Mann's novel *Mephisto* (which is itself based on the life and career of the twentieth-century German actor and director Gustav Gründgens, a contemporary of Bertolt Brecht). The Théâtre du Soleil's 2010 production *The Survivors of the Lost Hope* (*Les naufragés de fol espoir*), freely inspired by Jules Verne's little-known posthumous novel *The Survivors of the Jonathan*, is perhaps Mnouchkine's most complex and poetic reflection on the dance between artists, the societies they inhabit, and the performative representations they create and share.

For Mnouchkine such theater historical subject matter, unlike her take on Shakespeare's history plays, is always about implicit cross-historical metaphor and social commentary. The impulse to stage theater history was there from the very beginning of the company in its 1965 production based on Théophile Gautier's 1863 novel *Captain Fracasse*, which presents a vivid imaginary picture of the life of a company of itinerant actors in early seventeenth-century France: a rare representation of French theater *before* the age of Corneille, Molière, and Racine. This period of early French theater history reappears in the first half of Mnouchkine's epic film version of the life of Molière. One metaphor consistently embedded in Mnouchkine's repeated excavation and stage representation of the work of past theater artists is that these are both celebratory and critical self-portraits of the Théâtre du Soleil, as well as the naming and claiming of a theatrical heritage.

A key work in our unit on Mnouchkine's portrayal of Molière is *The Versailles Impromptu*, in which Molière satirically portrays himself and the members of his company as a cast of characters named after themselves. Mnouchkine's series of metaphorical stage self-representations similarly becomes literal in the portrayal of the director and the members of her company in the vast cycle of satirical one-man shows generated by her former leading actor Philippe Caubère (who played Molière in the film, among other roles on stage as part of the company). Thus the circle of representing theater history on stage is completed in a surprising way (Caubère in fact uses a quote from *The Versailles Impromptu* as an epigraph to the published text). Caubère created his eleven-part cycle over several years, and it ultimately runs around thirty hours in total performance time. He has both performed live and recorded it for distribution on video, with the complete text also available in print. Caubère's massive cycle is possibly the most exuberant example in contemporary theater of the "actor-creator" cultivated through Lecoq's pedagogy and Mnouchkine's subsequent practice.

Mnouchkine, like Charles Ludlam or Tony Kushner in American theater, is one of the great magpies of theater and film history. She does her homework with evident pleasure, and has consistently woven arcane archival materials into the company's productions such as street theater from the time of the French Revolution or sketches from Erika Mann's anti–Nazi Peppermill Cabaret.[9] She has also excavated and staged the histories of significant women in theater history such as Madeleine Béjart and Erika Mann. Comparisons between Mnouchkine and Kushner comprise one of the themes of the seminar, in particular the combination of their shared passion for the excavation and recycling of theater history and highly visible roles as public intellectuals. An early unit, for example, consists of reading Kushner's *The Illusion* (his adaptation of Corneille's *The Theatrical Illusion*, written in 1636) with the Théâtre du Soleil's early adaptation of Gautier's *Captain Fracasse* (works that all present complex defenses of actors and artists in society). A late unit similarly combines viewing *The Last Caravansary*, the Théâtre du Soleil's epic piece on displacement, the documentary film on the company's workshops in Kabul in 2005, with reading Kushner's *Homebody/Kabul*.

My seminar, therefore, is framed by the argument that Ariane Mnouchkine should be understood as a great contemporary theater historian, though one that has never taught the subject in a university classroom. We read theater history both through Oscar Brockett and Ariane Mnouchkine.

Mnouchkine's theme and inspiration is often theater history. But just as Shakespeare is unreliable as a social or political historian, Mnouchkine is also unreliable as a theater historian. As an artist, she selects, she has an appropriately subjective critical lens, she is creating the truth of an artistic work, not that of the historical record. Interestingly, she is perhaps more scrupulous about the details of social history that inform her works than of theater history. Her interest in theater history, like Shakespeare's histories of the English crown, is the creation of an enduring mythic history of the significance of theater and theater artists in society.

I am proud of the fact that my undergraduate theater students at Swarthmore may be the only ones in the country, if not the English-speaking world, who are introduced to the nineteenth-century French writer Théophile Gautier (1811–1872) as part of their education, an author whose collected works in French and English otherwise gather dust on the shelf of the Swarthmore library (our leather-bound sixteen-volume edition of his complete works in English dates from 1900). When Gautier's name is referred to in our annual viewings of Marcel Carné's 1945 classic film *Children of Paradise,* the students already know who he is.

Children of Paradise is another staging of a little-known period of French theater history, that of the early nineteenth century and the career of the renowned Czech-French mime Jean-Gaspard Duburau (b. Jan Kašpar Dvořák, 1796–1846). Duburau is of particular relevance to Lecoq and his writings, as well as to the entire tradition of *pantomime blanche* in French theater, through the performance of Jean-Louis Barrault in the film and into the post-war work of Marcel Marceau and others.[10] The making of the film in Vichy France and the post-war fate of the actress Arletty is yet another illustration of the seminar's theme of the political role of the theater artist in society.

Among the exercises that the students do in the seminar is imaginatively to retrace the steps of the theater-historical and dramaturgical process of a little-documented production such as *Captain Fracasse,* which at times is more generative than the parallel unit we do on the richly documented dramatization of *Mephisto.* Every year one student is assigned to read *Fracasse* and report on it to the group. That report includes a hypothetical discussion of how and why the novel would present an opportunity for theatrical adaptation and performance as our only way to get at what the 26-year-old Mnouchkine might have been thinking at the point she committed her company to this project. Among the unexpected collateral benefits of this exercise over the years was a student's decision to create precisely such a dramatization of another fascinating metatheatrical novel by Gautier, the gender-bending classic *Mademoiselle de Maupin,* as an honors thesis in production dramaturgy in 2011.[11] That thesis project earned a rare highest honors from the student's visiting examiner (Walter Bilderback, the resident dramaturge of the Wilma Theater in Philadelphia). Thus, students in the seminar can begin to apply the principle of engaging with the archive of theater history in the creation of new work, with Mnouchkine as a model of this practice.

On a larger scale, my teaching of the Mnouchkine seminar at Swarthmore since 1995 has exactly coincided with the history of Philadelphia's Pig Iron Theatre Company, whose core members have mostly studied at the Lecoq School in Paris (as did Mnouchkine in her youth), have participated in workshops with Mnouchkine and the Théâtre du Soleil in Paris, are avid followers of Mnouchkine and her company, and whose work Mnouchkine has seen in performance. Pig Iron is an example of an American theater company of a younger generation in the tradition of Chaikin, Lecoq, and Mnouchkine, that has for decades looked to Mnouchkine as an inspiration and model in the way that earlier American theater artists looked to Stanislavsky or Brecht. Pig Iron's work with performance text over the last twenty years has striking similarities to that of the Théâtre du Soleil (with the significant exception of Mnouchkine's collaboration with Cixous). As with the Théâtre du Soleil, Pig Iron's more than two-dozen productions, almost all original works, have typically been created under the direction of a self-effacing *auteur* director with a talent for company organization and management, Dan Rothenberg (b. 1973).

Pig Iron launched their Advanced Performance Training Program (APT) in 2011, which is North America's closest counterpart to the Lecoq School or to its English spin-off the London International School of Performing Arts (LISPA). APT is a two-year conservatory training program emphasizing physically-based devised ensemble theater. The influence of Mnouchkine and the Théâtre du Soleil is present both implicitly and explicitly in the curriculum and daily teaching of the Pig Iron school. My role as an occasional faculty member at APT is to provide a broader version of the historical and theoretical framework I use in my seminar on theater history and classes on performance theory at Swarthmore.

The example of the Pig Iron Theater Company and school is one way of affirming there is a resolution to the apparent contradiction of Mnouchkine as an *auteur* director and the Théâtre du Soleil's mission of experimental theater as research and development in the pursuit of *best new standard practices*. The issue for such experimental auteur directors and ensembles, defined as early as 1980 by Richard Schechner in *The End of Humanism*, is that of *transmission* to other artists, especially those of other cultures and younger generations.

With Mnouchkine as a model, the future practice of theater history should be bright.

SWARTHMORE COLLEGE

NOTES

1. Helen E. Richardson, *The Théâtre du Soleil and the Quest for Popular Theatre in the Twentieth Century*, diss., University of California, Berkeley, 1990.
2. See the 1999 documentary *Les deux voyages de Jacques Lecoq*, directed by Jean-Gabriel Carasso and Jean-Noël Roy.
3. Vasily Osipovich Toporkov, "*Tartuffe*" and "First Showing of *Tartuffe*," *Stanislavsky in Rehearsal*, trans. Christine Edwards (New York: Theatre Arts Books, 1979).
4. Théâtre du Soleil, *L'Age d'or: Première Ebauche*. Paris: Éditions Stock, 1976.
5. David Williams, ed., *Collaborative Theatre: The Théâtre du Soleil Sourcebook* (Lon-

don: Routledge, 1999). The production chronology that is an addendum to the text includes comprehensive attendance figures for all productions by the Théâtre du Soleil.

6. See articles by Mira Rafalowicz and Allen J. Kuharski in *Dramaturgy and American Theater: A Source Book* (Fort Worth: Harcourt Brace, 1997) and Roger Babb's book *Joseph Chaikin and the Winter Project* (Saarbrücken: Lambert Academic Publishing, 2010).

7. Ariane Mnouchkine, "AIDA," *Komedianci: Rzecz o bojkocie*, Zakłady Wydawnicze "Versus" 1990, 9–12.

8. *Swarthmore College Bulletin 2014–15*. CXII.1. The curriculum in art history at Swarthmore includes a total of 34 regularly scheduled courses and seminars in the following areas: six on Western architecture; six on Japanese and East Asian art; five on modernism in painting and photography; five on the Spanish Golden Age, colonial Latin America, and Native American art; ten on classical, medieval, and renaissance art; and a hand-full of broad survey courses. The Department of Theater, in contrast, is able to offer a total of four survey courses in theater history, performance theory, and production dramaturgy, all of which are by necessity comparative and (appropriately) emphasize methods and practices over knowledge of a cultural canon. A small number of additional courses in dance history and the history of opera are offered in the Department of Music & Dance. In the Department of Theater, it was decided decades ago that a course or seminar in twentieth-century American theater and drama would be too specialized an offering given the compression on our academic curriculum.

9. See Katrin Seig's chapter "The Cabaret: Erika Mann and the Peppermill" in her book *Exiles, Eccentrics, and Activists: Women in Contemporary German Theater* (Ann Arbor: University of Michigan Press, 1995), 50–80.

10. Jacques Lecoq, *Le théâtre du geste mimes et acteurs* (Paris: Bordas, 1987), 49–53.

11. Isa St. Clair, *Mlle*, Stage adaptation of *Mademoiselle de Maupin* by Théophile Gautier, Swarthmore College, Department of Theater, 2011.

WORKS CITED

Babb, Roger. *Joseph Chaikin and the Winter Project*. Saarbrücken: Lambert Academic Publishing, 2010.

Carasso, Jean-Gabriel, and Jean-Noël Roy. *Les deux voyages de Jacques Lecoq*. CNDP, 1999/2006. DVD.

Carné, Marcel, dir. *Les enfants du paradis*. Pathé Cinéma/Criterion, 2002. DVD.

Caubère, Philippe. *Le roman d'un acteur*. Provence: Éditions Joëlle Losfeld et La Comédie nouvelle, 1994.

Cixous, Hélène. *Drums on the Dam*. Trans. Judith G. Miller and Brian J. Mallet. *Selected Plays of Hélène Cixous*. Ed. Eric Prenowitz. London: Routledge: 2004.

_____. *L'Indiade, ou L'Inde de leurs reves*. Paris: Théâtre du Soleil, 1987.

_____. *The Perjured City*. Trans. Bernadette Fort. *Selected Plays of Hélène Cixous*. Ed. Eric Prenowitz. London: Routledge: 2004.

_____. *The Terrible but Unfinished Story of Norodom Sihanouk, King of Cambodia*. Trans. Juliet Flower MacCannell, Judith Pike, and Lollie Groth. Lincoln: Nebraska University Press, 1994.

_____, trans. *L'Orestie: Les Eumenides*. By Eschyle (Aeschylus). Paris: Théâtre du Soleil, 1992.

Flaszen, Ludwik. "After the Avant-Garde." Trans. Andrzej Wojtasik with Paul Allain. *Grotowski & Company*. Ed. Paul Allain. Holstebro/Malta/Wrocław: Icarus Publishing Enterprise, 2010.

Gautier, Théophile. *Le Capitaine Fracasse*. Paris: E. Fasquelle, 1905.

_____. *Mademoiselle de Maupin*. Trans. Patricia Duncker and Helen Constantine. London: Penguin Books, 2005.

Kuharski, Allen J. "Joseph Chaikin and the Presence of the Dramaturg." *Dramaturgy in American Theater: A Source Book*. Ed. Susan Jonas, Geoff Proehl, and Michael Lupu. Fort Worth, TX: Harcourt Brace, 1997.

Kushner, Tony. *Homebody/Kabul*. New York: Theatre Communications Group, 2004.

_____. *The Illusion*. New York: Theatre Communications Group, 1994.

Lecoq, Jacques. *Le théâtre du geste: Mimes et acteurs*. Paris: Bordas, 1987.

Mann, Klaus. *Mephisto*. Trans. Robin Smyth. New York: Penguin Books, 1977.

Miller, Judith Graves. *Ariane Mnouchkine*. London: Routledge, 2007.

Mnouchkine, Ariane. "AIDA," *Komedianci: Rzecz o bojkocie*. Ed. Andrzej Roman. Warsaw: Zakłady Wydawnicze "Versus," 1990.

_____. *Méphisto: Le roman d'une carrière d'après Klaus Mann*. Paris: Solin, 1979.

_____, dir. *Au soleil même la nuit/scènes d'accouchements*. Paris: Bel Air Classiques, 2011. DVD.

_____, dir. *Molière*. Screenplay by Ariane Mnouchkine. Paris: Bel Air Classiques, 2004. DVD.

_____, trans. *La Nuit des rois*. Paris: Solin, 1982.

_____, trans. *L'Orestie: Agamemnon*. By Eschyle (Aeschylus). Paris: Théâtre du Soleil, 1990.

_____, trans. *L'Orestie: Les choephores*. By Eschyle (Aeschylus). Paris: Théâtre du Soleil, 1992.

_____, trans. *Les Shakespeare: Henry IV, première partie*. By William Shakespeare. Paris: Théâtre du Soleil, 1984.

_____, trans. *Les Shakespeare: Richard II*. By William Shakespeare. Paris: Théâtre du Soleil, 1984.

Przybyszewska, Stanisława. *The Danton Affair*. Trans. Bolełsaw Taborski. *The Danton Affair & Thermidor: Two Plays*. Intro. Daniel Gerould. Evanston, IL: Northwestern University Press, 1989.

Rafalowicz, Mira. "Dramaturg in Collaboration with Joseph Chaikin." *Dramaturgy in American Theater: A Source Book*. Ed. Susan Jonas, Geoff Proehl, and Michael Lupu. Fort Worth, TX: Harcourt Brace, 1997.

Richardson, Helen E. "The Théâtre du Soleil and the Quest for Popular Theatre in the Twentieth Century." Diss. University of California, Berkeley, 1990.

Roman, Andrzej, ed. *Komedianci: Rzecz o bojkocie*. Warsaw: Zakłady Wydawnicze "Versus," 1990.

Schechner, Richard. *The End of Humanism*. New York: Performing Arts Journal Publications, 1982.

Seig, Katrin. "The Cabaret: Erika Mann and the Peppermill." *Exiles, Eccentrics, Activists: Women in Contemporary German Theater*. Ann Arbor: University of Michigan Press, 1994.

Swarthmore College Bulletin 1914–15. CXII.1. Swarthmore, PA: Swarthmore College, 2014.

Théâtre du Soleil [collective author]. *L'Age d'or: Première Ebauche*. Paris: Éditions Stock, 1976.

_____. *La dernier caravansérail: Odyssées*. Dir. Ariane Mnouchkine. Paris: Arte Video, 2006. DVD.

_____. *Les naufragés de fol espoir*. Dir. Ariane Mnouchkine. Paris: Bel Air Classiques, 2013. DVD.

_____. *La Nuit miraculeuse*. Dir. Ariane Mnouchkine. Screenplay by Hélène Cixous. Paris: Théâtre du Soleil, 1990. Videocassette.

_____. *1789: The French Revolution, Year One*. Trans. Alexander Trocchi. *Gambit* Summer 1972: 3–74.

_____. *1789: La révolution doit s'arrêter à la perfection du bonheur* and *1793: La cité révolutionaire est de ce monde*. Paris: Théâtre du Soleil, 1984.

Toporkov, Vasily Osipovich. "*Tartuffe*," "First Showing of *Tartuffe*." *Stanislavsky in Rehearsal*. Trans. Christine Edwards. New York: Theatre Arts Books, 1979.

Verne, Jules. *The Survivors of the Jonathan*. Trans. I. O. Evans. London: Arco Publications, 1962.

Wajda, Andrzej, dir. *Danton*. Gaumont/Criterion, 2009. DVD.

Wertenbaker, Timberlake, trans. *Mephisto*. By Ariane Mnouchkine. *Theater & Politics: An International Anthology*. Ed. Erika Munk. New York: Ubu Repertory Theater Publications, 1990.

Williams, David, ed. *Collaborative Theatre: The Théâtre du Soleil Sourcebook*. London: Routledge, 1999.

Norodom Sihanouk: The "Unfinished" Story of American Global Totalitarianism by Hélène Cixous and the Théâtre du Soleil

LES ESSIF

Abstract

Hélène Cixous's The Terrible but Unfinished Story of Norodom Sihanouk, King of Cambodia *enacts the tragic destiny of the Cambodian people, a dramatic chapter in the larger global story of U.S. foreign policy and its designs toward a new world order during the era of the Vietnam and Cold Wars. In view of the new world order of the twenty-first century (U.S. occupations of Iraq and Afghanistan and the global war on terrorism), thirty years after its original production, Cixous's prophetic story of "America" remains "unfinished." To date, scholarship has not sufficiently captured the play's depiction of the United States as the singular author of the Cambodian tragedy. This essay will show how the story of Sihanouk tells the story of American global totalitarianism through the cultural and moral comparisons and contrasts that it draws with respect to three principal characters and character-groupings: The highly cultured and cosmopolitan Sihanouk, the American politicians and diplomats, and the Khmer Rouge.*

Throughout the fifty-year existence of Ariane Mnouchkine's Théâtre du Soleil its *Frenchness* has been evident in its theatrical exploration of world history, from its production of *1789* (1970), to *The Last Caravanserai* (2003), to the recent revival of *Norodom Sihanouk* with a Cambodian cast. Originally produced in 1985, Hélène Cixous's *The Terrible but Unfinished Story of*

Norodom Sihanouk, King of Cambodia has a longer stage life than other Soleil productions, and this, I think, because it is so "unfinished." The work continues to expand its presence on the world stage. Since 2007 the Théâtre du Soleil has been collaborating with the Théâtre Phare Ponleu Selpak in Cambodia on a recreated Khmer-language version of the text. Under the co-direction of Georges Bigot (who created the original role of Sihanouk in 1985) and Delphine Cottu, the recreated performance continues to tour internationally.

Cixous wrote *Sihanouk* as one of her many collaborations with Mnouchkine's Théâtre du Soleil, a director and a company who have been collectively creating and/or commissioning socio-culturally relevant theatrical projects and texts since the late sixties. The Théâtre du Soleil is one of the most influential theatre companies in French and world history. Mnouchkine and her company are very French in their highly performative and creative theatrical presentation of sophisticated cultural discourse for a wide range of audiences, and in their commitment to social and political activism. *Sihanouk's* blatant denunciation of the U.S. role in global politics, at a time when the United States held sufficient control of the Western geopolitical sphere, reveals an admirable, courageous aspect of Cixous's and the Soleil's mission to interrogate history.

The play enacts the tragic destiny of the Cambodian people, a dramatic chapter in the larger global (his)story of U.S. foreign policy and its designs toward a new world order during the era of the Vietnam War, and the Eastern Block-Western Block Cold War framework within which it materialized. In view of the new world order of the twenty-first century (U.S. occupations of Iraq and Afghanistan, the Americano-global war on terrorism, and the aggressive expansion of an Americano-global and totalitarian form of corporate capitalism), thirty years after its original production, Cixous's prophetic story of "America" remains "unfinished." It makes clear that the story of the United States' global exercise of military and economic imperialism remains both incomplete and largely untold. The chapter of this story told theatrically by Cixous reveals the intricate bonds between U.S. imperialism, the story of Sihanouk, and the future of the globe. It lives the "unfinished" life of American imperialism. Cixous said that while writing the play, "I thought I was doing something forbidden, so I decided that when I finished it I would change all the names [...]. But I didn't" (cited in Judith Pike xviii). This decision to name names such as Kissinger and, in effect, to apply a heavy dose of history to theatrical fiction, to challenge fiction with historical reality (and vice versa), says something about the contrast between the French and American cultures. What is more, at the time she made the decision, Cixous would have been most apprehensive about the European and U.S. reaction to her explicit denunciation of U.S. imperialism.

To date, scholarship has not sufficiently captured the play's depiction of the United States as more or less the singular author of the brunt of the Cambodian tragedy. Juliet Flower MacCannell, for example, rightly compares the two "villains" of the play: Henry Kissinger (the U.S. National Security Advisor and the architect of the secret Cambodia bombings in 1969 and 1970) and Pol Pot (ruthless leader of the communist Khmer Rouge who was accused of organizing the genocidal purge that resulted in the murder of about two million people). MacCannell refers to Kissinger and Pol Pot as "these two avatars of fanatical and unreflected [*sic*] 'democracy'" who were "working to enforce the health codes of our time," the latter acting to purge Cambodia of "its noncommunist, traditional past" and the former, to cleanse the country of its communist influences (xi). For his part, David Graver insightfully affirms that "the story [Cixous] weaves is not one of good versus evil, but a shimmering tapestry of ambition, generosity, and fanaticism, threads which run through all the political camps portrayed" (212). MacCannell and Graver make excellent points about Cixous's strategy to take the broadest, most inclusive view possible on political corruption and fanaticism around the globe, especially as concerns the individual leaders involved in the decision-making of the time. Yet I believe that, in the end, the story tells us more about aberrant ethical and intellectual tendencies of national and world cultures than about personal portraits of diabolical historical figures. It does more to expose malevolent culture than malicious individuals.

This essay will focus on one particular aspect of the play: the way in which the text constructs and organizes the character portraits of the three principal characters/ groups: King Sihanouk of Cambodia; the American politicians and diplomats, with Henry Kissinger as their kingpin; and the Cambodian communist Khmer Rouge, with Pol Pot as its leader. This dramaturgical strategy ultimately tells the story of American global totalitarianism and exposes the United States as not just one of the "bad guys" but *the* bad guy in the story.

For a number of years now I've been writing on the subject of French plays that stage "America" in a variety of ways. I argue that French dramatists are primarily interested in, if not fascinated by, what Jean Baudrillard has referred to as American "unculture" and by a specific archetype of this unculture that I call "homo americanus." In reference to the United States, the French don't flirt with the term "unculture" to imply a lack of culture in the conventional sense of not being cultivated (or sophisticated). Instead the term suggests on the part of American culture a lack of potential or a disinclination to perceive or to address the dynamic contradictory nature of human culture and civilization. Terry Eagleton has developed this idea about the contradictory nature of human culture, saying that in the very act of realizing some human potentials, civilization also damagingly suppresses others. He makes the distinction between critical cultures and uncritical cultures, saying that critical cultures recognize this contradictory nature through the application of dialectical thought. Régis Debray would add that this critical, dialectical form of cultural thinking means to think not this or that, but this and that.[1] In essence, I argue that French culture (homo gallicus) is dialectical while homo americanus unculture is not. Soleil's and Cixous's theatrical exposé of American unculture reflects its dialectical Frenchness. With its conceptual and ideological emphases on "black or white" and "good or bad," the undialectical unculture of homo americanus generates America's uncritical "anti-"stance (in particular, in this case, anti-communism). This stance is the source for Cixous's text, which finds America responsible for the historical tragedy on which it is based.

Like many of Soleil's productions, the play is exceptionally long and complex. Even with cuts, its two-part performance lasted nearly ten hours in 1985. The play's plot dramatizes the history of Cambodia's political plight, its struggle for existence, in relation to King Sihanouk's political life from 1955 to 1979—his declining power, his diplomatic trips to China and Russia, his exile in China, and his detention following his return to Cambodia. It moves more or less chronologically from the onset of Cambodia's and Sihanouk's political disintegration, through Sihanouk's desperate quest to negotiate for the survival of an independent Cambodia, on the inside of his country's borders as well as outside. On the inside, he battles with representatives of diverse domestic political factions, some opposed to the ostensibly "undemocratic" royalist nature of Sihanouk's rule, others to his anti-capitalist (i.e., anti–U.S.) and socialist leanings. In the end he confronts his most daunting internal enemy, the extremist-communist Khmer Rouge led by Pol Pot. Externally, he pleads the cause of Cambodian neutrality concerning the Vietnam War with leaders of international political and military interests, ranging from Cambodia's robust and antagonistic neighbor Vietnam, to major players like China and Russia in the East and France and the United States in the West. Cixous's text has a supernatural component as it pays close attention to the Cambodian dead as well as the living, staging, for example, frequent interventions of Sihanouk's ghostly father, King Suramarit. It also enables the perspectives of women and of the more common people.

The twenty-five members of the cast play over fifty characters, which in the text's initial didascalia are arranged into groups representing the various geopolitical regions of the world that were involved in the story of Norodom Sihanouk's struggle to remain the leader of the Cambodian people, first as the king-monarch heir to the throne and then as the democratically elected prince-president. The groupings are "Cambodia," "Phnom Penh," "United States of

America," "USSR.," "China," and "Vietnam." Notwithstanding France's history of political control over Cambodia, which was its protectorate from the nineteenth century through the 1950s, the United States is the major player in this story, the one that to a certain extent ties together all the national groupings and the geopolitics, the one that orchestrates most fervently the Cold War political agenda leading to global political crisis, the one implicated in all the story's major themes—and the only Western culture of the major groups. To be sure, Cambodia's tragic destiny can be traced back to its colonial past, which necessarily marks the country as a "postcolonially traumatized" society.[2] Yet Cixous's text makes it clear that late twentieth-century American imperialism imposed itself as the major antagonist to Cambodia's future.

The individual characters of the play are fully representative of their respective groups. The groupings delineate distinct national cultures with signature behavioral patterns. In her analysis of the two "fanatical" villains of the play, Kissinger and Pol Pot—one seeking to make the world safe for American capitalism, the other for international socialism—MacCannell says that "Cixous shows them both as responding less to national political ideals than to the unconscious demands of an Ideal Ego, a malevolent Superego, commanding them to rid themselves of a persistent nagging 'stain'" (xi). I would take this argument further and assert that behind Kissinger's personal Superego lies the Superego of an aberrant national culture.[3] Erica Johnson has pointed out the "centrality of the figure of the [Cambodian] king to national identity" and how the character of Sihanouk provided Cixous "with a means of portraying national as well as personal identity" (120), and finally how "Sihanouk imagines himself to be coextensive with the nation that he represents" (124). One could say much the same for the figure of Kissinger but not for Pol Pot. While both Kissinger's and Pot's most salient character flaw is the masterminding of genocide on a grand scale in the name of a global geopolitical cause, Kissinger expresses his homo americanus national culture while Pot represents the aberrant ideology of extremist communism that conflicts with the national culture he shares with Sihanouk. Kissinger kills foreign "primitives" through a highly technocratic politico-military culture and with the use of high-tech bombs, while Pol Pot kills non-compliant members of his own culture through more primitive means and with more primal methods. There is something less blameworthy and less terminally tragic in Pot's behavior, especially since American imperialism is the global force that has survived and is still "unfinished." Kissinger reveals the uncultural egocentrism of an ostensibly non-violent homo americanus even as he refracts the savage brutality of Pot, a man whom homo americanus curiously perceives as lacking "culture."

The play draws cultural and moral contrasts that are especially strong between representatives of the domestically democratic but globally imperialist

United States and what appears to be the essential moral superiority of the Cambodian (popular) monarchy, that is, Sihanouk. Among Sihanouk's cultural-intellectual talents and virtues are his tactical naiveté, his outspoken directness, and the apolitical, disinterested simplicity and humanity of his judgment. From the very first scene of the play, Sihanouk shows the U.S. Ambassador McClintock how he personally ensures justice for his people by playing the role of a dispenser of justice in the manner of a King Solomon. During the "King Solomon" session, Sihanouk hears a case in which he sides with a group of peasant villagers against the interests of an American-Khmer (American-Cambodian) company. Following the session, Sihanouk's staunchly pro–American cousin Sirik Matak has a conversation with the U.S. ambassador, telling him that "Sihanouk is disgracefully anti–American," and "inimical to all progress and more concerned with schools and amusements than with industry and armaments" (23). McClintock voices his agreement with Matak, and he reveals his contempt for Sihanouk's refusal to follow a pro–American agenda by confiding to Matak that the Americans have "already set in motion a few very secret and very nasty little conspiracies" (24). One could safely argue that if Sihanouk's cousin represents a homo americanus perspective, Sihanouk, *accused* as he is of his humanitarian interest in education, tradition, and leisure to the detriment of industry, the military, and modernity, represents the French intelligentsia's point of view of the author of the play—education, tradition, and leisure being values that require a more dialectical perspective to maintain and having a higher priority in French culture than American "unculture." Shortly after this scene, Sihanouk demonstrates that he is not a dupe to either his cousin's subversions or the American conspiracies and double-speak. In his discussion with Sihanouk, McClintock says, "Doesn't our government give more and more aid to your tiny little country, day by day?" Sihanouk takes him to task for his use of the qualifier "tiny" as "a sign of malevolence, a mark of contempt" (37), and he winds up expelling the American ambassador.

Ashley Thompson takes interest in the predominance of the small/large dichotomy in this play. Summing up Sihanouk's witty reckoning as "the bigger the American aid, the smaller Cambodia becomes" (210), she casts her argument for the reversal of this small/large dichotomy in terms of the theatre and the cultural and dialectical depth within which theatre thrives. She explains how Sihanouk's portrayal of his country "operates theatrically to exemplify the small-that-is-large": "Cambodia is not a little country but a little world: it is the stage, the plot—the small is the large" (211). Theatre is both concentrated culture—a concentrated cultural activity and message—and culture writ large. Not only is "all the world a stage," as Shakespeare put it, but the tiny stage is all the world, a concentrated world—and a concentrated truth about culture in particular and the world in general. Likewise, in terms of global geopolitics, Cambodia should not automatically be judged as a less vital or valuable national culture simply because of its size (the state of Israel certainly is not). On the contrary, its size can imply cultural intensity and richness, a model or template of progressive civilization—something like theatre, but on a different cultural plane. Key to my argument then is that, if in this play the dichotomy is reversed so that Cambodia, theatrically, represents the geographically and demographically small that becomes the humanistically, culturally, intellectually, and theatrically large, then perhaps, from a theatrical, cultural, and humanistic perspective, the imperialistic, militaristic, and egocentric United States becomes the "large-that-is-small," that is, the vast geopolitical power whose culture is "small" in a cultural sense: "small culture" or the "uncultured small."

In her essay "An Inextinguishable Spark," which was included in the extremely informative program provided for the performance in 1985–86, Cixous insists on the profound theatricality of the historical figure King Sihanouk:

> [Sihanouk] seemed to us to be destined to be a theatrical hero. Sihanouk is "theatrical," that is to say worthy of Theatre [...]. Prince Sihanouk lives on the earth as he would on the theatrical stage. He takes the whole world aside and shows himself just as he is. He also shows others just as they are. He adopted for his own use the Shakespearian mischievousness of "All the world's a stage" [my translation].

The theatrical straightforwardness and authenticity of Sihanouk's character helps present him as more French than Cambodian. As a suitable response to the extremely complex geopolitical crisis that Sihanouk must face, Cixous projects onto his character a very French form of deep dialectical culture. For Cixous as for Mnouchkine, theatre provides a concentrated truth about the world, but, true to their dialectical approach, they question this truth at every turn, knowing full well its contradictory, uncertain status. The Prologue to Part 2 features a metatheatrical nod to the dialectics of Cixous and the French. A monologue by the "Chorus" addresses the importance of truth for world politics and for theatre: "Without ears, no truth./ Without truth, no theatre./ Aren't we all here out of a desire to hear/ And finally tear fragile Truth away from the furious tide of/ Falsehood?/ [...] And if you'd like, it's to truth that I dedicate our entire/ Performance including its errors and blindnesses" (109). Theatre equals culture. Unlike unculture which thrives on an undifferentiated, undialectical form of illusion reluctant to identify or acknowledge "errors and blindnesses," culture thrives on (dialectical) Truth, the antithesis of facile, uncontradictory, and predictable illusion. The play and its French author recognize the contradictions (the "errors and blindnesses") of all human culture, critical as well as uncritical versions. Cixous questions the truth of her text, its unstable state and her inexact understanding of history, and this coincides with Sihanouk's approach to truth and history as it contrasts with a homo americanus approach. We remember that in this play we are dealing with a French perception of a momentous confrontation between homo americanus and an Eastern culture.

To sum up the contribution of Sihanouk's character profile to the exposé of American unculture: American unculture is in large part implied contrastively by Sihanouk's cosmopolitanism and by his humanistic connection to the natural world, both of which coalesce with his broad knowledge of Western high culture. He frequently refers quite knowledgeably and poetically to icons of Western high culture such as Shakespeare, Mozart, Milton, Alfred Hitchcock, and Victor Hugo. Concerning the American profile, on the other hand, Sihanouk's principal political challenge is to try to maintain a position of neutrality in the Cold War military conflict in Asia—neutrality as it will ultimately be determined by the Americans. For the undialectical Americans, however, neutrality is not an option. Especially during the Cold War, the American ultimatum of "You're either with us or you're with the enemy" was very much alive and well. The Americans are not equal to or responsive to Sihanouk's humanistic (as well as complex and subtle) approach to rescuing his country from Cold War politics. The U.S. officials of Cixous's story expect to extend their influence and gain admiration as well as submission through a politics of fear; and they are quite blind to their own ambivalent intentions and contradictory behavior. They naively cannot apprehend that Cambodia and their other allies, as well as their enemies, see right through their political intrigues, and the contrast between the culture of the East and the unculture of the West intensifies.

In one telling conversation, U.S. General Abrams betrays the utterly simplistic, provincial (read: uncultured, undialectical) approach that too many Americans apply in their understanding of international affairs, an approach that betrays an inability to distinguish difference on a number of levels. He tells Kissinger, "Cambodia *is* Vietnam. Vietnam *is* Russia. So why wait? My planes have bellyaches" (51; author's emphasis). He wants to bomb Cambodia against the vigorous objections of the Secretary of Defense, Melvin Laird, the one clearly positive American character in the play, who speaks to the unqualified illegality of the threatened bombing of Cambodia and the utter cruelty and inhumanity of the act. The trigger-happy Abrams wins the "debate," and Kissinger orders "Free fire on Cambodia" (81). Getting unculturally carried away, he adds, "Give me cabinet members who are men! [...] And fire on Cambodia, Abrams! Free fire! [...] Let's get the job done! Bombs away. Bombs away! [...] Bombs away on Laird! Bombs away on the traitors. Let's get the job done. Fini! Fini!" (83).

This "machismo," evoked explicitly and implicitly by Kissinger, helps illustrate the feminine/masculine dichotomy that permeates this play. Judith Miller has perceptively pointed out how in Cixous's *L'Indiade* (1987), another of her historical epics for the Théâtre du Soleil, the character of "Ghandi—with his generosity and acceptance of the other—represented for Cixous a choice maternal figure, a Solomonic good mother in keeping with the Cixousian definition of 'the feminine'" (86). Miller remarks on Ghandi's "ability to partner the world, to give unselfishly of himself, and to metamorphose, if necessary, in order to make space for a fuller community" (86). But she could also have evoked Cixous's theoretical position that a feminine voice and sensibility was not limited to the female gender or body (see, for example, her groundbreaking essay "The Laugh of the Medusa"). As a voice of French culture, Cixous does not readily accept hard-and-fast dichotomies such as male vs. female. Instead, the thesis "male" and its antithesis "female" point toward some dialectically oriented synthesis such as "male *and* female" ("not this or that, but this and that"). Sihanouk too has his feminine side. His (and the East's) hybridized maternal nature adds to the opposition with the polarizing paternalistic "macho" character of the Americans. With this in mind, it is interesting to note that in the latest Khmer version of the play, Sihanouk's character is played by a woman, San Marady. It is also interesting to note that in Mnouchkine's original production of the Sihanouk story, the characters of Kissinger and Pol Pot were both played by the same actor.

Part 1 of the play concludes as Sihanouk makes trips to Russia (where he learns his government in Cambodia has been overthrown) and to China to plead the cause of neutrality. Part 2 pursues the portrait of Sihanouk and the biases of the American perspective, dealing in particular with homo americanus's virulent anti-communism, which unculturally encompasses anti-socialism. For homo americanus, any political system that is not grounded thoroughly on capitalism categorically equals communism ("this or that," one or the other); so the Americans label (and target) Sihanouk as a communist though he clearly is not. He seeks in his words "a socialist regime Sihanouk-style—moderate, Buddhist and monarchist" (120). In this play and in the Cambodian cultural context "monarchy"—contrasted as it is with U.S. uncultured "democracy"—has a beneficent, reassuring ring to it. What is more, we see once again the utterly complex, dialectical character of a "king" who embodies an amalgam of political perspectives.

As evidenced in the scenes between high-level historical figures such as Kissinger and Abrams outlined above, Cixous's story explores the American high command from the inside as well as the outside, allowing American administrators to incriminate themselves. In addition to the Secretary of Defense in his scene with Kissinger, Part 2 presents two additional American characters: the Head of the National Security Council Watts, and the new ambassador to Cambodia John Gunther Dean. They are clearly less uncultured and serve primarily to challenge—and therefore to reveal to the audience— the fundamentally malevolent nature of the American administration and Kissinger's patently inhuman crimes against humanity.

Cixous's "dialectically correct" story reveals that all politicians with a stake in the war in Southeast Asia partake in political double-talk throughout the play: not only the Americans but also those belonging to political cultures that the United States considers to be either clearly communist or unacceptably sympathetic to communism: the Chinese, Russians, Vietnamese, and even the French. All cultures are flawed (shall we say, "contradictory"?), but American unculture is truly remarkable in this regard, primarily because the key American characters in this play show themselves to be unwilling to even consider that America might be too categorical in its exceptionalist self-image, one which engenders its world view and which plays such a determinant role in the tragic fate of Cambodia and the world. The Americans' tremendous global power and influence is so unequal to the extent and the clarity of the stake they have in the geopolitical conflict. The audience is made privy to the private conversations of American officials, and we witness their uninspired, self-serving motives. The audience is not granted comparable access to the machinations of Pol Pot and the Khmer Rouge.

To complete the story, consistent with the historical chronology, Pol Pot and his Khmer Rouge cohorts will carry out the genocidal pogrom on their own Cambodian people. Pol Pot is the name taken by Solath Sâr when he orchestrates his putsch against the Cambodian political structure as head of the communist Khmer Rouge. Sâr makes an early appearance in the play as a political radical returning to Cambodia after his studies in Paris. Erica Johnson rightly points out the way in which this hateful character (Sâr, soon to be Pot) "appropriates the language of fragmentation and unity in an early soliloquy in which he reflects on the status of Cambodia" (122) and in which he expresses his profound "hatred for the world" (123). One might presume that Pot's antipathetic world view is anything but dialectical and that this aspect of his character would compare to that of the Americans. However, the character of the Americans, as reflected in the language of Kissinger and Abrams, is not really hateful, and this is what distinguishes them from Pol Pot and the Khmer Rouge. The Americans are, in essence, indifferent to either the plight or the future of the "targets" (I choose this word deliberately) of their lethal military power. In another scene that serves as a window to the U.S. bombing of Cambodia, William Watts accuses Kissinger of massive violence through criminal indifference: "Until now, Sir, I thought [you] were ambitious, meticulous. But this evening, studying this [plan to invade and bomb Cambodia], I saw you as indifferent as a tyrant, committing a crime, a truly great crime which goes beyond the human gaze to become invisible [...]. You're in the process of assassinating Cambodia" (129). Kissinger's immediate response is one of fear, an attribute and effect of unculture: "Don't lay a hand on me!" And following Watt's departure from his office, he exclaims his indignation: "My, such violence! Such violence! Why such violence?!" (130).

Beyond the great irony of Kissinger's response to Watt's virulent accusations of crimes against humanity, since Kissinger is alone when he utters his bewilderment, he has no one to convince but himself of his non-violent nature. Unlike the very serious Pol Pot who rationalizes his use of violence as an underdog fighting for the future unitarian goal of international communism, Kissinger's cry of "Bombs away!" sounds optimistic and even waggish, as if he were playing an easily winnable game to preserve the present global power structure. Radical as they are, Khmer communists are not "uncultured" in the same way as Americans. The rationale for their behavior lies not in indifference but in cultural passion, an obsession that generates not the plebian jargon of machismo but philosophical, poetic expression.

Given their declared devotion to communism, we presume the Khmer Rouge leaders to be vehemently anti–American—an antithesis that, interestingly, helps qualify the near-absolute evil of the American role in perpetrating this "truly great crime" against Cambodia. History has demonstrated the ultimately disastrous maneuvers of Pol Pot and the Khmer Rouge, and Cixous's text offers evidence of the consequences of their heinous crimes against the humanity of their compatriots. Yet unlike the *explicit* violence against the otherness of a very foreign culture evidenced by the Americans, especially Kissinger, the revelations of Pol Pot's motives are not all that incriminating. Pol Pot's language (as well as that of his chief spokesperson Ieng Sary), while far from non-violent, can be read as tactical and idealistic, even paradoxically or ironically non-violent, and never explicitly vengeful. He speaks explicitly of the positive, idealistic "uplifting wind of our [communist] Revolution" (155), while the disastrous consequences of the "ultimate uprooting" of Cambodia remain wholly implicit. In conversation with his immediate staff, Pol Pot's language can even be characterized as stirring and charitable: "The future is ours! Till tomorrow, beloved brothers!" (156). What is more, their condemnation of the Americans in this text seems to correspond to the categorical and uncultured nature of American anti-communism. The vehemently anti-communist United States has changed its mind about Sihanouk's politics and wants him to return to Cambodia before the communists take control of the capital, Phnom Penh. But once again the United States (through Kissinger) betrays Sihanouk by abandoning the capital prematurely (167–8). The United States continues to reveal itself as not just one of the bad guys but *the* bad guy.

So one must dare ask: To what extent do the Americans resemble Pol Pot's Khmer Rouge in this story? One answer would lie in the sheer scale of devastation they inflicted on the people of Southeast Asia as well as the apparent indifference with which they carried it out. Another response might consider the excess of their belief in their respective political systems and their sense of mission. The Prime Minister of communist China, Chou En-lai, opines that the communism of the Khmer Rouge under Pol Pot has a serious problem with excess and impatience. They are trying to "turn Cambodia into a prematurely and excessively communist country" (176). As the spokesperson for Pol Pot, Ieng Sary, puts it: "Our Revolution is going to give the world proof that one can achieve perfect communism in a single blow, and without mealy-mouthed hesitations. As Pol Pot says, it's Cambodia that's going to win the trophy in the Revolutions competition" (178). While the resemblances between the global superpower's chief spokesperson (Kissinger) and the sadistically potent yet poetic demagogue are numerous and deep, so are the divergence's of their motives. After all, the United States applies the bulk of its excess and impatience in its attempt to create a prematurely and excessively corporate-capitalist world.

Cixous's story begins by outlining the U.S./Kissinger opposition to Sihanouk. The story closes with Sihanouk's confrontation with the Khmer Rouge/Pol Pot, a confrontation that is paradoxically enabled by U.S. politics. So, what I'm saying is that Pol Pot's character is developed to a great extent —as is Sihanouk's—to serve as a foil for the uncultural cruelty of homo americanus. The dramaturgical weight of the number of unambiguously wrong-headed and inhumane bad-guy characters on the American side, associated with and concentrated within the exceptionally explicit malevolent (crime against humanity) motives of kingpin Kissinger, drive home the focus of the play. In large part because of its position of global hegemon, homo americanus is not simply just as bad as the commies. Referring to America's depiction in British drama, Una Chaudhuri affirms that the trope seemed to "transform other cultures into mere foils to or excrescences of its hegemonic reality" (*Staging Place* 128). To this extent, America's great crime against humanity has been its attempt to recreate the globe in its own uncomplicated uncultural image. This take on the "new world order" is what Cixous explores in this epic play, and that is what renders the story of Sihanouk as "unfinished" as it is prophetic.

UNIVERSITY OF TENNESSEE, KNOXVILLE

NOTES

1. For a more detailed account of my approach to theorizing "homo americanus unculture," see "Introduction: Part 1" of my *American "Unculture" in French Drama*, especially 1–20.

2. Erica Johnson briefly discusses Cixous's attempt to explore "the postcolonial situation of Cambodia—with an emphasis on the colonial" (123).

3. From a psychoanalytical point of view, Sigmund Freud has hypothesized the neurosis of a "cultural community" in the following terms: "If the development of civilization has such a far-reaching similarity to the development of the individual and if it employs the same methods, may we not be justified in reaching the diagnosis that, under the influence of cultural urges, some civilizations, or some epochs of civilization—possibly the whole of mankind—have become 'neurotic'? [...] I would not say that an attempt of this kind to carry psycho-analysis over to the cultural community was absurd or doomed to be fruitless" (91).

WORKS CITED

Chaudhuri, Una. *Staging Place: The Geography of Modern Drama.* Ann Arbor: University of Michigan Press, 1995.

Cixous, Hélène. "L'Etincelle inextinguible." Program for *The Terrible but Unfinished Story of Norodom Sihanouk, King of Cambodia.* Dir. Ariane Mnouchkine, Théâtre du Soleil, Paris, France. October 1985–June 1986.

_____. "The Laugh of the Medusa." Trans. Keith Cohen and Paula Cohen. *The Critical Tradition: Classic Texts and Contemporary Trends.* Ed. David H. Richter. New York: St. Martin's Press. 1090–1102.

_____. *The Terrible but Unfinished Story of Norodom Sihanouk, King of Cambodia.* Trans. Juliet Flower MacCannell, Judith Pike, and Lollie Groth. Lincoln: University of Nebraska Press, 1994.

Essif, Les. *American "Unculture" in French Drama: Homo Americanus and the Post–1960 French Resistance.* New York: Palgrave Macmillan, 2013.

Freud, Sigmund. *Civilization and Its Discontents.* Trans. James Strachey. New York: W. W. Norton, 1961.

Graver, David. "The Théâtre du Soleil, Part Three: the Production of 'Sihanouk.'" *New Theatre Quarterly* 2.7 (1986): 212–216.

Johnson, Erica L. "Incomplete Histories and Hélène Cixous' *L'Histoire terrible mais inachevée de Norodom Sihanouk, roi du Cambodge.*" *Texas Studies in Literature and Language* 42:2 (2000): 118–134.

MacCannell, Juliet Flower. "Cixous and Modern Consciousness." In Hélène Cixous, *The Terrible but Unfinished Story of Norodom Sihanouk, King of Cambodia.* Trans. Juliet Flower MacCannell, Judith Pike, and Lollie Groth. Lincoln: University of Nebraska Press, 1994. vii–xvi.

Miller, Judith G. *Ariane Mnouchkine.* London: Routledge, 2007.

Pike, Judith. "Sihanouk and Contemporary 'Epic' Theater." In Hélène Cixous, *The Terrible but Unfinished Story of Norodom Sihanouk, King of Cambodia.* Trans. Juliet Flower MacCannell, Judith Pike, and Lollie Groth. Lincoln: University of Nebraska Press, 1994. xvi–xix.

Thompson, Ashley." Terrible but Unfinished: Stories of History." *New Literary History* 37.1 (2006): 197–215.

Oedipus King / Oedipus Pig: Nanos Valaoritis's Ludic Politics

Vassiliki Rapti

Abstract

This paper sheds light on the recent political interventions of noted Greek author Nanos Valaoritis in his effort to denounce the dangerous neo–Nazi methods used by members of the increasingly appealing extreme rightist party Golden Dawn in Greece. I argue that such political activism is the natural reaction of an intellectual who consistently fought through his writings against three fascist regimes. The essay examines two of his unpublished and unperformed dramatic texts written in personal exile during the Greek Junta, Oedipus Pig *or* Oedipig *and* King Hogdacus the First *or* In Hog We Trust, *accompanied by some of his drawings. By deconstructing the language of a canonical text such as* Oedipus King *and by interjecting some episodes from the Gospel of John, Valaoritis creates his own "piggish" metalanguage reminiscent of the Barthesian "writing degree zero" of language in an effort to create both language and myth anew and destabilize canonical works of Western civilization. This process constitutes Valaoritis's ludic politics.*

> Enter the Generals:
> Hail to Nation! Hail to Eternal Hellas
> All this filth, their [the Oedipus family's] rottenness
> We will clean it up for your sake—
> We will achieve catharsis for the nation's soul
> By means of fire and iron—
> Nanos Valaoritis, *Oedipus Reversed or the Dilemma of a Man of Unknown Identity* (1969)[1]

[Golden Dawn] is a transvestite mixture of Hitleric gestures, such as the raised hands, the insignia, the swastika, the protests in military form and the black semi-militaristic uniforms and parades with fireworks and torches at night, as in the appalling ceremonies of the Nazis in Germany.
—Nanos Valaoritis, *Either of the Height or of the Depth* (2013)

The two passages above, written over a span of forty years, provide a glimpse into the direct political intervention of noted Greek writer Nanos Valaoritis. This intervention took the form of an open letter to the Prime Minister of Greece in which he urged him to act immediately against the dangerous practices of the increasingly appealing neo–Nazi Golden Dawn party. This gesture raised strong reactions, ranging from praise to mocking scorn for the response of an aging 93-year old elitist intellectual.[2] Anti-authoritarianism, as both a theme and a concern, has long preoccupied—almost haunted—this long-standing political activist. The first passage comes from the unpublished and unperformed play *Oedipus Reversed or the Dilemma of a Man of Unknown Identity* (1969). Reminiscent of the notorious "trap scene" from Alfred Jarry's *Ubu Roi* (1896), it echoes the Nazi ideology and alludes to the dictatorship of the Colonels in Greece (1967–1974). The second passage above directly attacks the Golden Dawn party as a grotesque imitation of Nazism and comes from Valaoritis's recent book of essays Ἡ τοῦ Ὕψους ἤ τοῦ Βάθους (*Either of the Height or of the Depth*) (2013). This collection consists of all the articles that Valaoritis initially published in various newspapers and blogs throughout 2013, immediately after his letter to the Greek Prime Minister Antonis Samaras on 30 April 2013 on his Facebook page. In that letter, he strongly urged Samaras to take immediate action against the Greece's worrisome tolerance of racism before it was too late.[3] After referring to their common friend, Nobel laureate Odysseas Elytis, who once freely walked the Athens streets at night, he wrote,

Besides having suffered the most unjust, humiliating moral and cultural attack in our history for two years now in the German media, and its systematic and convincing spread to the rest of the world, to such a degree that it became persuasive even among Greek citizens outside Greece, we also have witnessed the creation of a barbaric construct that calls itself Golden Dawn, and, thanks to adverse circumstances, has managed to enter the Greek Parliament with the symbols and deportment of neo–Nazis. That this is not a "Greek" phenomenon is evident from the ideology and symbols and ceremonies that it so roughly and clumsily imitates. Many of my colleagues and intellectual writers seem not to take it seriously. "Don't worry about it," they say lightly. "We have seen this before, and this will pass."

Anticipating evils to come, Valaoritis has been proven right. Since that open letter, to which the Prime Minister offered counter-arguments in response,[4] horrific developments have rapidly ensued in Greece. Several murders and the subsequent imprisonment of the majority of Golden Dawn's parliamentary members, including its leader, remains a hotly unresolved issue to this day.[5] Yet Golden Dawn's popularity has not diminished; on the contrary, it has increased, as the latest results of the European elections have shown, where it ranked third.[6]

In this essay I will defend Valaoritis's recent political intervention as a thoughtful, intuitive, and genuine act of political activism. More importantly, by linking his recent outcry against the Golden Dawn party with the plays he wrote more than forty years ago as satires of the regime of the generals from 1967 to 1974, I will offer a hypothesis to explain his long-standing political activism. I refer to his unpublished English plays, *Oedipus Pig or Oedipig* and *King Hogdacus the First or In Hog We Trust*, which were written in English concurrently (with the aforementioned *Oedipus Reversed or the Dilemma of a Man of Unknown Identity*) in 1969. Due to the Greek Junta, Valaoritis was self-exiled in the United States, teaching creative writing at the San Francisco State University. Regardless of the fact that these unknown plays were never performed or published (due to practical impediments, as he admits in a recent interview to the author of this article[7]), I argue that they bear evidence of his consistent struggle against any type of authoritarian form, manifested either in society or in the canonical works of Western tradition.

This struggle in Valaoritis's case took the form of a ludic experiment with the English language as part of his overall experiment with writing itself and its revolutionary impact on society. He desperately attempts to reach the core of writing, where there is no gap between sign and referent, where the flesh-like materiality of language resurfaces. Longing for freedom from a pre-ordained state of language and oppressive preconceived ideas, Valaoritis committed himself to create an entirely new language, one that would possibly de-mythologize the traditionally inherited and socially instituted forms of writing and particular discursive orders that found their culmination in the pillars of the Western Canon, particularly the Greek classics and the Bible. This is why he sought to create an entirely new language, a piggish language that could be achieved through the rules of play and its various mechanisms such as substitution, inversion, displacement, and reversal, among others. By so doing, he would accomplish another equally important goal: abhorrence and negation of any fascist ideology that was rooted in dangerous discursive practices such as those used by Nazis and Golden Dawn.

The provocative if not sacrilegious use of the "pig" in order to subvert Sophocles's idealist tragedy and the Gospel of John constituted a revolutionary act. Valaoritis borrowed animal hierarchy from George Orwell's influential *Animal Farm* (1945), which "was the first book in which [he] had tried, with full consciousness of what [he] was doing, to fuse political purpose and artistic purpose into one whole" in order to satirize the Stalinist era.[8] Valaoritis reached far beyond Orwell's use of allegory and satire toward the same end. In order to satirize the dictatorship of the Colonels in Greece (1967–1974) and its supporters, he attempted to contrive a new language emerging out of a lexicon centering upon the pig as a *dramatis persona*. The Pig as a character seemed ideal for Valaoritis's play, given the derogatory appellation "pigs" used in major American cities (including San Francisco) during the late 1960s and early 1970s as a taunt to the police. Valaoritis was of course aware of this derogatory appellation, but he further specified its use: "I wanted to create a language in its lowest possible level, to downgrade a myth and a hero to a grotesque figure, something that fitted perfectly the Junta; the pigs were the Colonels and their supporters."[9] Lately, in the context of the European economic policy of austerity, PIGS resurfaced in common discourse, this time as an acronym in the mass media for the economically troubled countries of Portugal, Ireland, Greece and Spain. In regards to this ironic coincidence, Valaoritis comments, "Interestingly enough, I find here a parallel to what I accomplished in my first novel *Απ' τα κόκκαλα βγαλμένη* (*Rising from the Bones*) without me being aware of it, that is, the spirit of Rabelais before I knew it. Likewise, my pig plays can be read in light of the latest developments in the European Union of the crisis *avant la lettre*."[10] The present essay is located at the intersection of all these pig-driven discourses. I would like to stress Valaoritis's unknown yet remarkable experiment with the derivatives of the word "pig." He rejoiced in the richness of this lemma, as it allowed him to test the limits of his experimental political game. This new language contains references to pig, hog, swine, boar, piglet, etc., in both *King Hogdacus the First* (or *In Hog We Trust*) and in *Oedipus Pig* (or *Oedipig*).

Interestingly, the construction of this new language was complemented by the playwright's own telling drawings, some of which are incorporated in this article. These images are comparable to those of Kurt Vonnegut, Valaoritis's well-known contemporary, who also included drawings to accompany his works.[11] What immediately captures our attention in these drawings, apart from their vividness and their satiric power, is the interplay between image and text. Consider the depiction of a boar intruding vehemently onto the page [Figure 1]. It is as if the referent attempted to displace the signifier foregrounding its bestiality, as if the image attempted to replace the text to make it as transparent as possible. Another arresting technique is the use of puns in both titles of the plays. For instance, notice the wordplay in the title *Oedipus Pig*, echoing and resonating with, yet denigrating, Sophocles's *Oedipus King*. Also notice the subversion of the name Labdacus, Oedipus's grandfather, when turned into *Hogdacus*; or the parody of the inscription associated with the American dollar ("In God We Trust") in the alternative title of this play, *In Hog We Trust* [Figure 2]. The title *Oedipus Reversed* in the opening passage neatly encapsulates the ludic strategies operative here. My goal is to demonstrate how these ludic strategies (play, witticism, and experiment with language) are manifested in both these plays, and how they fermented into his act of political intervention in his open letter to the Greek Prime Minister.

Valaoritis's ludic politics are influenced by Roland Barthes's notion of "Writing Degree Zero," a very influential theory in the revolutionary decade of the 1960s during which Valaoritis wrote his English Oedipus-centered plays. Barthes defined this type of writing as "a colorless writing, freed from all bondage to a pre-ordained state of language" (82). As Jean-Michel Rabaté puts it, "writing degree zero" is "an attempt to create a neutral literary style deprived of all traditional markers that heralds an encounter with language as such, while stressing the gap between language and the world" (69). Valaoritis, who had attended many of Barthes's lectures in Paris, gave me his own definition of writing degree zero:

Figure 1. "A Boar Intruding Vehemently onto the Page" (courtesy of Nanos Valaoritis).

> It must become clear that this notion can be understood in different manners. In my own view, it refers to a common language that is easily accessible, that is, utterly transparent, one that everyone can understand without the need of any dictionary, one that does not use any metaphor. In other words, it is a language that has been degraded to its lowest degree.[12]

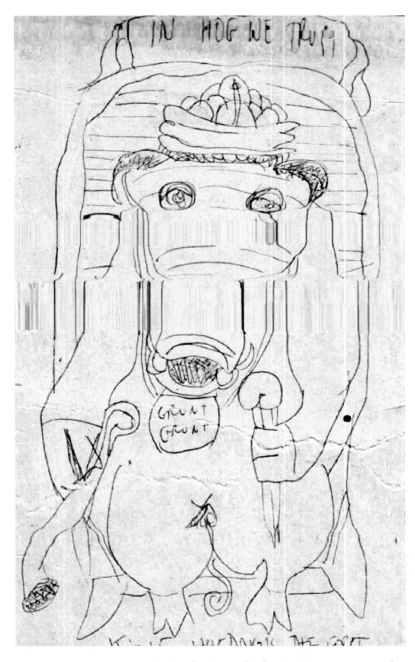

Figure 2. "In Hog We Trust" as "In God We Trust," a drawing opening Nanos Valaoritis's unpublished play *King Hogdacus the First or In Hog We Trust* (courtesy of Nanos Valaoritis).

Following in Barthes's footsteps, Valaoritis attempted to undo the Western canon and to denounce all authoritarian discourses and practices. Nevertheless, his ludic playwriting strategies are best understood in the context of the Western Canon, to which his own prolific, variegated "canon" owes its existence. Indeed, Valaoritis's avant-garde work, consisting of a myriad of genres, is mobilized by a desire for constant subversion of the European literary tradition and by constant preoccupation with the role of writing within society. Among his writings, besides the aforementioned recent volume of essays *Either of the Height or of the Depth*, he also published two volumes of essays, entitled *Towards a Theory of Writing* (1990) and *Towards a Theory of Writing B* (2006), where one can see his constant preoccupation with the undoing of the Western Canon. The following section will demonstrate how Valaoritis specifically challenges the traditional authority of classical texts including *Oedipus King* and the Gospel of John.

In *King Hogdacus the First* or *In Hog We Trust*, Valaoritis attempts a deliberate mutilation of the Sophoclean tragedy by focusing on what he calls the "Hogocaust," an obvious allusion to the Holocaust, which he foregrounds in order to excoriate anti–Semitism. After replacing all Sophocles's characters with their pig-related analogues, he creates his cast of

Figure 3. "Oedipuspig/Oedipig/King PigOedipus?" Playing with the name of Oedipus (courtesy of Nanos Valaoritis).

characters belonging to the dynasty of Labdacoswines: Laiospig the Hogdacus, father of Oedipuspig or Oedipig [Figure 3]; Josowcasta or Josaocasta, mother and wife of Oedipuspig and Queen of Pigthebes [Figure 4], bearing visible hams and tail; and Antigonesao or Antisaogone, the swine princess or Princess Antigoneshepiglet. Valaoritis transforms Sophocles's characters into pigs, ruthlessly reversing everything and treating Christian doctrine sacrilegiously when incorporating the scenes "The Last Supper of King Pig" and "Pig and Crucified Pigtrilogy."

The play opens with an imposing drawing of a boar hanging as a poster on which is written [Figure 1], bearing the inscription: "Wild Boar is Ravaging the PIGDOM OF OEDIPIG / Whoever will get his head and bring IT TO PIGTHEBES / will be rewarded with the paw/ OF / PRINCESS ANTIGONESHEPIGLET." The chorus of humans, headed by two butchers, reacts with agitation to this announcement: "The paw? Only the paw? What the heck, that's nothing: I want at least a whole thigh of ham." The play continues

Figure 4. "Josowcasta, Queen of PigThebes" (courtesy of Nanos Valaoritis).

with the portrayal of the Last Supper of the King Hogdacus (alias Oedipus Pig or Oedipig the First, son of Labdacus) who announces that he launched an investigation about an alleged pollution into Far Land and that his hogs have gone to Pighorinth and to Porkphokis and are expected anytime soon. At the same time he has promised his daughter to anyone who would rid them of that pest to his pigdom, the wild boar.

Antisaogone or Antigoneshepiglet reacts boldly against her father whom she calls a real chauvinist pig while declaring overtly her love for Aimonswine.

Her father counters by telling her that her love for her cousin is prohibited by law as incest. Antisaogone's unbridled speech continues by confronting her father as an intruder to the throne of Pigthebes where her mother and, by succession, she herself have the sovereign rights. Her sister Isaosmene intervenes in an attempt to resolve the quarrel between father and daughter, but Antisaogone remains obstinate. Then Kreonswine intervenes asking Oedipus Pig to punish Antisaogone to set an example. Oedipus Pig appoints Tireasopig, the pig that unravels the mystery of male and feminine pleasure, as Chief Prosecutor, but he does not accept this officialdom.

In a telling passage, Antisaogone confronts Oedipig and Tireasopig, expressing the right of the female sows to sexual pleasure. Oedipig reprimands her: "ANTISAOGONE, my daughter, please do not beaspig against the HIGH HOGA and his SERVANT THE PIGSEER TIRESAOPIG, the only one of the Hampandic race who experiences both the male and female pigness." Notice here that the language contrived by Valaoritis extends beyond the names of the protagonists to the verb "bespeak," which is transformed into "beaspig," and the noun "highness," which becomes "pigness." This deconstructive game continues throughout the play to an astonishing degree. Valaoritis keeps the original motivation of each character but in new circumstances. In the end, it is revealed that Oedipus Pig has committed an incestuous union with his mother Josowcasta who, in turn, hangs herself. At the moment Kreonswine orders his guards to arrest Oedipus Pig he manages to blind himself, bidding farewell to his light and his sister/daughter. That is how the play ends. Clearly this play is a grotesque caricature of the original, yet it keeps the bare bones plot. Valaoritis treats the themes of greed, incest, racism, sexism, battle of sexes, power, and authority—all at the heart of the post–May 1968 period.

A particularly arresting scene occurs just before the arrival of the messenger from the Oraclepig. Antisaogone talks with her father about the arch Hog, JUPIGHOG, Herasao's husband. At the mention of the sound "Jew," authoritarian Kreonswine gets irritated and asks:

KREONSWINE: Did I hear the word JEU? Guard my sword...
OEDIPIG: She said JUPIGHOG not JEW.

Kreonswine's son Hemonswine comments: "Grunt grunt, my father is an anti–Jupig: this is hubris." This is exactly what causes the fight between the twin piglets:

ETEOPIGLES: Forget it. He is just an old man ... grunt grunt...
POLYPIGNIKES: Forget it? If we forget this and then that ... in the end you have Pigshitism ... Hogism and all the rest...!
(They both draw swords and face each other) (The guards separate them).
ETEOPIGLES: I Support my PIGLAND and its tradition.

POLYPIGNIKES: And I'll seek justice in foreign lands. HE LEAVES WITH
FLOWERS: I'll not stand in this PRIGISHNESS.
<u>The Gates slam shut.</u>

This moment is one of the most successful effects of Valaoritis's piggish language. Polypignikes stands up with Hemonswine against authoritarian Kreonswine's anti–Jupism which Polypignikes cannot stand, sending a clear
message against Hogism that equates with racism and sexism, and leaving
Pigland to seek justice elsewhere. Like Polypignikes, Valaoritis could not stand
the triptych of "fatherland, religion, family" that was full of xenophobia and
fascist ideology in the dictatorship of the Colonels in 1967, so he sought justice
in the Far Land.

Valaoritis's second play, *King Hogdacus the First*, is more elaborate and
borrows some ideas from science fiction. Its action is set in the future circa
2400 AD in the Pigsty City. The protagonists are again a family of pigs: the
male chauvinist pig or Machapig, the female altruist sow and their piglets, a
male chauvinist piglet and a female chauvinist sowlet, and a chorus of women
bearing pig masks. The action centers on a garbage can located at the center
of the stage, a clear allusion to Samuel Beckett's *Endgame*. Machapig confronts
some extraterrestrial parachutists who have been able to convert garbage into
energy. Pigs fall from the sky wearing pig masks and pig suits and ultra violet
pistols that shoot processed garbage. Machapig argues he has done nothing to
deserve this fate, but a grocer tells "his Pigness" he has transgressed the Law:
"Thou shall not <u>ham-a-pig or bacon or lard it!</u> For only the gods can do this!"
Then he sets up an investigation, and when he questions his attendants, they
deny everything. Then he condemns them immediately to slaughtering for
fear of downfall of his pigdom: "It will cause the downfall of Pigdom and civilization: A barbaric anarchy will inevitably follow: And we shall all be cooked
by the Aliens."

When Machapig's butcher tells him that his attendants are good only for
canned sausages, he starts lamenting for the decline of his Pigdom. At that
moment a miracle happens: the ultra-pigs bring a pulsating can with processed
garbage turned into energy. They place it before the palace of Machapig and
take away the old empty one. The new garbage can pulsates with light and
green energy. The chorus of naked women holding pig masks slowly ascend
on stage, addressing Machapig: "Machapig Machapig you luckiest of all kings
come forth and see your fortune: the Gods have rewarded Your Constance
with an extraordinary gift: this is a heaven-sent garbage can, which will provide
garbage forever: as long as you don't pronounce the forbidden word." At the
moment Machapig opens the lid of the new garbage can, some ultrapigs
descend from the sky and give Machapig the Nazi hail amidst martial music:
"ULTRAPIGS: HEIL, MACHAPIG you are the chosen leader."

The golden age arrives with pig dances, and the family of Machapig indulges in garbage delights until Machapig reveals his true tyrannical face towards everyone, even his own family. Femalesow reveals to her female piglet: "Yes my daughter your Father is already a great tyrant: The greatest in all history." Machapig's tyranny takes on a new, religious nuance when Machapig kneels before the image of Ultrapig and, like a caricature of Jesus Christ, he utters these words: "Ah, God, Give the courage to be a pig!" At that moment, a procession of beautiful female chorus slaves enters, bearing a bowl and preparing to wash Machapig's feet, while singing and performing an ode to his honor in soulful style. The scene continues with a caricature of the biblical episode between Jesus Christ and Mary Magdalene—now Mary-Magdalen Piggins—washing his feet, washing away her sins, addressing him as follows: "Oh Master, your faithful slave hath purified and restored your divine feet." At the sight of Mary-Magdalen Piggins, Femalesow begins a scene of jealousy that leads Machapig to order the imprisonment of both women along with the female piglets who are on their mother's side, after consulting with his Counsellor in German accent.

Death is brought up during this conversation. Valaoritis deconstructs the word "Death" in a manner that introduces confusion into the scene:

MACHAPIG: Correct! De-ath.
KLINGSORE: But that is different: De-ath means to de-athanatize or de-immortalize!
MACHAPIG: It's all Greek to me—which is the best?
KLINGSORE: Both are equally good: One means that you are deprived of life. The other deprived of immortality.
MACHAPIG: Oh yea?
KLINGSORE: Yes, yes, Majesty.
MACHAPIG: Good. Good: De-ath then: De-immortalize them then....
KLINGSORE: How would your Majesty like it done?
MACHAPIG: What's the most economical?
KLINGSORE: The ovens! In this manner they will be cooked as well for consumption by the garbage-producing slaves who will pay generously for such a treat.

The direct allusion to the ovens is a chilling one and represents a stark denunciation of the Holocaust.

What follows in this play is further complicated by references to many other canonical texts both Shakespearean and classical. Lysistrata becomes Pigistrata, and the Eumenides-Amasaozones come to Femalesow Queen's rescue. The Queen's royal line would continue with her son, King Porkypig the Second, who under his mother's firm hand was expected to rule the Pigdom. The scene ends with a march of the victorious Amasaozones.

What we find in both *Oedipus Pig* and *King Hogdacus the First* is an attempt by Nanos Valaoritis at a radical undoing of the Western Canon both thematically and stylistically. Just as he wanted to eradicate every possible oppressive authority and with it every aspect of abhorred totalitarianism, Valaoritis also attempted to rebel against every literary tradition rendered oppressive by its cultural institution. In the process he turned language upside down. He also introduced radical plot transformations. For example, Polyneices heads off for permanent voluntary exile because he can't stand the prejudice of Creon (which Eteocles accepts). In the end, one must admit that Valaoritis's new "bestial" language constitutes his Barthesian "writing degree zero." This language can be readily understood by everyone with no need of further explanations, as it was distilled down to the lowest degree—while simultaneously corresponding perfectly to his immediate targets: the Colonels and their supporters. One might well argue that this new piggish language was ultimately ineffective because it did not reach an audience, remaining unpublished and unperformed to this day. However, I would counter that it nevertheless functioned as a necessary stage in the playwright's trajectory in order for him to cope with horrible realities in the guise of gallows humor. Through this new piggish language and for his own sake, he grotesquely expressed the horrific atrocities of the three fascist regimes he had experienced up to that moment in Greece: first by Metaxas, then by Mussolini and Hitler, and finally by the Colonels. Valaoritis explains,

> Well ... in my life, because I have lived many years, when I was a student we had the first fascism from 1935 to 1939, in 1940–1941 we had Metaxas, who had dressed us in uniforms in an organization called EON, he forced us to do parades, to hail in a fascist manner and this was required in the entire school [...]. It was a detestable regime. [...] Then the Occupation came. Second Fascism, much worse. Back then in order to go to the University, you had to cross the corpses on Solon Street and outside the University was also the morgue, where the Court had carts, full of corpses that had gathered the previous evening. Athens had turned into a cemetery, a medieval spectacle. This spectacle certainly ignited the Resistance of young students, but unfortunately resulted in the Civil War, as we were divided into left and right groups that began to fight each other. [...] The third time was the Junta. And during the last two, the Occupation and the Junta, I left Greece and from there I was many years abroad, without finding myself anywhere.[13]

Valaoritis's traumatic experiences from the spectrum of fascism found appropriately grotesque expression in his Oedipus pig plays. Yet these tensions remained unresolved and assumed another form under the current rise of the neo–Nazi Golden Dawn party in Greece. His anti-fascist principles accumulated steadily over a span of nine decades, finally making it urgent for Valaoritis to cry out in as clear a voice as possible against Golden Dawn. At the threshold of another life, he felt the urge to act publicly. Valaoritis's ludic writing strategies may well have started as a degree zero game that targeted the Colonels of the years 1967–1974 in Greece. Yet they also explain his outspoken direct encounter with today's real dangers. He confirms, "Now to face for the fourth time the rise of fascism under a democratic—supposedly—regime and within the European Union? It is improbable and unbelievable [...]. I feel as if the Second World War was never won despite the huge sacrifice of people: 600.000 in Greece alone, millions everywhere."[14]

HARVARD UNIVERSITY

NOTES

1. Nanos Valaoritis wrote this play along with all the other mentioned here in Oakland, California, circa 1969. They remain unpublished, unperformed, and lack pagination. I am deeply grateful to Nanos Valaoritis for granting me permission to publish some excerpts of these plays with some of their accompanying drawings here. Likewise, I am grateful to *Text & Presentation* for the feedback I received for this paper. Special thanks also go to Julia Dubnoff for her invaluable suggestions.

2. For a sense of the spectrum of responses, see the scores of comments that accompany Valaoritis's letter in this link: http://www.tovima.gr/culture/article/?aid=515206.

3. Valaoritis's open letter to the Greek Prime Minister Antonis Samaras was reprinted in the newspaper *To Vima* on 29 May 2013. Here one can access the letter: http://www.tovima.gr/culture/article/?aid=515206. All translations from the Greek original are mine.

4. Here one can read the entire reply of the Prime Minister to Valaoritis: http://www.tovima.gr/politics/article/?aid=515451. And here Valaoritis comments on Samaras's reply: http://www.tovima.gr/politics/article/?aid=515646, where he insists that Samaras did not denounce Golden Dawn.

5. Everything started with the murder of the rap musician Pavlos Fyssas, known as Killah P, on 18 September 2013, by a member of Golden Dawn, and since then two other murders occurred with two Golden Dawn victims. The chronicle of the murder of Pavlos Fyssas is given in this link: http://el.wikipedia.org/wiki/Δολοφονία_του_Παύλου_ Φύσσα.

6. For more details, see: http://greece.greekreporter.com/2014/05/27/final-greek-results-of-the-european-parliament-elections/#sthash.wL22PvbV.dpuf.

7. In an interview with me on 14 July 2014, Valaoritis admitted that he never published this play because he never transcribed the manuscript and because he never found any support in his environment to do so in regards to his theatrical attempts.

8. See George Orwell: http://www.netcharles.com/orwell/essays/why_i_write.htm

9. I refer to my 14 July 2014 interview with Valaoritis.

10. Ibid.

11. Cf. Kurt Vonnegut (e.g., *Breakfast of Champions*). In fact, a comparative study examining the work of Nanos Valaoritis and Kurt Vonnegut would reveal a much deeper connection between the two authors and activists, as both experienced the horrors of the Second World War—especially Vonnegut, who recorded his dreadful Dresden experience in 1969 in his novel *Slaughterhouse-Five*. Their affinities are also evident by the same writing style they both use during the early 1970s: a combination of black humor

or gallows humor; witticism as a reaction to a hopeless situation. Finally their outspoken political activism against war and corporate greed, especially at the end of their lives, is another connecting thread. One can find more information on Vonnegut's legacy in this link: http://www.vonnegutlibrary.org/about/. However, as Valaoritis informed me in an email communication dated 31 August 2014, all these affinities are not influences at all. They are due simply to the spirit of the time.

12. I refer to my 2014 interview with Valaoritis.

13. Here is the Greek text where Valaoritis talks openly about the scars fascism left upon him throughout his long life:

"Λοιπόν ... στη ζωή μου, διότι έχω ζήσει πολλά χρόνια, όταν ήμουν μαθητής είχαμε τον πρώτο φασισμό από το '35 μέχρι το '39, το '40–'41 είχαμε τον Μεταξά, ο οποίος μας είχε ντύσει με στολές σε μια οργάνωση που λεγόταν EON, μας έβαζε να κάνουμε πάνω-κάτω παρελάσεις, να χαιρετούμε φασιστικά και αυτό ήταν αναγκαστικό σε όλο το σχολείο. [...] Ήταν άθλιο καθεστώς [...] Μετά ήρθε η Κατοχή. Δεύτερος φασισμός, ακόμα χειρότερος. Εκεί, για να πας στο Πανεπιστήμιο, περνούσες πάνω από πτώματα στην οδό Σόλωνος και έξω από το Πανεπιστήμιο ήταν και το νεκροτομείο, εκεί στο Δικαστήριο, που είχε κάρα γεμάτα πτώματα που είχαν συλλέξει το προηγούμενο βράδυ. Η Αθήνα είχε μετατραπεί σε ένα νεκροταφείο, μεσαιωνικό θέαμα. Αυτό το θέαμα βέβαια ξεκίνησε την Αντίσταση στους νέους, τους φοιτητές, αλλά δυστυχώς κατέληξε στον Εμφύλιο, διότι χωριστήκαμε σε δεξιές κι αριστερές ομάδες που άρχισαν να πολεμούν η μία την άλλη. [...] Η τρίτη φορά ήταν η χούντα. Και τις δύο τελευταίες, στην Κατοχή και στη χούντα, έφυγα από την Ελλάδα κι από κει έμεινα πολλά χρόνια έξω, χωρίς να βρίσκομαι πουθενά." This excerpt comes from the interview Nanos Valaoritis gave to Christina Linardaki on 24 April 2013 for the electronic journal *Stigma Logou*: http://stigmalogou. blogspot.com/2013/04/blog-post_24.html.

14. http://stigmalogou.blogspot.com/2013/04/blog-post_24.html. The original reads: "Τώρα να αντιμετωπίσουμε τέταρτη φορά άνοδο φασισμού κάτω από δημοκρατικό— υποτίθεται—καθεστώς και με σύνδεσμο στην Ευρωπαϊκή Ένωση; Είναι τόσο απίθανο και απίστευτο... Αισθάνομαι σαν να μην κερδήθηκε ο Β΄ Παγκόσμιος Πόλεμος με τόση τεράστια θυσία ανθρώπων: 600.000 στην Ελλάδα μόνο, εκατομμύρια παντού."

Works Cited

Barthes, Roland; *Writing Degree Zero.* 1953. Trans. Annette Lavers and Colin Smith. London: Jonathan Cape, 1967.

Orwell, George. "Animal Farm." *Orwell and Politics: Animal Farm in the Context of Essays, Reviews and Letters Selected from* The Complete Works of George Orwell. Trans. Peter Davison. London: Penguin Books, 2001. 231–321.

Rabaté, Jean-Michel. "Barthes, Roland." *The Johns Hopkins Guide to Literary Theory and Criticism.* Ed. Michael Groden and Martin Kreiswirth, 68–72. Baltimore and London: Johns Hopkins University Press, 1994.

Valaoritis, Nanos. E-mail Communication. 31 August 2014.

_____. *King Hogdacus the First or In Hog We Trust.* Unpublished Play, 1969.

_____. *Oedipus Pig or Oedipig.* Unpublished Play, 1969.

_____. *Oedipus Reversed or the Dilemma of a Man of Unknown Identity.* Unpublished Play, 1969.

_____. Personal Interview. Athens. 14 July 2014.

_____. *Για μια Θεωρία της Γραφής* (*For a Theory of Writing*). Athens: Exantas, 1990.

_____. *Για μια Θεωρία της Γραφής Β* (*For a Theory of Writing B*). Athens: Electra, 2006.

_____. *Ή του Ύψους ή του Βάθους* (*Either of the Height or of the Depth*). Athens: Psychogios, 2013.

Friends Dying Before Our Eyes in Annie Baker's *The Aliens*

Thomas Butler

Abstract

In her plays, Annie Baker, winner of the 2014 Pulitzer Prize for The Flick, *consistently seeks to examine how friendship takes place in the course of quotidian life. In* The Aliens *(2010), an unlikely friendship comes uneasily together for three characters who spend their days loitering outside the back door of a coffee shop. One character dies between the play's two acts, and the play then pivots to question the relation between friendship and death. This essay argues that Baker makes use of plentiful silences and the evanescence of performance to present a kind of friendship that flourishes when distance separates individuals. Drawing on Maurice Blanchot's and Jacques Derrida's conceptions of friendship, the essay maintains that, in Baker's art, live theater, where live, mortal actors perform before spectators, is capable of presenting a vision of friendship marked by both separation and intimacy.*

The official announcement of the 2014 Pulitzer Prize in Drama is remarkably tepid and lapidary, which presumably has more to do with the Prize's journalistic roots than with the selection committee's level of enthusiasm:

> Awarded to "The Flick," by Annie Baker, a thoughtful drama with well-crafted characters that focuses on three employees of a Massachusetts art-house movie theater, rendering lives rarely seen on the stage [Pulitzer].

Nevertheless, this brief justification for the award points to the central conceit of the play: It is a piece of live theater about life in a movie theater. And that juxtaposition succeeds in "rendering lives rarely seen on the stage." How is the presence of film—once thought to mark the death of live theater—able to bring theater to life?

The Flick runs over three hours and is set in a movie theater whose seats face the audience of the play. It features three characters who work in the theater and finds its dramatic energy in their understated interactions with each other. Critic Patrick Maley writes that "*The Flick* sets itself up as a mirror on reality, crafting characters who are moving in their very mundane ordinariness. It is a play that finds poetry in the everyday, through and amongst the utterances of 'like,' 'I mean,' and 'whatever' that pepper the characters' speech as much as they do everyday speech." The slow-paced ordinariness of the lives on stage counters the common presentation of characters in contemporary entertainment. Critic David Cote notes, "This hypnotic, heartbreaking micro-epic about movies and moving on is irreducibly theatrical; it could never be adapted for the big screen." Theater, as Baker conceives of it, is distinctive in its ability to present life in real time. Michael Feingold finds that Baker "believes in the stage as a place where things take their natural time. In a different play, she'd undoubtedly employ stage shorthand without a qualm, but this one's all about the work the two men do: Every square inch of popcorn they sweep up is a precious minute in their disjunctive, perplexed lives."[1]

The Flick works with ideas and techniques Baker consistently practiced in her earlier plays. Baker entered the New York theater scene with *Body Awareness*, which ran at the Atlantic Theater Company in 2008. Since then she has found critical and popular success with *Circle Mirror Transformation*, which, according to *The New Yorker*, was the second-most produced play in the United States in the 2010–2011 season (Heller 30). Her work also includes a well-received adaptation of Chekhov's *Uncle Vanya*, produced at the Soho Rep in 2012. Drawn to mundane, undramatic life, Baker acknowledges that Chekhov lurks behind much of her writing. In a 2009 interview, Adam Szymkowicz asked Baker who her heroes are. She responded, "Chekhov. Chekhov. Chekhov. Chekhov."

It is, however, Baker's *The Aliens* (2010) that most forcefully complements and prepares the ideas raised in *The Flick*. In this essay, I show how *The Aliens* presents friendship as a counterintuitive experience of distance between individuals. That distance hinges on an awareness of mortality, which is distinctive in theater where there are, among other things, live (and, therefore, dying) bodies performing on stage. Theater is both an ephemeral and a mortal experience, and enables a presentation of friendship that bears the marks of life and mortality.

Friendship in *The Aliens*

All of the action of *The Aliens*, which premiered at the Rattlestick Playwrights Theater in New York in 2010, takes place in what Baker describes as *"the desolate back patio of a coffee shop in Vermont"* (5). A trash bin, a recycling bin, a picnic table, and a few plastic chairs fill the space. Two men in their early 30s, KJ and Jasper, smoke, sip tea, sing songs, and while the day away. A welcome distraction comes when Evan, a worker from the coffee shop, emerges from the backdoor to throw out a bag of trash. He is 17 years old and terrified by the prospect of social interaction. Since he cannot possibly avoid KJ and Jasper when taking out the trash, Evan reluctantly talks to the two loiterers, and eventually the three form an unlikely bond of affection. Their friendship culminates at the end of the first act when Evan turns up for KJ and Jasper's Fourth of July party, which, much to Evan's surprise, consists of only the three of them and some brownies and schnapps Evan stole from his parents' liquor cabinet. Against the backdrop of the city's elaborate fireworks display, these three dejected characters enact their own off-beat celebration. Countering the fireworks, KJ lights a sparkler and joyously dances, waving it in his hand as Jasper and Evan happily watch him.

In the second act, this feeling of joy gradually dissipates. In Evan's first two appearances in this act, he sees only KJ behind the coffee shop. With much difficulty, KJ eventually admits to Evan that Jasper died a week earlier from a heroin overdose. At the end of the play, KJ says he's going to move to another city, and he gives Jasper's guitar to Evan. At KJ's urging, Evan plays it and sings a "slightly out-of-tune" version of Lee Hays and Pete Seeger's song "If I Had a Hammer." The final stage direction reads: *"Evan tries not to smile. But then he does"* (84).

Nathan Heller's 2013 *New Yorker* profile of Baker notes that Baker's plays tend to center on mentorship, but a kind where "the teachers are never people one might entirely admire" (35). Certainly in *The Aliens* KJ's fondness for tea infused with psychedelic mushrooms would be enough to startle any prospective protégé. Baker's portrait of such imperfect characters underscores the differences among them, most emphatically between Evan and the pair, KJ and Jasper. Early in the play, as Jasper smokes and KJ sips his doctored tea, Evan explains that next week he will work as a counselor-in-training at a music camp for Jewish children. Clearly, the differences are stark. Yet the play shows how a friendship develops in virtue of such differences.

In the first act, KJ tries to impress Evan by telling him that he and Jasper used to play in a band that over the years had assumed many names. After KJ rattles off a sampling of the band names, including The New Humans and Hieronymous Blast, Jasper interjects, "I wanted us to be called The Aliens"

(29). Jasper explains that this name, which KJ found too boring, comes from a poem by Charles Bukowski, a writer Jasper admires because "he cuts away all the bullshit" (30). Bukowski's poem "The Aliens" describes with a measure of baffled disdain the lives of people who go through life blissfully free of troubles.

The poem places the speaker and indirectly the addressee against the rest of the world, and they take pride in their marginal status. Clearly the play's three characters assume a similar position, which Evan succinctly describes while explaining his dislike of Fourth of July celebrations:

> Yeah. You know. I don't know. It's like all these families spread out on the football field? With the glowsticks? And they have that crappy local marching band. I don't know. It's like anticlimactic I guess? Like afterwards everyone seems a little disappointed. And I don't know: it's like, kind of random. Like we explode stuff in the sky and we look at it in like a group? *(pause)* And like, I kind of hate America. So I don't feel this like urgent need to celebrate it or anything [30].

With this speech Evan first expresses his connection with Jasper and KJ as a band of outsiders or "aliens" apart from others, namely, the flag- and glowstick-waving society. Together they have carved out their marginal space beside the dumpsters behind the coffee shop, as the rest of society sips cappuccinos inside and heads down to the football field to watch the fireworks.

More important, however, is the distance the friends maintain between each other so that they are aliens to each other. Baker uses pauses and silences throughout the play to create a speech rhythm that underscores the gulfs between characters. In a note at the beginning of the script, she writes, "At least a third—if not half—of this play is silence. Pauses should be at least three seconds long. Silences should last from five to ten seconds. Long pauses and long silences should, of course, be even longer" (3). The script can only go so far to indicate the extent of silence Baker has in mind, but it is readily apparent on stage. Critic Stephen Kaliski, for example, writes of the 2010 Rattlestick production, "One simple word captures the prevailing style of the play: silence. Baker expertly navigates the life lived between the lines, allowing her characters to process each other without heaps of forced dialogue." The play's first scene brilliantly uses silences to highlight the gulf between KJ and Jasper. For example, after a long silence, KJ asks Jasper if he'd like to talk about his recent break-up with his girlfriend:

> KJ: Hey. Uh. Do you wanna talk about it? Or would you rather just, uh …
> *KJ trails off.*
> JASPER: Andrea?
> *KJ nods.*
> JASPER: Not really.
> *KJ nods again. A pause.*

JASPER: She's crazy, man.
KJ nods again. A pause [7–8].

And so the conversation goes, filled with silences that reveal the distance between the friends.

Against a philosophical tradition that has tended to view friendship as a unity between individuals, Baker's play may seem misguided. Montaigne is perhaps the leader of this friendship-as-unity tradition. He famously described his own friendship with Etienne La Boétie as ideal: "In the friendship I speak of, our souls mingle and blend with each other so completely that they efface the seam that joined them, and cannot find it again" (192). Or, as he puts it later in the same essay: "he is myself" (195). The goal of friendship, it would seem, should be for friends to become as alike as possible. Intimacy stems from closeness and harmony, and distance between friends is ultimately ruinous to their bond. Versions of Montaigne's position, albeit less spirited, continue to hold sway today. In an influential essay on friendship from 1970, the philosopher Elizabeth Telfer emphasizes the value of shared experiences between friends: "[F]riendship can enlarge our knowledge throughout the whole gamut of human experience, by enabling us in some measure to adopt the viewpoint of another person through our sympathetic identification with him" (240). Certainly more tempered than Montaigne, Telfer nonetheless underscores identification as a hallmark of friendship.

A different perspective, however, can help us get a handle on the kind of friendship at work in *The Aliens*. After the death of his friend Georges Bataille in 1962, Maurice Blanchot suggested that it is in fact distance and not unity between friends that sustains a friendship. In his essay entitled "For Friendship," which concludes his book *Friendship*, Blanchot writes, "We must give up trying to know those to whom we are linked by something essential; by this I mean we must greet them in relation with the unknown in which they greet us as well, in our estrangement" (291). A friend, then, for Blanchot, is someone who is fundamentally unknowable. But the friend's position outside of cognitive categories creates an experience that has something in common with Blanchot's experience of certain forms of recalcitrant, modernist literary texts. In *Friendship*, for example, he includes an essay, "Idle Speech," prompted by "a few words that were said to me, shortly before his death, by Georges Bataille concerning [René des Forêt's novel] *Le Bavard*" (117). Read alongside Blanchot's essay "For Friendship," his response to this novel illuminates an affirmative upshot of an experience of estrangement in which "a verbal expanse all of a sudden gives way to something that no longer speaks but that one sees" (127). This relation with a text or with a friend takes place where logic and language fall to the side: "A wondrous moment without wonders, the spectral equivalent of silence, and perhaps death, death being the pure visibility of what escapes all grasp" (128).

The experience of friendship, like the experience of reading texts by authors like des Forêt, Kafka, and Celan, takes hold where speech and knowledge come up short. In place of speech and knowledge, Blanchot finds a revelatory distance between two friends. Blanchot explains, "It is the interval, the pure interval that, from me to this other who is a friend, measures all that is between us, the interruption of being that never authorizes me to use him, or my knowledge of him (were it to praise him), and that, far from preventing all communication, brings us together in the difference and sometimes the silence of speech" (291). The distance and silence between friends bring them together in their relationship. Or as critic Patrick ffrench puts it, "The most intimate is also the most distant" (35). Intimacy in friendship results from the individuals' openness to the kind of experience Blanchot describes in his reading of des Forêt.

In *The Aliens*, this conception of intimacy through distance informs the wisdom of KJ's mother, Sandy Jano, who never appears on stage but who, in Jasper's estimation, is something of a sage. Jasper recalls a difficult time in his life when he was crashing on a couch at KJ and Sandy's house. At that time, Sandy encouraged Jasper to accept, in his words, "this in-between state, this being unstable or whatever" (21). He then goes on to express her nugget of wisdom in his own idiom: "She was like: the state of just having lost something is like the most enlightened state in the world" (21). Upon the news of Jasper's death later in the play, these lines resonate as they suggest a relation between the distance between friends and the prospect of their death. Blanchot admits such a relation in his essay on Bataille when he views the interval between friends as a commendable form of discretion. He acknowledges that "at a certain moment this discretion becomes the fissure of death" (291). Though he says that when the death of a friend takes place, "all that separates, disappears," he notes that in life, death, "this imminent presence," was already tacitly in place (292, 291). Further, the inevitability of a friend's death nourishes the intimacy the friends share. He says, "[I]t is on the basis of this discretion that the precaution of friendly words calmly affirmed itself" (291).

The Aliens presents friendship as an experience marked by distance. Jasper's death at the center of the play—indeed, between its two acts—haunts the relationships presented on stage. This haunting, however, is not a menace; rather, it secures a relationship between individuals in a space that affirms their difference from each other and, at the same time, prohibits their becoming one. If friends were identical, not only difference but life would be drained from their relationship. *The Aliens* presents friendship as an experience of mourning, but one in which liveliness edges out dolor.[2]

Liveness and Performance

Or perhaps it's liveness that edges out dolor. To flesh out this suggestion, I recall Philip Auslander's *Liveness: Performance in a Mediatized Culture*, which has sparked considerable discussion about the concept of liveness since its publication in 1999. Auslander argues—with a touch of an iconoclast's relish—that there is nothing inherently distinctive about live performance vis-à-vis television. In fact, he maintains "live" only makes sense in relation to "recorded," as demonstrated, for example, by the Oxford English Dictionary's dating of the first usage of "live" in reference to performance in the 1930s, well after recording technology was in wide use: Shakespeare's plays were not "live" theater, they were simply theater. Auslander contends that "live" is not so much opposed to "recorded" as both terms are part of the same economy which, at present (in 1999, at least), televisual media dominates: "Far from being encroached upon, contaminated, or threatened by mediation, live performance is always already inscribed with traces of the possibility of technical mediation (i.e., mediatization) that defines it as live" (53). There is no such thing as pure, live theater; it exists only in relation to mediatization, which is a term Auslander borrows from Fredric Jameson to underscore that live performance and technical media are part of "the same cultural economy" (5).[3] Auslander is not interested in making an ontological argument. Instead, he seizes on Walter Benjamin's idea that "human sense perception [...] is determined not by nature but by historical circumstances as well" (qtd. in Auslander, *Liveness* 34). What that means for Auslander is that audiences experience live performance in relation to the dominant televisual meditization. Just as sports fans at live events watch the Jumbo Tron as much as the game, theater audiences increasingly find validation for their experience by anticipating its reproducibility. He cites the close connection between Broadway musicals and their film counterparts, which together form a mutually reinforcing entertainment commodity. Although Auslander does not say all live theater events are reproducible, he argues that theater can in fact be a "mass medium," which then quashes its assumed privileged, original position.

Auslander argues against a formidable critical tradition that has made special claims for theater, but he engages most fully with Peggy Phelan, who in *Unmarked: The Politics of Performance* (1993) contends that live performance resists the dominant culture in both its technological and capitalist guises. He cites a passage from *Unmarked* that makes clear the special status Phelan accords to performance:

> Performance's only life is in the present. Performance cannot be saved, recorded, documented, or otherwise participate in the circulation of representations *of* representations: once it does so, it becomes something other than performance.

> To the degree that performance attempts to enter the economy of reproduction
> it betrays and lessens the promise of its own ontology [Phelan 146; Auslander
> 39].

For Auslander, there is no escape from "the economy of reproduction" because
live performance is always already caught up in it. Further, performance is not
the only evanescent form of art. Auslander notes that every time he plays a
film on his VCR, the quality of the tape is compromised, making it, therefore,
impossible to replicate that experience of watching the film. (*Liveness* first
appeared when VCRs were still commonplace. Auslander writes in a footnote
it is "worth wondering about the implications of digital reproductions [...]
since at least some digital media ostensibly do not degrade" [45n.].) Television
also passes in time insofar as "scan lines replace one another" (45). Auslander
asserts, "Disappearance, existence only in the present moment, is not, then,
an ontological quality of live performance that distinguishes it from modes
of technical reproduction" (45). Theater and live performance in general,
therefore, are not ontologically different than other popular forms of media.

As Auslander criticizes Phelan for not fully considering the technological
aspects of performance, he understates Phelan's focus on the body in performance. Phelan argues that the embodied evanescence of performance allows it
to operate in opposition to the dominant politics of reproduction, which is
complicit with patriarchal inequality. Performance creates a space that culti-
vates a non-identical openness between stage and audience, character and
actor, and, most important, presence and absence: "Performance uses the performer's body to pose a question about the inability to secure the relation
between subjectivity and the body *per se*; performance uses the body to frame
the lack of Being promised by and through the body—that which cannot
appear without a supplement" (150–51). The body stands in the way of interpretative efforts to reduce the performance to a settled narrative fit for the
economy of reproduction. Phelan cites Angelika Festa's *Untitled Dance (with
fish and others)* (1987), in which Festa hung from a pole with her eyes covered
for 24 hours. To Auslander's point, an enlarged image of Festa's feet was projected behind her, a video documenting the embryology of fish played on a
monitor, and a time-elapsed video of the performance played on another monitor. For Phelan, however, the technological elements are ancillary to the presence of Festa's suspended body: "The work is primarily a spectacle of pain"
(153). In order for spectators to see the images, they must either look past
Festa or turn their back to her. The entire work underscores the performing
body's paradoxical place as both present and absent. "The spectator's inability
to meet the eye *defines* the other's body as lost; the pain of this loss is underlined
by the corollary recognition that the represented body is so manifestly and
painfully there, for both Festa and the spectator" (156).

Even as different as Festa's performance surely is from a piece of theater like Baker's *The Aliens*, I would like to take up Phelan's emphasis on the body as a way to resuscitate an understanding of theatrical liveness from Auslander's critique of it. In doing so, I will show that an important part of liveness entails an acknowledgement of evanescence, or mortality, which is precisely what characterizes friendship in *The Aliens*. I will leave to the side the rich theoretical issue of the relation of the body and technology in performance to focus instead on the body's part in a performance's passage of time. Even if, as Auslander points out, films were once seen as evanescent, that does not affect theater's temporality; it merely casts doubt on theater's ontological distinctiveness. In an essay written after the publication *Liveness*, Auslander considers the possibility of liveness in entirely technological performances featuring "Internet chatterbots," which are programs that respond to human conversation. Chatterbots can perform live, Auslander contends, insofar as they "perform in the moment" responding to unscripted and unpredictable conversation ("Live" 21). He concludes, therefore, that liveness does not depend on human activity, let alone on bodies: "The ability to present performances that can be watched as they occur, or, to switch to a technological vocabulary, to perform in real time—the heart of the concept of liveness—is an ability shared by human beings and chatterbots" (21). Auslander does not continue to explain the concept of "real time" and how it differs for a chatterbot and a human being. Undoubtedly, however, time experienced in an audience's relation to the theoretically interminable (and, as Auslander says, "immortal") chatterbots is categorically different than its relation to living performers (20).

Herbert Blau forcefully argues that such a difference would have to center on the mortality of the performer. In his *Take Up the Bodies*, for example, he writes, "When we speak of what Stanislavski called Presence in acting, we must also speak of its Absence, the dimensionality of time through the actor, the fact that he who is performing can die there in front of your eyes; is in fact doing so. Of all the performing arts, the theater stinks most of mortality" (83). Therefore, it seems that what is distinctive, if not categorically definitive, of theater is the human actor whose presence bespeaks an acknowledgment of death. The body of the actor introduces a sense of passing time foreign to Auslander's chatterbots. Baker's *The Aliens* underscores this effect with its plentiful silences that call to mind some of the experimental work of John Cage. Recall, for example, Cage's account of his attempt to find pure silence in an anechoic chamber at Harvard University in the 1950s. All external sound was eliminated, but his own body stymied his attempt to find silence. He reports that he heard "two sounds, one high and one low. When I described them to the engineer in charge, he informed me that the high one was my nervous system in operation, the low one my blood in circulation. Until I die there will be sounds" (8). The experience of silence is possible only to the extent that it is shadowed by markers of mortality. The bodies of performers and the silence (impure as it is) in the theater together smell of mortality, and can, therefore, effectively present the experience of friendship, which, for Blanchot and Baker, is animated by distance and the immanence of death.

Performer and Spectator

Walter Benjamin found this aspect of an actor's presence to be wanting in the early days of film. In "The Origin of the Work of Art in the Age of Its Reproducibility," he describes how the theatre actor's aura dissipates on screen because the actor's physical (dying) presence is lost:

> [F]or the first time—and this is the effect of film—the human being is placed in a position where he must operate with his whole living person, while forgoing its aura. For the aura is bound to his presence in the here and now. There is no facsimile of the aura. The aura surrounding Macbeth on the stage cannot be divorced from the aura which, for living spectators, surrounds the actor who plays him [3: 112)].

The experience of theater, unlike that of film, centers on a shared sense of mortality between the performer and the spectator. Theater's liveness carries with it the prospect of the end of the performance, a passing from "the here and now," which can never be replicated when the lights go up.[4] That temporal awareness creates a hothouse effect regarding the passing of time for the actors and spectators alike: as the play's time passes, so does the actors' and audience's time. Perhaps this is what Christopher Isherwood is getting at in his review of *The Aliens* when he says the experience of the play is like a painting by "a less-heralded old master" which you would overlook in a quick tour of a museum. "Its magic is too subtle for that. But the longer you look, the more you see and the more you feel." And what you feel is the passing of time.

Benjamin writes that film reduces the distance between spectator and work and, therefore, satisfies people's desire "to 'get closer' to things spatially and humanly" (4: 255). He argues that at the time when he was writing, people were willing to sacrifice uniqueness for reproducibility. Aura, however, exists through a work of art's uniqueness and distance from its spectator. In his essay "Little History of Photography," Benjamin asks, "What is aura, actually? A strange weave of space and time: the unique appearance or semblance of distance, no matter how close it may be" (2: 518). As close as the audience may feel to the actors, the aura of the performance safeguards a distance through which their proximity is made possible. That is, presence in performance effects a relation between actor and spectator that unfolds in space and time.

In his review of the San Francisco Playhouse's 2012 production of *The Aliens*, Charles Kruger notes how the distancing experience of silence paradoxically creates a sense of proximity: "Baker takes the extraordinary risk of writing intensive silences into the play—some lasting two or three minutes. The effect is amazing. We seem to be experiencing this relationship in real time, not theatrical time at all. As each tiny revelation of character and insight is given, we are allowed ample time to reflect upon it as though we had actually heard it from a personal friend." For Kruger, the silences between the characters on stage produce in spectators a sense of intimacy with the characters. The characters' silences and the passing of real time in this case demonstrate, as Blau puts it, the mortality of theatrical performance.

In his essay "The Storyteller," Benjamin declares, "Death is the sanction of everything a storyteller can tell" (94). By this, he means that the life of the storyteller grants authority to the stories he tells. "Thus traces of the storyteller cling to the story the way the handprints of the potter cling to the clay vessel" (92). The absence of the potter, present only in his traces, brings the work of art into being. Art comes into being bearing traces of death and absence. Thus, in theater the presence of the actor emerges at the same time as his absence, which manifests itself as his dying before our eyes. Live theater can present a non-identical relation of proximity and distance that accords with the kind of relationship friendship achieves in *The Aliens*. The climax of the play comes at the end of the first act during the Fourth of July party when KJ, Jasper, and Evan all seem finally, albeit uneasily, to come together as friends. KJ begins an erratic, joyful dance. As the others watch his performance, Jasper asks Evan if he has any friends at his high school. In response, *"Evan shakes his head peacefully"* and says he doesn't (50). At that moment, without missing a beat in his solo dance, KJ says, "I NEED A SPARKLER" (50). Jasper lights one, hands it to KJ, who now continues his dance waving his lit sparkler. In this scene, as Evan admits he has no other friends, this friendship takes hold. Yet the gap constitutive of this friendship is apparent in the spectacle of KJ's dance. The act concludes with KJ exclaiming, "It's going out it's going out!" (50). It does, and then darkness fills the stage. The image of the sparkler, which is festive and exciting because of its evanescence, affirms the mortality at the heart of friendship. The presence of friendship is possible only in relation to the distance between the friends, and that is most saliently represented by their mortality.

Surely one of the most penetrating legacies of late twentieth-century literary theory is the insight that presence depends on its relation to absence. *The Aliens* shows that in live theatre this relation can take the form of presence appearing alongside an acknowledgment of mortality. The performance will end, as will our lives. Perhaps this is not the best way to advertise the offerings of a local theater, but it need not be a gloomy assessment. Heidegger, for example, maintained that an authentic life is possible only when one embraces what he calls "Being-towards-Death," which philosopher Simon Critchley has glossed: "If our being is finite, then an authentic human life can only be found by confronting finitude and trying to make a meaning out of the fact of our death." In *The Aliens* friendship has a place in such an authentic life: if friendship is to be meaningful, it must happen in relation to mortality. Derrida made a similar point in even starker terms: "To have a friend, to look at him, to follow him with your eyes, to admire him in friendship, is to know in a more intense way, already injured, always insistent, and more and more unforgettable, that one of the two of you will inevitably see the other die" (137). Live theater, in Baker's art, is just the place to see the other dying before our eyes.

EASTERN KENTUCKY UNIVERSITY

NOTES

1. In his complimentary review of the play, Patrick Maley samples some of the comments he overheard from audience members, which echo Vladimir and Estragon's dialogue about the tedium of waiting for Godot and (here's Beckett's humor) of the audience's experience watching the play. For example, Maley reports, "'Good God,' muttered the woman sitting behind me at Saturday's matinee, 'I hope the next three hours are more fun than this.' 'Where do they get their nerve,' another chatty audience member grumbled as the play slowly wound to its conclusion, 'it's twenty-to-six for Christ's sake!'" Critic Jeremy Gerard may have been one of those grumbling spectators, as he concludes his review in *Bloomberg News*: "After three-and-a-quarter hours of excruciating tedium, escaping into a miserable winter night felt like liberation."

2. The idea of haunting has in recent years received much critical attention in theater scholarship. Jacques Derrida's *Specters of Marx* begins with a reading of *Hamlet* and goes on to trace the haunting presence of Marx—spectral insofar as his presence is shot through with absence—in modern Western thought. Focusing more specifically on theater practice and drama history, Joseph Roach's *Cities of the Dead: Circum-Atlantic Performance* (1996), Marvin Carlson's *The Haunted Stage: The Theatre as Memory Machine* (2003), and Alice Rayner's *Ghosts: Death's Double and the Phenomena of Theatre* (2006) are particularly significant.

3. Jameson defines "meditization" as "the process whereby the traditional fine arts [...] come to consciousness of themselves as various media within a mediatic system" (qtd. in Auslander 5).

4. Discussing his first play, *The Day Room*, Don DeLillo notes how the evanescence of theater distinguishes a play from a novel:

For one thing, when you're finished with a play, you don't have an object you hold in your hand and say, "This is what I've done." You're not quite sure what you've done. Rehearsals vary, performances vary. The play will be in book form, but that's not really the play—this is the play. And yet it's very elusive to try to determine a definitive performance, even a definitive moment, because they change all the time [21].

I thank Graley Herren who brought to my attention DeLillo's comments on theater at the 2014 CDC.

WORKS CITED

Auslander, Philip. "Live from Cyberspace: Or, I Was Sitting at My Computer This Guy Appeared He Thought I Was a Bot." *PAJ* 24 (2002): 16–21.

_____. *Liveness: Performance in a Meditized Culture.* New York: Routledge, 1999.

Baker, Annie. "I Interview Playwrights Part 38: Annie Baker." Interview with Adam Szymkowicz. Web. Accessed 15 May 2014.

_____. *The Vermont Plays.* New York: Theater Communications Group, 2012.

Benjamin, Walter. *Selected Writings.* Ed. Michael W. Jennings. 4 vols. Cambridge: Belknap, 1996–2003.

Blanchot, Maurice, *Friendship.* Trans. Elizabeth Rottenberg. Stanford: Stanford University Press, 1997.

Blau, Herbert. *Take up the Bodies: Theater at the Vanishing Point.* Urbana: University of Illinois Press, 1982

Cage, John. *Silence.* 50th Anniversary ed. Middletown, CT: Wesleyan University Press, 2011.

Cote, David. "The Flick." 12 March 2013. *Time Out New York.* Web. Accessed 19 May 2014.

Critchley, Simon. "*Being and Time* Part 6: Death." *The Guardian* 13 July 2009. Web. Accessed 5 May 2014.

DeLillo, Don. "A Novelist Faces His Themes on New Ground." Interview with Mervyn Rothstein. *Conversations with Don DeLillo.* Ed. Thomas DePietro. Jackson: University Press of Mississippi, 2005. 20–24.

Derrida, Jacques. *The Work of Mourning.* Eds. Pascale-Anne Brault and Michael Naas. Chicago: University of Chicago Press, 2001.

Feingold, Michael. "*The Flick* and *Talley's Folly* Meet New People." *The Village Voice* 13 March 2013. Web. Accessed 19 May 2014.

ffrench, Patrick. "Friendship, Asymmetry, Sacrifice: Bataille and Blanchot." *Parrhesia* 3 (2007): 32–43.

Gerard, Jeremy. "Baker's 'The Flick' Is Slow-Motion Torture." *Bloomberg* 12 March 2013. Web. Accessed 19 May 2014.

Heller, Nathan. "Just Saying: The Anti-Theatrical Theater of Annie Baker." *The New Yorker* (25 Feb. 2013): 30–35.

Isherwood, Charles. "Outsiders, Tender and Troubled." *New York Times* 23 April 2010. Web. Accessed 28 July 2014.

Kaliski, Stephen, "The Aliens." Review. Nytheater.com 17 April 2010. Web. Accessed 28 July 2014.

Kruger, Charles. "SF Playhouse: Annie Baker's 'The Aliens' Is a Masterpiece and Not to Be Missed." *Theatrestorm* 26 March 2012. Web. Accessed 28 July 2014.

Maley, Patrick. "Unconventional Beauty in Playwright Horizon's *The Flick*." *Stage Magazine* 10 March 2013. Web. Accessed 19 May 2014.

Montaigne, Michel de. "Of Friendship." *Other Selves: Philosophers on Friendship.* Ed. Michael Pakaluk. Indianapolis: Hackett, 1991.

Phelan, Peggy. *Unmarked: The Politics of Performance.* New York: Routledge, 1993.

The Pulitzer Prize Winners. "Drama." Web. Accessed 21 May 2014.

Telfer, Elizabeth. "Friendship." *Proceedings of the Aristotelian Society* 71 (1970): 223–241.

A Comparative Analysis of
Three Plays on Disasters:
Omnium Gatherum, Carried Away
on the Crest of a Wave, and *Radio 311*

YUKO KURAHASHI

Abstract

Over the past decade, a number of plays that focus on recent catastrophic events and their aftermaths have appeared. My essay examines three such plays—Omnium Gatherum, Carried Away on the Crest of a Wave, *and* Radio 311—*which deal with the responses, views, and experiences of survivors of human-made and natural disasters in the twenty-first century. This essay discusses how these plays narrate, memorialize, and invoke traumatic events in order to bring a nightmare out of the margins to the center of public discourse, giving both its victims and bystanders a legitimate space to reflect and process their experiences.*

Disasters or other traumatic events often propel theatre artists to create works that address the experience of victims and survivors. This reflects the role of theatre as a medium for gaining psychological insight. As Peter Elsass, a professor of clinical psychology at the University of Copenhagen, argues, both actors and psychotherapists "share the aim of creating new insights or making implicit knowledge, explicit for the audience and patients" (333). Applied theatre scholar Penny Bundy goes further to state that drama can be used in the counseling process as a tool to "redress some of the ongoing problems experienced by survivors" (7).

This cathartic function of theatre is not limited to psychodrama or special therapeutic projects. A scripted play performed by actors also has the potential to provide a space and tool for healing in the aftermath of a disaster or traumatic event. Writing about a shadow puppet performance that responded to the bombing of a night club in Kuta, Bali, in 2002, I Nyoman Sedana argued that the performance provided the Balinese with a cultural space for "healing through performance" (73). He stressed that this performance promoted "the correct relations between the gods, humans, and nature in spatial terms" (83) because the performers could "[step] into a place of power where disorder can be mediated by the active power of performance" (85).

Elsass, Bundy, and Sedana all examined theatre projects that were intended to mediate, mitigate, memorialize, and heal psychological wounds and pains of victims and survivors of traumatic events. Over the past decade, a number of plays that focus on recent catastrophic events and their aftermaths have appeared. My paper examines three such plays—*Omnium Gatherum*, *Carried Away on the Crest of a Wave*, and *Radio 311*—which deal with the responses, views, and experiences of survivors of human-made and natural disasters in the twenty-first century. Theresa Rebeck and Alexandra Gersten-Vassilaros's *Omnium Gatherum* (2003) is set at a dinner party in New York City, after the 9/11 attacks. David Yee's *Carried Away on the Crest of a Wave* (2013) uses the 2004 tsunami off the west coast of Sumatra, Indonesia, as a motif to deal with issues of loss, redemption, survivor's guilt, responsibility, and self-justification. Ryosei Kajiwara's *Radio 311* deals with victims and bystanders of the 2011 earthquake in Fukushima, Japan. This paper discusses how these plays narrate, memorialize, and invoke traumatic events in order to bring a nightmare out of the margins to the center of public discourse, giving both its victims and bystanders a legitimate space to reflect and process their experiences.

Omnium-Gatherum

After the attacks of 9/11, the media coverage became the primary bridge between the attacks themselves and people throughout the United States (and beyond), acting not only as the main source of information but also as an agent to orchestrate, represent, and stage the tragedy. Ruth E. Propper and her colleagues researched how the media influenced people's reactions to 9/11. They found that media exposure had a great influence on the "levels of stress and trauma in response to the September 11 attacks" (335). In "9/11, Afghanistan, and Iraq: The Response of the New York Theatre," Marvin Carlson explored the effects of experiencing catastrophic events solely through the mass media. He argues that even the actual witnessing of the burning Trade Center had a "theatrical, simulated quality and the feeling of something already experienced in visual fiction" (3). This innate theatricality, Carlson continues, was "solidified by the endless replaying of the catastrophe on television in the following days" (4).

In the aftermath of the tragedy, people began to look, beyond media reporting, to understand and critically analyze the response of the government and media. The theatre community was no exception. For example, a special issue of *Theatre Journal* (2002) devoted over forty pages to "the concept of tragedy in the context of these world-changing events" (Taylor et al 95). One contributor, Una Chaudhuri, saw the destruction of the World Trade Center as the fall of the symbol of "the West's exemplary metropolis" (97). Diana Taylor viewed the tragedy as one in a continuum of tragic events, which "banished and blinded the witnesses" (96) with the help of the media and the government's focus on consumerism after 9/11.

While the media discourse and its counter-discourse continued to permeate, a number of therapists and social workers engaged in various healing programs for those who were wounded or who lost loved ones. Many of the

Figure 1. The cast of *Omnium-Gatherum*: Melanna Gray, Edward A. Hajj, Robert Lee Simmons, Kristine Nielsen, Philip Clark, Richard Furlong, Roma Maffia and Dean Nolen. Humana Festival of New American Plays, Actors Theatre of Louisville, 2003 (photograph by John Fitzgerald).

healers expressed the need to understand the complexity of events, including ambiguity (many of the victims' bodies were not recovered), differences in race, culture, and ethnicity, different approaches to closure, and the rift between mainstream media discourse and actuality. Documenting the work of a team of therapists from Minnesota and New York who worked with labor union families of workers gone missing on September 11, 2001, Pauline Boss and her co-authors illuminate the importance of recognizing these variables in "systematic interventions to the community level" in the time of a catastrophic event (456).

Those who tried to help the community were not only clinicians, psychotherapists and social workers. After several months of mass media presentations of the event, theatre artists began to attempt, metaphorically, to recover the lives and voices of those who had disappeared in the attacks. Rather than "replaying the catastrophe," theatre artists looked for alternative ways to share experiences, grief, and insights. Examples of such 9/11 plays, discussed by Carlson, include Anne Nelson's *The Guys* (2002), Neil LaBute's *The Mercy Seat*, and the 2003 Theatre Against War project.

In spite of successful runs at the Humana Festival and off Broadway, *Omnium Gatherum* has remained less familiar to theatre goers than the plays examined in Carlson's article.[1] This may be due in part to harsh criticism by *New York Times* critic Frank Rich, who wrote, "The scenario is Tom Wolfe for dummies," and "this glib play" congratulates, instead of criticizes, "a complacent audience on its own moral superiority to the nattering nabobs onstage" (Rich 2). In Rich's opinion, the play "is part of the problem, not the solution, at a time when America, arguably, is waltzing into what the former C.I.A. Director James Woolsey has called the next world war" (Rich 2). Whatever were the merits of Rich's criticism, the play did provide opportunities for self-reflection and self-criticism as America was "waltzing" into wars in Afghanistan and Iraq. The play also poignantly points to ambiguous differences in responses to the 9/11 attacks.

The title *Omnium Gatherum* means a "miscellaneous collection." The miscellaneous collection here is a dinner party with the seven characters, hosted by homemaker/entrepreneur Suzie several months after the 9/11 attacks. In her luxurious Manhattan apartment with a long table and chair, Suzie, who reminds us of Martha Stewart, entertains her guests with exquisitely prepared dishes. Suzie's Babbittian guests are eager not only to taste them but to use them to exhibit their sense of self-importance and righteousness. Her guests are the reactionary novelist Roger (a Tom Clancy type), a pro–Palestinian British intellectual Terrence (a Christopher Hitchens character), an Edward Said-reincarnation named Khalid, an African American minister Julia, the vegan Lydia, and Jeff the fireman. Toward the end of the evening, Suzie surprises her guests with her last guest, a terrorist named Mohammed.

As *New York Times* critic Ben Brantley states, the familiar dramaturgical setting of a dinner party provides a "too-familiar frisson of irony," as seen in such popular works as Tom Wolfe's "Radical Chic" and *The Bonfire of the Vanities*, and Luis Buñuel's *The Discreet Charm of the Bourgeoisie*, with "the sending up of pretentiously poetic descriptions of food" and "the weightier subject under discussion" (Brantley E1). Brantley praised its "radical yet perfectly organic shifts in tone" which helped to mix "tragedy and triviality, ponderousness and pettiness" into "a salad so deliriously tossed that you can't separate the individual ingredients" (Brantley E1). Different tones, tunes, and rhythms in the dialogue between the guests, which are constantly interrupted by the arrival of a new dish, vividly illustrate the universality of human greed, conquest of others, and narcissism in Suzie's dining room. During the course of dinner, Suzie's fashionable guests reveal their shallowness and superficiality by debating the world's tragedies without much sympathy for victims. Their self-righteous attitudes are occasionally peppered with a sense of guilt and kindness, making the characters more human and less caricature.

Khalid states that "if we could but shrink the earth's population to a village of precisely 100 people" "57 are Asians, 21 are Europeans, 14 from the Western Hemisphere, 8 are Africans, 52 are female, 48 are male, 70 are non-white, 70 are non–Christian, 30 are Christian, 89 are heterosexual, 11 are homosexual, and six people would possess 59 percent of the entire worlds' wealth and all six would be from the United States" (Rebeck 339–40). While this helps to inform the audience about the world population's makeup of race, ethnicity, sex, and the distribution of wealth, Rebeck and Gersten-Vassilaros also use it to underscore the self-serving arrogance of Khalid, who talks about poverty and exploitation just before he indulges himself in an elaborate dinner. This contrast between talk and action is illuminated by Suzie's descriptions of the elaborate dishes which she constantly interjects into the contentious arguments during her dinner party. Her stylish descriptions are ignored by the characters who are concerned only about themselves. They ask questions about food and fashion only to take a break from heated debate:

> KHALID: Unbridled capitalism has long been a concern to the global community—
> SUZIE: (To Julia.) I love your jacket, is that Donna's?
> KHALID: Warnings have been made again and again and the resistance in America—
> JULIA: I got it at Lohman's. They cut the tag out.
> KHALID: —to the simplest examination of this basic question has been rather absolute. We must reflect.
> LYDIA: Americans, reflect?
> ROGER: Hey. You don't get to criticize us after you blew up the World Trade Center. (They all protest at once.) [343]

This alternation between the serious and frivolous underscores American arrogance, self-righteousness, and self-indulgence. As Robert Brusetin observes, *Omnium Gatherum* "strongly indicts the unthinking hedonism of a consumer society in which, as one character observes, 'our spiritual response to any catastrophe should be to go out and shop'" (27).

Toward the end of the evening, Suzie's special guest, Mohammed the terrorist, arrives. It initially seems that her intention is to add extra spice to her party: "I did manage to tempt a rather interesting young man to stop by, for just a few minutes" in order to "answer some of the many questions we've all been discussing tonight in such a lively fashion" (376). An argument between Mohammed and Khalid follows. Mohammed accuses Khalid of siding with "infidels" by supporting the United States, "the first terrorist in the history of mankind." Khalid then accuses Mohammed of being a "barbarian, a scourge, part of a group of rejects of the Noble Muslim civilization" (376). Rather than continuing this argument with Khalid, Mohammed attacks him with a fork, leading the male guests to grapple with Mohammed and then tie him to a chair.

The arrival of Mohammed, who turns out to be one of the hijackers from a plane that struck the World Trade Center, serves as a dramaturgical device that evokes the voice of the voiceless "other" in the media presentation of 9/11. His claim that "everything you do" is "to silence the Arab community," to take "our oil" and "our wealth," is not normally heard in the mainstream media. Here the playwrights question and criticize the mainstream media image of the entire Muslim world as an enclave of terrorists. Mohammed's presence and his comments also provoke a response from soft-spoken Jeff, the fireman, revealing that Jeff actually died during his rescue mission on September 11, 2001. The arrival of Mohammed and the following scene thus contrast those who are aware of where they are—Mohammed and Jeff—and those who continue to fail to grasp their situation. While the audience begins to wonder if the other characters are also dead and whether the dinner party is actually an "omnium gatherum" of the dead, the characters themselves refuse to see that possibility. This act of denial also suggests that these characters are not only engaged in a meaningless dinner party but are actually trapped in a kind of purgatory. Their shallow consumerist intellectualism blinds them to the extent that they do not even realize that they died in the very event they have been discussing.

In the final tableau, Terrence is completely drunk; Suzie and Roger dance; Khalid and Julia stare at each other; Lydia reflects on her stomach (she is pregnant); Mohammed, who is eventually offered Suzie's dishes, continues to eat; and the sound of helicopters grows louder to the extent that the chandelier is shaken and the play ends with the sudden sound of a loud explosion. This final scene leaves an impression that these characters, even after their deaths, remain completely ignorant of others and of their present circumstances.

Rebeck and Gersten-Vassilaros's characters represent the scholars, writers, ministers, and businessmen who shape world opinion and blind us to reality. Writing about Luis Buñuel's *The Discrete Charm of Bourgeoisie*, Rebecca Pauly states that Buñuel "deftly dismembers the niceties of life, turns the cracks in the façade of social manners into epistemological rifts," revealing "the monsters slumbering beneath" (233). In *Omnium Gatherum* beneath their intellectual and fashionable façades, Suzie's guests reveal their own slumbering monsters manifest as the hypocrisy of hyper-intellectualized discourse on 9/11 events. The audience is reminded that these characters are all familiar through television, radio, newspapers, academic journals, panel discussions, and books. Rebeck and Gerten-Vassilaros's characters represent the commentators who shape the public's view of events. As Sonia Ambrosio de Nelson argues, the public treats "news as objective facts" and take "the information and interpretations passed on by the media" at face value, especially when "'authoritative' analysts, commentators and eyewitnesses" adroitly "arrange the knowledge" in accordance with "a scheme of relevance prescribed by the social order" (334). Rebeck and Gerten-Vassilaros position the audience as media targets through the characters' remarks, lectures, and random thoughts about the 9/11 attacks. The guests particularly highlight American ignorance, arrogance, and indifference to the suffering of others outside their circumscribed world. Rebeck and Gersten-Vassilaros's point is not to make the audience feel superior to these characters but to see itself through them.

Carried Away on the Crest of a Wave

While *Omnium Gatherum* portrays a futile discussion by a self-righteous and self-indulgent group, Canadian playwright David Yee's *Carried Away on the Crest of Wave* presents different responses by survivors of a natural disaster.[2] The play portrays a series of vignettes in response to the Indian Ocean tsunami of December 2004, where a massive earthquake off the west coast of northern Sumatra in Indonesia triggered a tsunami that killed over 280,000 people. Yee's episodic structure of unconnected stories explores a variety of consequences of the disaster. While I encountered many plays about 9/11 and 3/11, Yee's is the only play that I am aware of dealing with the disaster of the December 26, 2004.

Yee felt a personal connection to the Indian Ocean tsunami disaster. On the day of this post–Christmas disaster, Yee was driving through northern Ontario, "along icy and unpaved roads, alongside cliffs and rivers and Lake Supe-

Figure 2. *Carried Away on the Crest of a Wave.* **The Hub Theatre, Fairfax, Virginia, 2013. Ed Christian, Hedy Hosford, Andrew Ferlo, Ryan Sellers, Nora Achrati, and Rafael Sebastian Medina (photograph by Melissa Blackall).**

rior." There was limited cell phone service or radio reception in the area, so he didn't hear about the disaster until he pulled over at a rest-stop. As soon as he reached his destination, Yee began to call his friends living in South-East Asia. Everyone was safe—except for one friend who was seriously injured and lost both of her parents in the tsunami. Later she told Lee that her father was washed away while lifting her up into a tree to save her (Yee Interview). This personal relationships with some of the survivors prompted Yee to collect stories from other survivors to create a play, the artistic form with which Yee had been most familiar. He spent five years researching and interviewing survivors, discovering that "not a single person" he spoke to told him "the story [he'd] expected to hear" (Macfarlane). Yee's poetic and symbolic vignettes based on actual survivor stories offer a theatrical collage of different world views and personalities.

Yee describes *Carried Away* as neither "purely fiction" nor "strictly fact" of the tragedy (Macfarlane). Celia Wren, theatre critic for *The Washington Post,* observed that as the "vignette gives way to vignette, world view to world-view and personality to personality," Yee's play "musters a good deal of cumulative profundity and an impressively seeping vision," providing "a methodical probing for the social and existential meaning behind pain and randomness."

Yee shows survivors as "victims" who continue to deal with loss, pain, and guilt. Emma Varley and her colleagues who researched the Indonesian Ocean tsunami's psychosocial impacts on survivors argued that the "scope of mental health and psychosocial problems" among the survivors was one of the most serious problems in its aftermath (657). Yee's characters' different responses to the tragedy allow the audience to understand, rather than judge, the choices that survivors made.

The play also includes scientific explanations of the earthquake and tsunami, providing a context for the event. This is evident from the first vignette which reflects Yee's exploration for a scientific "meaning behind pain and randomness." In the play's only monologue, "The Leap Second Story" sets a tone for the rest of the play, providing a linkage between nature and humans. At a press conference for the International Earth Rotation and Reference Systems Service, a scientist named Beckett explains that every eighteen months the IERS adds a "leap second" to Coordinated Universal Time to accommodate changes in the Earth's speed and position. This reminds us the natural fact that an earthquake is part of life on earth and affects the entire globe.

The following scene, "The Swimming Child Story," introduces two siblings, Swimmer and Runner. They are in a house floating on the ocean, throwing items out of the window to keep the house from sinking. They toss out the television, their running and swimming trophies, photo albums, books, CDs, and toys—all filled with their memories—in a desperate effort to survive. Finally Swimmer jumps into the ocean to find a sea turtle which, according to myth, could carry the house on its back. This vignette illustrates the transitory nature of existence and our relationship to materiality. Swimmer's action of jumping into the water to save her brother reflects those who sacrificed themselves to save their family and friends during the disaster.[3]

The third episode, "The Saint Story," raises the question of how one can explain survival. Whether they see it as a reflection of their own good fortune or mere chance, people look for meaning in their survival. In this episode a church and its congregation survived the tsunami after taking shelter in their church. Afterwards the priest hires an architect to find the reason for their survival. The architect, who is a Muslim, investigates and finds evidence that the density of the soil around the church was what saved the church and its congregation. However, the priest insists that God chose to save them because they were Christians. The architect challenges the priest: were the people who died condemned just because they were non–Christian?

> And now you want me to say that God worked a miracle on your Catholic Basilica because someone put a string of beads on the statue of a woman? You want me to say those 2,000 people standing on a breakwater were better than the 200,000 who died in Aceh? Is that what you're asking me to do? [18].

"The Saint Story" echoes "one of the primary psychological tasks" that would follow negative experiences, "that is "mak[ing] sense out of them" and "render[ing] them meaningful" (Adler 904). Yee challenges this urge to make sense by framing it as the priest's prejudice and sense of a religious superiority over others. Through the character of the architect, Yee challenges the temptation to "render" tragic experiences "meaningful" by bringing the facts of nature to reframe survival as random as death. As Wren observes, randomness lies at the core of this play.

The next vignette, "The Water Story," is about a man who lost his wife in the tsunami. This vignette illuminates the survivor's need for telling a story to find closure in the aftermath of the disaster. The scene opens in a hotel room with a man and a prostitute known for her ability to listen to survivors' stories. The man tells her about his wife and their life together. As he tells his story, his memory of his wife grows stronger. When he finally has the clearest memory of his wife, he submerges himself in a bathtub and with the help of the prostitute, as he arranged, he drowns himself. The symbiosis of the two deaths reflects Yee's compassion for those who continue to suffer from "intrusive memories or flashbacks," "psychic numbing," and other symptoms of PTSD (Smith 520).

"The Millimeter Story" introduces another way to come to terms with one's loss after disaster. In this vignette a mother copes with the loss of her son in the tsunami by taking a child who did survive and claiming him as her son. Several years have passed since the woman returned to her home, Salt Lake City, with that child. One day a detective visits her house with an official death notice of her son. His visit is also to question her about the child whom she claims is hers. In the end the woman confesses that she took the child but defends her action by saying, "We were both orphaned that day, but we found each other. I provided for him, I am not negligent or abusive, I am a woman of means and I love him. He has the opportunity to be anything if he's with me. What would his life had been there? A fishing village? He deserves so much more" (58). In this vignette, Yee highlights the struggle of a survivor and her desperate choice after the disaster, while placing her act in an ethnical context. Although it is clear that what the woman did was wrong, Yee allows the audience to ask themselves a question of "who are we to judge her," because instead of being there on that day we were safely "11,000 miles away" from the disaster site, where "the ground shifted upwards by one millimeter" (58).

The next vignette is set at an arrival lounge at Bandaranaike International airport, where a girl and a man wait for her uncle to arrive. The girl lost her parents in the tsunami while she was saved by the man who is waiting with her. While waiting, the man tells her about his own childhood and how he was able to fight back when a bully teased him about being an orphan. This advice is another gift from the man to the girl; he tries to help her to understand that losing her parents does not mean she is meant to be a victim. This vignette was inspired by the story of Yee's friend who lost her parents to the tsunami. This friend was saved by her own father, but she also rescued a girl who happened to be the niece of a woman who went to school with her. The chain of saving and being saved is, through Yee's dramaturgy, transformed into one of the most moving vignettes because of its focus on selflessness and the beauty of human connection in the time of disaster.

The last vignette, "The Vermin Story," introduces a Burmese survivor, Vermin, who is brought to a hospital in Thailand. He steals the identity card of a Thai tsunami victim to avoid deportation when he recovers. Several years after the tsunami, he encounters a character, Diego, on the beach. Diego tells Vermin that he used to work at the PTWC (Pacific Tsunami Warning Center) in Hawaii and his erroneous report that there would not be a tsunami as a result of the earthquake contributed to the deaths of many people. In this story we have the combination of someone who has profited by the disaster, Vermin, by taking advantage in the chaos of the disaster to escape deportation and another, Diego, who suffers from a form of survivor's guilt and a sense of responsibility. Both Diego and Vermin thus represent many survivors who feel they might have caused someone's death or profited from it.

The characters' stories illustrate the different responses of human beings to disaster. Some actions reflect an early stage in the process of adjusting to disaster as well as reintegrating the self into a pattern of denial afterwards. The man in the hotel cannot continue to face the fact that his wife is dead. The woman who claims an orphan child as her own cannot accept the death of her own child. As Collin Murray Parkes states, denial is a "stage of bereavement reactions" (62). One of the ways to mitigate the pain of grieving for one's loss is "not to believe that the loss has occurred" (Parkes 62). Yee highlights this "stage of bereavement reactions" by showing the difficulties that psychologically impacted survivors face in a way that the audience can identify and sympathize with.

Radio 311

The 3/11 Tohoku earthquake, tsunami, and meltdown of the Fukushima nuclear reactors disaster, its aftermath, and people's responses have been explored in a number of theatre projects. Masataka Matsuda wrote and staged *Record of a Journey to Antigone, and Its Performance* (2012), Akira Takayama presented *The Referendum Project* for Festival/Tokyo 2011, and Toshiki Okada and his theatre company Chelfitsch staged *The Current Location* in 2012.

These theatre artists attempted not only to give voice to victims but also to find a bridge between direct victims and those affected less directly. Royosei Kajiwara's *Radio 311* (2013) goes beyond creating this connection, suggesting that people in Tokyo not directly affected by the disaster can help those who were.

Prior to the premiere of *Radio 311*, Kajiwar and his co-writers Itaru Era and Yuki Maeda had already written another play on 3/11, *Hikobae (Rebirth)*, which was staged both in Japan and the United States in 2012 and 2013. *Hikobae* was based on recorded interviews with physicians and nurses at the Soma City Hospital, a medical center in the Fukushima evacuation zone. While interviewing the medical personnel, Kajiwara and his co-creators also talked to orphans who had lost their parents in the tsunami. Kajiwara has described his need to write a play about the earthquake and tragic aftermath: "When the earthquake happened, I couldn't do anything. [...] I was suffering some sense of guilt maybe because I couldn't do anything. And I still feel that way whenever I go to Soma City. [...] I wrote this play for myself to ease my mind. Because I don't think I can heal the victims" (Swanson). *Radio 311* marks

Figure 3. *Radio 311.* **Kamakaji Lab, Woody Theatre, Tokyo, 2013. Mariko Tomi (female office worker), Ryunosuke Kawai (groom), Hiroshi Takahashi (manual laborer), Ruriko Kariya (manual laboler's wife), Sayaka Tsukahara (public servant's wife), Kohei Miyajima (public servant) (photograph by Ryosei Kajiwara).**

Kajiwara's mixed sense of a helplessness, mission, and responsibility to examine the disaster's impacts.

A need to help and support the victims was nation-wide after the 3/11 earthquake and tsunami. The urge to help was heightened by Japanese leaders' inappropriate and ineffective responses to the disaster. Prior to the disaster, the government of Prime Minister Kan was already in trouble because of funding scandals, problems with public pension programs, and "continued floundering in U.S.–Japan relations" (Matsumura 22). These problems and the resulting political instability contributed to the central government's extremely slow response to the disasters in East Japan after the 3/11 earthquake and the inadequate emergency measures. In addition, the remarks made by the Governor of Tokyo further infuriated the public. On March 14, just three days after the crisis, Tokyo Governor Shintaro Ishihara stated that he saw the disaster as "divine punishment or *tenbatsu*." According to Ishihara, the tsunami, "produced by Japan's largest-ever recorded earthquake," was a divine "means of washing away the 'egoism' (*gayoku* in Japanese) afflicting the Japanese people" (McLaughlin 291). Though he apologized for his remarks the next day, this response from one of Japan's leaders to a disaster of this magnitude has continued to trouble the public. The government's persistent withholding of information—regarding the damage to nuclear power plants and the release of radioactivity and its effects on humans, animals, and other natural resources— has triggered mistrust of the government and contributed to a sense of personal mission and responsibility among the public.

Kajiwara's two main characters reflect those who took action despite the failures of the government and companies which operated the nuclear power plants. One character is Ando, a nuclear plant employee who is assigned to inspect the damaged nuclear facilities, leaving his wife and pregnant daughter in Tokyo. The other is Kunio, a young man who lives in Tokyo with no specific purpose or plan for the future. When the play begins, Ando is looking forward to his retirement at the end of March 2011 because his only daughter is expecting a child. He and his wife also look forward to having more time together after his retirement. Soon after the quake and tsunami in East Japan, Ando receives a call from the Tokyo Electric Power Company, to report to the Fukushima reactor control building. Ando and other workers attempt to cool the reactors but the overheated reactors explode, exposing the workers inside the building to radiation. Injured by the explosion, Ando cannot escape the building. As he is dying he calls his wife and daughter to express his regret that he will never see his first grandchild. At the end of the play, Kajiwara projects a series of photographic images showing the birth of this grandchild.

The character Kunio is jobless and apathetic. He has little money and cannot even afford a television. He sleeps all day, showing little interest in others, including his mother in Sendai with whom he has not talked for a long time. Kunio's life changes drastically when, just after the Fukushima Earthquake on March 11, 2011, six strangers appear at his apartment. The three men and three women are all dressed differently. One young man wears a tuxedo, while another man wears a worker's uniform. The visitors are surprised to find themselves in Kunio's apartment, and all express in Fukushima dialect their concerns about their family members who might have been injured in the disaster. They gather around Kunio's small radio, which is the only source of news, hoping to obtain information about their families.

The audience soon realizes that the strangers are actually victims of the disaster, unable to move on because of their uncertainty about their loved ones. This becomes apparent when a young woman in a wedding dress enters and is reunited with the man in tuxedo. As they embrace and the others congratulate them on their wedding, the sound of a helicopter is heard approaching and a beam of white light shines on them. After a quick blackout, the wedding couple disappears from the stage. This sequence continues; whenever one of the strangers discovers the whereabouts of their loved ones, they disappear. The last couple to disappear is the man in a worker's uniform and his wife, who ask Kunio to give the photo of their son, which he was carrying, to let their son know how much he and his wife loved him.

Left behind in his apartment, Kunio decides to visit the disaster site to deliver the photo and also to visit his mother in Sendai, the closest city to the center of the quake. When he arrives there he meets his father, who is painting on the beach, for the first time since he abandoned Kunio and his mother. Kunio speaks to his father quietly and lets him know who he is, how he is doing, including his strange visitors, while his father continues to paint. His encounter with his father completes his rite of passage, enabling him to he accept the choice his father made. Kunio also finds a meaning in his life through his witnessing of a number of volunteers cleaning the disaster sites.

In the characters of Ando and Kunio, Kajiwara is able to explore two meaningful responses to the disaster. Ando is a man who had a purpose and role when the disaster occurred which he fulfilled. He would be like the firefighters and other emergency responders who entered the Twin Towers during 9/11. That he failed to stop the reactor explosion does not demean his effort. He was a hero. This is the traditional heroic narrative that the media gives us with respect to 9/11. Kajiwara's genius is his creation of the non-heroic character of Kunio, who goes through a rite of passage. Previously unable to find meaning in his life, he discovers a sense of purpose through his encounter with the six victims. This process of transformation through an experience outside of the everyday is what Joseph Campbell, borrowing Toynbee's words, called the birth of "something new" that would "nullify the unremitting recurrences of death" (16).

Kunio's journey in the play reflects that of Kajiwara himself, who searched for a way to overcome his own depression and shock at the time of the disaster and to find a way to serve the survivors. Though different in circumstance and result, both Ando and Kunio provide a stark contrast to the Japanese government and plant officials who seemed only concerned with their own survival. Kajiwara proposes that, while we should acknowledge and honor the heroes who confront disasters and risk their lives, this is not the only response we should make. Rather, like Kunio, we should look beyond our own limitations and needs to find ways to help.

Both *Carried Away* and *Radio 311* focus on traumatic natural disasters through different stories of victims and survivors. Examining psychotherapy and theatre, Peter Elsass argues that the therapist (or playwright) brings the past into the present, shuffles cause and effect, and mediates life and death (333). Elsass states that the healing power comes not from seeing the actual causes of misfortune, but from creating a particular image that gives one an opportunity to reflect on disasters and draw meaning from them. Both Kajiwara and Yee provide their audiences with this particular image by bringing the past to the present through stories of victims and survivors. While *Omnium Gatherum* focuses on the intellectual but meaningless debates and discussions after 9/11, it also addresses how we cope with disaster by paradoxically illuminating those incapable of sharing their experience of trauma.

The three plays serve as vessels for personal memories and stories about the disasters. In the midst of the media blitz after a disaster, an official memory would overpower individual memories. Writing about memory and nostalgia in relation to the tenth anniversary of 9/11, Jack Zevin argues that contemporary culture is "increasingly dependent on visual representations from media." As we "spend a great deal of time viewing screens," we have become part of a "theater of memory" (141). Things remembered through a "theater of memory" are, however, sustained for a limited amount time. As soon as the media stops broadcasting images, the tragedy, disaster, and their victims are sent into oblivion.

In addition to bringing personal memories and stories of victims and survivors to the forefront, *Omnium Gatherum*, *Carried Away*, and *Radio 311* also point to the inevitability of disasters. Bonnie Henderson's new book *The Next Tsunami: Living on a Restless Coast*, quotes geologic oceanographer Chris Goldfinger: "It seems that the more advanced a society becomes, the shorter its memory." Native Americans "have a memory of the last Cascadia earthquake 311 years ago" and even "of the explosion of Mount Mazama about 7,600 years ago" (287). Meanwhile, with all our technology, we forget and seem to think such things will never happen to us. These three plays help the audience to examine our responsibilities as part of the global community that unfortunately possesses numerous causes of disasters in the future.

KENT STATE UNIVERSITY

NOTES

1. My first encounter with this significant theatre work by the two female playwrights was at the Humana Festival in the spring of 2003 and my second was its off–Broadway production in fall 2003. At the Humana Festival in particular, the audience was genuinely moved by this insightful, fateful, provocative, and self-reflexive play.

2. It premiered at Tarragon Theatre, Toronto, in April 2013. I attended the U.S. premiere at the Hub Theatre in Fairfax, Virginia, in November 2013.

3. Both Swimmer and Runner are written as brothers. However, a female actor played the character of Swimmer in the Hub Theatre production, giving the audience as an impression that they were a brother and sister.

WORKS CITED

Adler, Jonathan M., and Michael J. Poulin. "The Political Is Personal: Narrating 9/11 and Psychological Well-being." *Journal of Personality* 77.4 (2009): 903–32.

Boss, Pauline, et al. "Healing Loss, Ambiguity, and Trauma: A Community-Based Intervention With Families of Union Workers Missing After The 9/11 Attack In New York City." *Journal of Marital & Family Therapy* 29.4 (2003): 455–467.

Brantley, Ben. "A Feisty Feast of Wicked Wit." *New York Times* 26 September 2003: E1.

Brustein, Robert. "Shotover's Apocalypse." *New Republic* 229.20 (2003): 27–30.

Bundy, Penny. "Using Drama in the Counselling Process: The Moving on Project." *Research in Drama Education* 11.1 (2006): 7–18.

Campbell, Joseph. *The Hero with a Thousand Faces*. Princeton, NY: Princeton University Press, 1972.

Carlson, Marvin. "9/11, Afghanistan, and Iraq: The Response of the New York Theatre." *Theatre Survey* 45.1 (2004): 3–17.

De Nelson, Sonia Ambrosio. "Understanding the Press Imaging of 'Terrorist': A Pragmatic Visit to the Frankfurt School." *International Communication Gazette* 70.5 (2008): 325–337.

Duncan, Barry. "Remembering 9/11 a Year Later." *Australian Screen Education* 30 (2002): 44.

Elsass, Peter. "The Healing Space in Psychotherapy and Theatre." *New Theatre Quarterly* 8 (1992): 333–42.

Henderson, Bonnie. *Next Tsunami: Living on the Restless Coast*. Corvallis: Oregon University Press, 2014.

Kajiwara, Ryosei. *Radio 311*. Unpublished Manuscript. 2013.

_____. *Radio 311*. Dir. by Ryosei Kajiwara. Kamakaji Lab, Woody Theatre, Tokyo, Japan. 1 June 2013. Performance.

Macfarlane, David. "Moving Beyond the Crest of the Wave: Pop Culture Weighs in on 2004 Tsunami." *The Toronto Star* (25 April 2013).

Matsumura, Masahiro. "Japan's Earthquake: The Politics of Recovery." *Survival* 53.3 (2011): 19–25.

McLaughlin, Levi. "In the Wake of the Tsunami: Religious Responses to the Great East Japan Earthquake." *Cross Currents* 61.3 (2011): 290–297.

Parkes, Collin M. *Bereavement. Studies of Grief in Adult Life.* Harmondsworth: Penguin, 1980.

Pauly, Rebecca. "A Revolution Is Not a Dinner Party: The Discrete Charm of Buñuel's Bourgeoisie." *Literature Film Quarterly* 22.4 (1994): 232–237.

Propper, Ruth E., et al. "Is Television Traumatic? Dreams, Stress, and Media Exposure in the Aftermath of September 11, 2001." *Psychological Science* 18.4 (2007): 334–340.

Rebeck, Theresa, and Alexandra Gersten-Vassilaros. *Omnium Gatherum. Humana Festival 2003: The Complete Plays.* Eds. Tanya Palmer and Amy Wegner. Hanover, NH: Smith and Kraus, 2004. 335–388.

_____. *Omnium Gatherum.* Dir. by Will Frears. Humana Festival of New American Plays, Actors Theatre of Louisville. 28 March 2013. Performance.

_____. *Omnium Gatherum.* Dir. by Will Frears. The Variety Arts Theatre, New York. 13 Sept. 2013. Performance.

Rich, Frank. "Where's Larry Kramer When We Need Him?" *New York Times* (5 October 2003): 2.

Sedana, I. Nyoman. "Theatre in a Time of Terrorism: Renewing Natural Harmony after the Bali Bombing Via Wayang Kontemporer." *Asian Theatre Journal* 22.1 (2005): 73–86

Smith, Martin, David Lees, and Kay Clymo. "The Readiness Is All: Planning and Training for Post-Disaster Support Work." *Social Work Education* 22.5 (2003): 517–528.

Swanson, Abbie Fentress. "Play about Japan Tsunami First Responders Staged for Anniversary." 9 March 2012. http://www.wnyc.org/story/191220-hikobae/. Accessed 31 May 2013.

Taylor, Diana, et al. "A Forum on Theatre and Tragedy in the Wake of September 11, 2001." *Theatre Journal* 54.1 (2002): 95–138.

Varley, Emma, Wanrudee Isaranuwatchai, Peter C. Coyte. "Ocean Waves and Roadside Spirits: Thai Health Service Providers' Post-Tsunami Psychosocial Health" *Disasters* 34.4 (2012): 656–675.

Wren, Celia. A Review of *Carried Away on the Crest of a Wave. The Washington Post,* 6 December 2013.

Yee, David. *Carried Away on the Crest of a Wave.* Unpublished Manuscript. 2013.

_____. *Carried Away on the Crest of a Wave.* Dir. by Helen Pafumi. The Hub Theatre, Fairfax, Virginia. 17 November 2013. Performance.

_____. Email Interview. 27 August 2014.

Zevin, Jack. "Memories Slipping Away: The Tenth Anniversary of 9/11." *The Social Studies* 102 (2011): 141–46.

Perceptions of Memory and Mechanisms of Power: Beckett, Williams and Pinter A Review Essay

DOUG PHILLIPS

Gordon, Robert. *Harold Pinter: The Theatre of Power*. Ann Arbor: University of Michigan Press, 2013. Pp. 216. Paperback $26.95.

Murphy, Brenda. *The Theatre of Tennessee Williams*. London: Bloomsbury, 2014. Pp. 307. Paperback $27.95.

Weiss, Katherine. *The Plays of Samuel Beckett*. London: Methuen Drama, 2012. Pp. 286. Paperback $27.95.

For those who teach in modernized classrooms—what we, at my university, call "smart" rooms—you have no doubt found yourself in a situation where something doesn't work, and whatever advanced technological skill set or power of divination you've brought with you (on this particular Tuesday morning, say) is punishingly useless. The damn thing still won't turn on. There's no sound. Your password doesn't work. You're choking. After much frustration and major time ticked off the clock—during which your students happily fiddle with their smart phones while your lesson plan burns—you beseech one of your phone-fiddling, hip-on-tech students to help save the day, or at least what's left of the hour, but she too is nonplussed by the inexplicable lack of light or sound or power, and so finally, after even more wasted time (and your authority now in tatters), you wave your white flag of incompetency before proceeding unhappily with Plan B.

If indeed you were smart enough to come to the smart room with a Plan B.

And so it is that Katherine Weiss's recent study, *The Plays of Samuel Beckett*, thrums a familiar if unpleasant chord of experience. For here she shows the various ways in which the presence of technology in Beckett's stage, radio, and teleplays reflect, confound, constrain, undermine, or otherwise put into question the authority of characters who find themselves in the clutches of a sometimes comic, sometimes tragic, mechanization.

Given its title—and the series to which it belongs, Methuen Drama's *Critical Companions*—Weiss's book would appear, *prima facie*, to be one of broad overview, pitched to students and theatregoers in need of smart commentary or a quick précis. And that it is, sort of. Absent, however, a scope-narrowing, right-of-the-colon subtitle common to academic books of this kind, *The Plays of Samuel Beckett* suggests in name that *everything* Beckett wrote for the stage (as well as for radio and television) will be put onto slides, peered into, and neatly summarized under the usual "umbrella of absurdism or existentialism" (9). And that it isn't, not at all. Instead, Weiss approaches her material from a fresh angle, the degree of which is neither existential nor absurd. "The unifying element," she announces in her introduction, "is Beckett's uses of and references to technology" (9). In his later works especially, writes Weiss, Beckett "is using technology" to show that "characters' repetition and cyclical movements are part of a vast machinery" (10). She then adds: "However grim Beckett's thematic approach to modern technology may seem, his extensive and innovative use of technology surely points to a more complicated understanding of its role in modern life" (12). While we are left mostly on our own to piece together what's meant by a "surely [...] more complicated understanding," we are also made aware, by the implications of Weiss's analyses, of the similarities between our own surroundings and Beckett's world of "decomposition brought on by technology" (11). As a contribution to Beckett studies—and to those of us for whom the delightful adjective *Beckettian* most accurately describes the day-to-day absurdity of our tech-bespattered lives—Weiss's work is timely.

Which suits, given the attention she pays to time, whether *mechanical* in the form of Pozzo's pocket watch or *ontological*, in the way that virtually every one of Beckett's characters is suspended between a past that won't quite go away and a future that doesn't ever seem to arrive. Whether measured by a watch's hand or a foot's fall or a thought's recording or a rocking chair's aged and repetitive creak—time, Beckett reminds us, both flees and never leaves. Technological objects such as recorders and music boxes are repositories of remembrance, and remembrance, we might say, is a *ronde* into which the likes of Ru, Vi, and Flo come—and go. Ever haunted by the once-was, they—like Krapp, like the characters in *Play*, like us—"struggle to gain control over their narratives" (11). The condition is as much Hamm's as it is Hamlet's; Gogo's as it is Gatsby's; the Ancient Mariner's as it is Mouth's. Memory persists, Beckett insists; and paralysis waits in the wings.

There's more to tech than time and memory, however. And more to time and memory than characters who tramp to nowhere in particular but the past. For Weiss, technology in Beckett's plays is entwined with time and paralysis, yes, but also with the status of one's authority, the state of one's isolation, the legitimacy of one's story, and the effects of one's personal hauntings. In prose sometimes less felicitous than one would wish, Weiss goes so far as to show— or attempt to show—that a character's interior state is intimately bound up with whatever technological object is closest at hand: "With this in mind, we can see that Krapp's inability to produce fecal matter further aligns him with his tape recorder" (37). In turn, these thematic considerations are buttressed by Beckett's specific instructions for using technology in production, be it the tortuous shine of a spotlight, the cough and rumble of a city soundscape, or the voyeuristic leer of a roving camera. Altogether, Weiss's project entails a rather complex weave of ideas, and if there are loose ends in the telling, it may have something to do with the over-arching concept of *technology*, itself a complex weave of etymology and historical evolution. For this reason, a more detailed explication of the manifold ways in which the word "technology" may be understood would perhaps point readers toward a "more complicated understanding" of technology's role in modern life. Here, I think, Heidegger might help, in particular his essay "The Question Concerning Technology," first delivered as a lecture in 1953, the very year of Beckett's *Godot*.

Vital to Heidegger's argument—and which would usefully support Weiss's own—is the way he first traces *technology* to its root (*techné*), before showing how the word split into two different trajectories of meaning, the most familiar of which today is *technology as instrumentality*. This, it appears, is Weiss's general use of the word throughout her study, though she doesn't name it as such. For Heidegger, *instrumentality* describes the way we use technology to *order* our world, which he in turn calls *enframing*. This in effect describes every literary critic's use of the pen to order and master (*enframe*) another author's work. Understood this way, technology or *techné* is instrumental as a *means to an end*, especially if that end is power and control (which is the upshot of Weiss's analysis of Pozzo and his pocket watch). And while it is true we make use of technology (often destructively) as a way to master and control our natural world, it's increasingly the case that technology has come to master and control us (often destructively), whether through our smart phones and smart rooms, or, in the case of Beckett's characters, through their tape recorders and alarm clocks and music boxes.

There is, however, another way to understand technology, also derived from the ancient Greek word *techné*, which has everything to do with artistic creation, in particular poetry (*poiesis*) and its power to *reveal* truth (*alētheia*). While Weiss seems to be in tune with Heidegger's thinking on this point (the sheer number of times that Weiss deploys the verb "reveals" makes me think she's onto this Heidegger business already), she again neither mentions him by name nor does she elaborate directly on the significance of her observations. For example, in her discussion of *Krapp's Last Tape*, she identifies a tension between the deleterious effects of machine technology and the implied enrichment that comes with artistic creation, but seems unaware that both of these things—by Heidegger's account, anyway—count as distinct forms of technology or *techné*: "Krapp cannot produce written texts because he hoards memories of love and loss onto a machine which ultimately leads to an unproductive artistic life" (38). In light of Heidegger's two definitions of technology, Weiss has basically written that Krapp cannot produce technology ("written texts") because technology ("a machine") prevents a productive technological ("artistic") life. In her discussion of *Endgame*, she encounters the very same tension and draws a similar conclusion: "When creating order on stage, Clov undermines artistic creation" (29). In other words, *techné* undermines *techné*.

The point I'm trying to make here—and which Heidegger is making— is that technology is a part of who we are, not just since the industrial revolution, but as far back as when flint was first formed into tools. For Heidegger, we can no more opt out of technology than we can opt into it. Technology simply *is*. But not all forms of technology point to "decomposition." Through their *techné*, artists seek to enlarge life, not impoverish it. Plus, argues Heidegger, the *techné* of art may be our best, perhaps *only*, hope for truth.

Along with suggestions for further reading and a chronology of the playwright's life, the latter half of Weiss's book contains supplementary material (a common feature of the Methuen Drama series) to acquaint readers with recent thought in Beckett studies. This material includes transcripts of interviews between performers of Beckett's work and Weiss (herself a director) on the various challenges and complications—as well as gratifications—that come with staging Beckett's plays. There are also critical perspectives by leading contemporary specialists whose latest research points to new ways of thinking about textual and performance issues. Regarding the former, Graley Herren's contribution deserves special mention for the way in which he takes on philosophy's current darling, Alain Badiou, in relation to love and Beckett. With prose lapidary enough to cut stone, Herren contests Badiou's conception of love when applied to Beckett's late teleplays. "To endow such meagre efforts with the bravery, hope, and redemption that Badiou associates with love," writes Herren, "is to burden them with more philosophical weight than they can bear" (175). As for Weiss, she welcomingly bears the philosophical weight of not just Herren's but of all the contributors' perspectives, engaging each in her own heavy take on Beckett's drama.

* * *

Brenda Murphy's *The Theatre of Tennessee Williams* belongs also to the Methuen Drama series, and so will appeal to the same audience as Weiss's book, namely students and theatregoers who, in this case, wish to deepen their understanding of and appreciation for Williams's work, especially in light of his published letters and, more recently, notebooks. In this, her eighteenth book, Murphy also points to the burgeoning interest among scholars in Williams's lesser known works—as well as new insights borne out of gender and queer studies about both the playwright and his plays—as reason to revisit his dramatic oeuvre. The latter third of *The Theatre of Tennessee Williams* offers the same kind of supplementary rigging as Weiss's, minus the interviews. Of the critical perspectives, Bruce McConachie's "All in the Timing: The Meanings of *Streetcar* in 1947 and 1951" is especially fascinating for the way in which he considers the differences between how audiences and critics responded to the first stage production of *Streetcar*, and how they responded to the later film adaptation, both of which McConachie frames through the lens of cognitive science.

"While his sexual identity, and his sex life generally, were very important to Williams," writes Murphy, "it is also important to see these elements in the larger perspective of his self-declared identity as an artist and bohemian" (3). Like many a bohemian artist, Williams lived much of his life on the outside (among the so-called "fugitive kind"), the price for which was loneliness, addiction, misunderstanding, and the wretched impossibility—to paraphrase Beckett—of ever knowing and being known. Regarding the latter, Murphy writes in her brief but brilliantly executed introduction (a small exercise in clarity and grace) that the complexities of identity—of knowing ourselves and others—are but one of four principal themes she will consider in relation to "the plays that have proven most significant to the theatre and to critics" (5). The other themes—all of which she faithfully addresses and thoroughly sources—concern Williams's family life, his sister especially; his spiritual quest and search for God; and his engagement, explicitly or implicitly, with other literary works, characters, or authors. Working chronologically through his plays, Murphy provides critical commentary for each, her own as well as commentaries from other leading scholars in the field. These in turn are pitted against the backdrop of what reviewers had to say back in the day upon seeing Williams's work when it was first produced. From start to last, Murphy's summaries are generous without being overwritten; her explications insightful and accessible, the way in fact a *really* good teacher's are.

What students and theatregoers will also enjoy about Murphy's book—apart from her authoritative ease and crystalline prose—are the many curiosities about Williams and his works that seem to pop-up on every other page. While scholars will no doubt find some of these details (here paraphrased) old hat, others less familiar with Williams's life will be literarily roused:

- At the age of 32, when at last Williams had achieved some financial security, his "greatest enthusiasm" was working on an adaptation of Browning's poem "My Last Duchess," entitled *The Balcony in Ferrara*.
- Williams's last produced play on Broadway was *Clothes for a Summer Hotel* (1980), about Scott and Zelda Fitzgerald. Opening to an onslaught of negative reviews, it closed after 15 performances.
- During the 1961 production of *The Night of the Iguana*, Williams continuously revised the script, often giving the actors their rewrites only hours before the night's performance.
- *A Streetcar Named Desire* was originally titled "*Blanche's Chair in the Moon*." (Don't ask)
- Prior to her lobotomy, Williams's beloved sister, Rose, was making noise about having been abused by her father.
- "Blue Devils," Williams referred to his depression as.
- In 1938, after completing his early play *Spring Storm*, Williams wrote in his journal: "I see plainly now that I'm a distinctly second or third rate writer—and I wonder how I ever got into it so deep—now what?"
- Williams wrote an early play called *Spring Storm* (Who knew?)
- While it is generally well known that Williams's initial title for *The Glass Menagerie* was *The Gentleman Caller*, what's less known is the unthinkable third option: *The Fiddle in the Wings*.
- *The Fiddle in the Wings* (!)
- To the question *Why does a man drink?* Williams replied: "There's two reasons, separate or together. 1. He's scared shitless of something. 2. He can't face the truth about something." (Indeed)
- By 1964 Williams was drinking nearly a quart of liquor a day, as well as popping a mélange of pep and sleeping pills. However, he told Paul Bowles he was quitting cigarettes because he feared lung cancer.

Regarding the last note above, Williams's late work was no doubt compromised by the downward spiral of his last two decades. But there is reason enough, argues Murphy, to take another look in the wide critical clearing since the day he swallowed the cap [his accidental swallowing of a pill bottle cap, it turns out, may or may not have been the cause of his death]. And if, say, *In the Bar of a Tokyo Hotel* (1969) remains as difficult as ever to ingest, it will at least now go down with a good deal more perspective.

*   *   *

While the three playwrights considered in this review have much in common (not least of all their avant-gardism), there is a particular shared aesthetic that Murphy points to in her discussion of *The Glass Menagerie*. In a sentence which, intentionally or not, looks forward to both Beckett and Pinter, she has this to say: "What made *The Glass Menagerie* unique as a play in 1944 was its overt presentation to the audience as a work of art, a play that made the subjective perception of memory into an aesthetic approach to truth" (59). Not only is the "subjective perception of memory" central to Weiss's study of Beckett's own aesthetic approach to truth, but it's also a thematic cornerstone of Robert Gordon's recent *Harold Pinter: The Theatre of Power*.

No study of Pinter would be complete, of course, without a thorough unpacking of the power grabs that appear pretty much everywhere in his plays, and Gordon certainly works this angle throughout, claiming, "The ceaseless desire for power is the prime motor for the action in almost all of Pinter's drama" (1–2). But the word *power*, like *technology*, is complex and tricky, and pursued or deployed for many different ends, not all of them nefarious or menacing or cruel. One such end is to take control of one's past—in the case of Blanche or Krapp certainly, but also Max in Pinter's *The Homecoming*. As Gordon writes in his introduction, Pinter raises "questions of time and memory" whereby he "addresses the radical subjectivity of memory, exposing the attempt to retrieve the past as a struggle for power and control" (3). On this score—what Gordon refers to as "Pinter's persistent themes of truth, time, and memory" (148)—readers will note marked similarities to Weiss's and Murphy's own truth/time/memory arguments.

Time and memory together, however, are but one of four vectors that Gordon traces from the central theme of power. The other three concern (1) the "territorial imperative" (that is, "the struggle to defend one's territory and protect one's identity"); (2) "the exercise of power through the language of authority" (that is, "how language functions both to disguise and to authorize the operations of power"); (3) "Sex, gender and the construction of identity" (that is, "how the performance of gender is formative in the construction of identity"). For those getting newly acquainted with Pinter's work, this is ideal. Gordon provides a range of focused instruction, crucial to first-timers.

If more experienced readers of Pinter find these plantings to be well-furrowed already, then know there's something fresh in the fertilizer. On his critical approach, Gordon explains:

> I have attempted as far as possible [...] to trace how the meaning of key plays might unfold in putative performance. This is a phenomenological approach that aims to capture the way that each drama is conceived as a pattern of lived experience to be grasped by the audience in its moment-to-moment presentation in space and time [9].

Though he makes clear that "every reader will construct a somewhat different interpretation" (10), Gordon (not unlike Weiss in *Samuel Beckett*) emphasizes throughout the ways in which audiences might be affected by what they see and hear on stage. For this reason, directors and performers of Pinter's work may also find a great deal of value in what Gordon has to say.

The pleasure of reading all three of these books in succession—apart from gathering renewed inspiration for next semester's syllabus—is to note the many observations that might be easily mapped on to any one of the three playwrights' work. In the case of Gordon's book, for example, consider the following: "The image provides a haunting metaphor for the ghostly experience of an existence between life and death, where no action occurs, but people wait—either to die or go on merely waiting" (121). It's not *Godot* that Gordon is describing here, but rather Pinter's *No Man's Land*. Elsewhere he compares Pinter's *Betrayal* to Beckett's "observation of the duplicity endemic in social existence" (129), though he might have made the same point by referencing Williams's (via Big Daddy's) persistent worrying over *mendacity*. And Gordon rounds out his discussion of *The Birthday Party* with a concluding reference to the "mechanism of power" (48), a phrase which, at the risk of sounding reductive, encapsulates Weiss's take on Beckett.

Together, Gordon and Murphy and Weiss offer handy, informative, readable guidebooks to their respective authors, the whole sweep of which points to a wondrous crisscrossing of modern theatre's biggest acts.

UNIVERSITY OF ST. THOMAS

Review of Literature: Selected Books

Penny Farfan and Lesley Ferris, eds. *Contemporary Women Playwrights: Into the Twenty-First Century*. New York: Palgrave Macmillan, 2013. Pp. 306 + xvi. Hardcover $105, paperback $33.

Penny Farfan and Lesley Ferris's edited collection, *Contemporary Women Playwrights*, is a far-reaching yet focused book that brings a renewed sense of urgency to the study of women playwrights writing from the 1960s to the 1980s and since the 1990s. Thoughtfully culled essays from previous publications mixed with new essays make for an organized and thorough collection. In the spirit of studying the (almost) canonized women playwrights from the 1960s to 1980s alongside the up-and-coming women playwrights of the new century, the contributors to this collection are appropriately a mix of long-standing leading scholars and promising future leading scholars. Despite the too-often-times celebratory tone, this book does indeed "support, promote, and advance the world of women playwrights by providing a resource for researching, teaching, producing, and appreciating it" (5). This clear, concise, organized, and thought-provoking collection does justice to the immense talent of the women playwrights discussed.

In the Introduction, co-written by Penny Farfan and Lesley Ferris, the editors state the predicament of the contemporary woman playwright: despite huge strides in both the production of plays by women from the 1960s to 1980s and the outpouring of scholarship surrounding these plays in the late 1980s, access to the stage is still tremendously limited for women playwrights (2–5). Farfan and Ferris take the reader around the world to look at the less-than-equal opportunities women playwrights have in trying to stage their plays: Off-Broadway staged four times as many plays by men in the 2008–2009 season; regional theatres in the United States, despite now staging many African American playwrights since the 1990s, still only produce a small number of plays by African-American women; Canadian women still lag behind men in status in the theatre; in the U.K. women playwrights still receive fewer commissions than men, and their commissioned plays are produced at a lower rate; and in Egypt, parity for women playwrights is almost unthinkable (3–4). This short yet powerful tour around the world reinforces the urgency that the rest of the book aims to instill. Organized into three parts—"Histories," "Conflicts," and "Genres"—the essays form a clear line of thought, naturally flowing from one essay to the next.

In the first section, "Histories," Elaine Aston begins the collection with her essay, "Feeling the Loss of Feminism." Aston argues that since the mid–1990s contemporary women dramatists do not align themselves with feminism—nor a "new" type of feminism—but, instead, write plays that make the audience feel the loss of feminism (19). In her essay, "Female Alliances and Women's Histories in Contemporary Mexican and Argentine Drama," Ana Elena Puga then looks at how individual efforts become collective. By examining the works of four important Latin American female playwrights, Puga argues that "they stage the tensions and negotiations intrinsic to the formation of alliances between and among women" (35). In "Chronic Desires," Sara Warner examines why women choose to write plays. She suggests that women, and lesbians in particular, have a "chronic attachment to the theatre," in that it is "fear that motivates women to choose [playwriting]" (51). Discussing a group of women playwrights who could certainly fall into Warner's aforementioned group, Nehad Selaiha and Sarah Enany provide a linear history of the emerging Egyptian playwrights in "Women Playwrights in Egypt." In "Transcultural Dramaturgies," Natalie Alvarez demonstrates how "third wave" Latina playwrights write about cultural collisions and lived experience in that they write about the "uneasy navigation between cultures" (82). Soyica Diggs Colbert's essay, "Black Women Playwrights Making History," concludes the "Histories" section by reading Katori Hall's *The Mountaintop* as a means of "signifying on the form of the African American history play" by linking to it and distinguishing itself from "the black aesthetic practice of recuperation" (98).

"Conflicts," the second section, opens up with an essay by Sharon Friedman entitled "The Gendered Terrain in Contemporary Theatre of War by Women." Friedman examines plays that deal with war by "[unsettling] familiar perspectives by giving voice to those often silenced or ignored in official stories by politicians and the mass media" (115). Telescoping a specific conflict, Amelia Howe Kritzer looks at plays that "present viewpoints that have been unheard or ignored" in order to "give audiences the kind of direct and immediate experience of the conflict" (131) in her essay, "Enough! Women Playwrights Confront the Israeli-Palestinian Conflict." Moving to another section of the globe, in "Women Playwrights in Post-Apartheid South Africa" Yvette Hutchinson considers how two playwrights, Yael Farber and Lara Foot-Newton use theatre to encourage the public to consider "diverse, ubiquitous, and often disavowed stories," giving post–Apartheid South Africans a new way to interact (149). Diana Looser, in "Writing Across Our Sea of Islands," provides an overview and survey of Pacific Islander women's playwriting as a "way of identifying the major trends, concerns, and strategies [...] while demonstrating its stylistic and cultural reach" (165). The "Conflicts" section closes with an essay by Wendy Arons and Theresa J. May entitled "Ecodramaturgy in/and Contemporary Women's Playwriting." Arons and May read a diverse number of plays through the lenses, vocabularies, and analytical modes of ecocriticism, ecofeminism, and queer ecology (182).

The third section, "Genres," begins with Katherine E. Kelly's essay, "Making the Bones Sing," which explores the feminist history play. In a survey of plays from 1976 to 2010, Kelly argues that from the 1970s onward there is an affinity between Western feminist historiographers and creative works by women playwrights (199). Continuing to look at the history play, Lesley Ferris and Melissa Lee examine the role of the actress in history plays in their essay "Performing (Our)Selves." Ferris and Lee read two contemporary history plays set in crucial, transformative historical moments and argue that these two plays both "illuminate and interrogate the 'roles' of women [...] by staging the real and symbolic power of the actress as a site for struggle, change, and future possibility" (217). Penny Farfan continues the section with her essay "Historical Landscapes in Contemporary Plays by Canadian Women," in which she examines the national landscape. Reading three plays, Farfan shows how playwrights "reconceive nation" through the portrayal of cross-cultural alternative relationships that suggest new futures and celebrate inter-generational community by a connection to landscapes (232). In "Asian American Women Playwrights and the Dilemma of the Identity Play," Esther Lee Kim discusses the "identity play" of the "Asian American," showing how three contemporary playwrights both write about their own identity and simultaneously reject the limitations and expectations imposed upon it (245). The section and the book end with Elin Diamond's essay, "Deb Margolin, Robbie McCauley, Peggy Shaw." Diamond reads the new work of Margolin, McCauley, and Shaw through the lens of affect theory, arguing that "the performers dig deep into shame to deepen their audience's response to—their interest-enjoyment in—a shared bodily life" (263).

As I read through this impressive collection, however, I could not ignore the elephant in the room: despite their remarkable qualifications and biographies, a look at the list of contributors revealed *only* women's voices writing about women playwrights. This is not necessarily a problem, but what is significant is that this is never acknowledged or commented upon. I hesitate to play the role of cultural commentator, so I will only pose two questions that

I wish were either answered, or, at the very least, addressed: 1) what does it say about contemporary women playwrights that they are studied, presumably, almost exclusively by women scholars?; and 2) what does the fact that all of the contributors to the collection are women say about opportunities for women in academia? Despite this occlusion (whether it was a choice or an oversight), this book is still an admirable and important collection that is a most welcome addition to the study of contemporary women playwrights.

MICHAEL Y. BENNETT
University of Wisconsin-Whitewater

Arturo J. Aldama, Chela Sandoval and Peter J. García, eds. *Performing the US Latina and Latino Borderlands*. Bloomington: Indiana University Press, 2012. Pp. xv + 504. Paperback $35.

U.S. Latina/o cultural productions cross between and beyond conventional academic disciplines. U.S. Latina/o poets have infused American poetry with Latin American and African American traditions like the Mexican *corrido* [lyrical ballad], Caribbean musical rhythms, and the oral declamation associated with hip hop culture. U.S. Latina/o theatre borrows from the *actos* and *carpas* of the farmworkers' movements [short, migratory, political plays often performed in tents] as well as from the iconography of the Catholic mass and the melodrama of *telenovelas* [soap operas]. Latina/o scholars have had to develop their own transdisciplinary analytical tools: for instance, *rasquache* for understanding the way that Chicana/o artists subversively recycle the castoffs of the dominant material culture; *mestiza* consciousness for examining the different worldviews that clash and commingle in Latina/o *mestizaje* [racial and cultural hybridity]; and borderlands for highlighting the productive yet often violent friction of cultural contact zones.

Arturo Aldama, Chela Sandoval, and Peter García's recent collection, *Performing the US Latina and Latino Borderlands*, is true to all of these border-crossing impulses. The collection stretches the definition of performance beyond the stage to include recorded music, television, everyday acts (from anxiety disorder to *cholo*/gangster fashion), and static visual forms (like painting and photography). The 26 contributors build from analytical traditions that will be familiar to most scholars of theatre and performance (such as Judith Butler's theory of the performative "nature" of identities and Augusto Boal's account of theatre as a collaborative rehearsal for real-world activity) as well as culturally-specific frameworks for understanding Latina/o texts (such as Gloria Anzaldúa's theories of writing as shamanism and nepantla, Frances Aparicio's work on tropicalization and transnational musics, and Charles Ramirez Berg's work on the deployment of Latina/o stereotypes in Hollywood film). The lively performances these essays cover—community celebrations, film and television, painting, reading, stand-up comedy, and more hybrid forms like *ranchera*/punk *corridos*, photography/essay, and fashion/melodrama—alone make this collection an engaging read. Most important is the book's attention to a broad variety of ways that Latina/os perform cultural and political resistance.

The genesis of this collection was a conference panel on Latina/o music that led to a trans-disciplinary discussion about a "methodology of the oppressed" (Sandoval's term) that is shared across Latina/o media: practices that deconstructively challenge dominant conventions and undermine preconceived notions about both dominant and marginalized cultures. In her preface to the collection, writer/art critic/literary critic Alicia Gaspar de Alba calls this book a "crash course in a new field that the editors call Borderlands Performance Studies" and a lesson in the "artistic interventionism" (xiv) that occurs at the many borderzones Latina/os inhabit (international and local, cultural and linguistic, rural and urban, disciplinary and epistemological). If this book represents a new field, what makes it new is the breadth given to terms like borderlands and performance and the transnational and transdisciplinary archive these essays draw upon. Their heterogeneity is dazzling, sometimes disorienting. The collection as a whole is a bit uneven, with some essays that take readers down new critical pathways with flawless prose and some that are less original and more clumsily written. But they are all held together by an understanding of what the editors term the "emancipatory aesthetics of Borderlands Performance," "de-colonizing performatics" and "performantics" (1–2). These antics put viewers in a position of critical witnessing, shocking them out of their "conditioned mind-body-affect matrix" with scripts unlike those established by colonial powers (20).

I would like to draw attention to a few of the collection's noteworthy contributions. The first is the opening essay, Micaela Díaz Sánchez's comparison of the works of a Mexican and a Chicana performance artist. Díaz Sanchez follows a new trend in transnational dialogue among Mexican origin scholars and artists in the United States and those in Mexico, particularly around issues like feminism and sexuality. Her argument, strikingly, borrows the figure of the Aztec codex (an indigenous pictographic text) for understanding postmodern, embodied performance on both sides of the U.S./Mexico border.

Tiffany Ana López compares productions of Josefina López's play *Real Women Have Curves* in two different locations, Josefina López's Chicana/o neighborhood in East Los Angeles (where the play is set) and Las Ramblas in Barcelona, Spain. This transnational comparison reveals that the culture of garment workers in Los Angeles failed to translate to the Spanish audience, despite their shared language. The play, which was intended to engage in a pedagogy of social justice, lost its political valence when the Spanish director chose not to historicize the story or to invoke parallel situations in Spain (like Moroccan street vendors).

Yolanda Broyles-Gonzales focuses on an earlier period, when the Tejana bolero singer Chelo Silva rose to prominence within the new transnational "imagined communities" enabled by radio in the 1930s. Her music spoke to Mexicans and Mexican Americans experiencing a new romantic morality in urban, cosmopolitan communities of peoples displaced by the Mexican Revolution and poverty. Silva's lyrics—presenting stories of failed love, adultery, and promiscuity—appealed to audiences whose altered geo-cultural locations challenged the ideal of domesticated women and middle-class families. Her melancholic singing modeled ways for women to have independent voice, command attention, and value their inner lives and emotions.

Roberto Hernández turns borderlands study on its head by focusing on "anti-border musics" that resist the cartography and national narratives established by the U.S./Mexico border. He chooses three songs that incorporate the same line, "We didn't cross the borders, the borders crossed us!" and analyzes how this anti-border statement resonates in the different musical genres of the Mexican ska/rock band Tijuana NO, the Chicano band Los Tigres del Norte (which favors traditional Mexican styles like the *corrido*), and the hard punk band Aztlán Underground. The "sonic geographies" Hernández traces demand "alternate spatiotemporal frames" rather than colonial origin stories (251).

Some of the essays use unconventional forms, performances in themselves, to express their critical messages. Philosopher Maria Lugones proposes that tango can be seen as an alternate theoretical mode, an erotic and embodied way to account for mutual agency, the call-and-response of different axes of identity (gender, class, sexuality, and race). Her essay is written as an embodied solicitation, inviting the reader to dance. William Anthony Nericcio creates a "rasquache semiotic whatsit" (165), coupling images captured with his Kodak camera in Laredo, Texas, with prose semiotic analysis of the uncanny juxtapositions that occur in the borderlands.

The final essay, Berta Jottar-Palenzuela's analysis of a New York rumba circle, is one of my favorites, closing the book with an account of how a group of Afro-Cuban, Dominican, Puerto Rican, African American, and Jewish drummers claimed a portion of Central Park for rumba performances. When the police tried to cast the drummers in the role of Black criminals creating a public disturbance, the drummers shifted the discourse, with one man arriving at the park wearing a gas mask, making this a story about police brutality and pan-ethnic resistance.

I would recommend this book for scholars interested in learning about diverse ways that marginalized populations seize the tools of performance and alter them to shift the story: in this case, to make the story about the mixtures, migrations, subversions, recombinations, and persistent political resistance of U.S. Latina/os. Each chapter contains enough cultural context for scholars unfamiliar with Latina/o Studies and enough entertaining performance for everyone.

SUZANNE M. BOST
Loyola University Chicago

Tony Jason Stafford. *Shaw's Settings: Gardens and Libraries*. Gainsville: University Press of Florida, 2013. Pp. 170. Hardcover $74.95.

Tony Stafford's *Shaw's Settings: Gardens and Libraries*, the latest addition to the Florida Bernard Shaw Series edited by R. F. Dietrich, provides a systematic study of a vital but often overlooked aspect of Shaw's plays. The book shows how Shaw's settings, whether they are fully materialized on stage or simply imagined from the dialogue, enrich his plays' meanings in a variety of ways, adding new dimensions to his characters, themes, and ideas. Recognizing that a comprehensive study of all of Shaw's settings would be impossible, Stafford makes an inspired decision to focus on a pair of settings that appear in many of Shaw's plays: the library and the garden. These settings recur with surprising frequency in Shaw's work, and Stafford's analysis of the library-garden motif provides insight not only into individual plays but also into Shaw's development as a playwright as he moves from a more realistic style in *Widowers' Houses* to a more fantastic one in *Back to Methuselah*. Through the book's nine chapters, each focused on a different play, Stafford explores the variety of ways in which the two settings function, delivering on his promise that the reader will "gain a sense of the depth, flexibility, resourcefulness, and complexity of [Shaw's] genius" (3).

The first three chapters emphasize the social function of gardens and libraries in Shaw's early plays. Shaw begins using the library-garden motif as early as his first play, *Widowers' Houses*, the subject of the first chapter. At this stage in Shaw's career, both gardens and libraries serve to highlight their owners' social aspirations and pretensions. As Stafford perceptively observes, gardens may superficially appear to serve as a peaceful and picturesque refuge, but in the early plays they are places where "appearances, acceptability, and proper conduct prevail" and "the rules of respectable British society are most powerfully enforced" (12). In *Widowers' Houses*, Shaw uses the library and garden to enhance his critique of hypocrisy, as the appearance of culture, civility, and propriety implied by these settings masks an underlying vileness and greed. In *Mrs. Warren's Profession*, the garden once again represents conventionality and hypocrisy, but here the emphasis lies on Vivie's desire to escape from this confining and corrupt space. Stafford vividly illustrates this point through a revealing moment when Crofts forcibly prevents Vivie from opening the latch of the gate—a good example of how Stafford's careful attention to setting draws attention to Shaw's playwriting skill. Vivie eventually succeeds in moving beyond the enclosed garden; for her, freedom ironically means moving into an office space. The third chapter turns to *Arms and the Man*, where libraries and gardens serve to accentuate the Petkoffs' social pretenses as well as the play's central conflict between realism and idealism. The Petkoffs pride themselves on their library, but the library itself—a single shelf of cheap, well-worn novels—reveals the naïveté of their pretensions. Similarly, the garden, with the stables encroaching and the washing spread out to dry on fruit bushes, serves as a reminder of the Petkoffs' peasant roots, making it an appropriate setting for a crucial scene exposing the falseness of Sergius's and Raina's romantic illusions.

Chapters Four and Five emphasize the relationship between space and character. In both *Candida* and *Man and Superman*, Shaw locates his characters politically and intellectually through specific books in their libraries. The "garden" in *Candida*, Victoria Park, also has political resonances: patronized by working-class East Enders, the park has numerous speakers' corners where orators would speak on a variety of subjects, including socialism. Stafford finds a harmonious relationship between the library and the park in *Candida*—one that clarifies the popularity of Morell's Christian socialist beliefs within his environment. In *Man and Superman*, on the other hand, the contrast between the library and the garden suggests a movement away from the enlightened but ultimately conventional world of Roebuck Ramsden toward a more natural, vibrant world associated with Jack Tanner. In the final act, the garden in Granada, with its fecund and Edenic resonances, provides an appropriate setting for one of Shaw's "most explicit and elaborate discussions of the Life Force" (70). As Stafford's chronological approach makes clear, this garden represents a significant departure from the gardens in Shaw's earlier plays, which were used primarily to indicate social status.

In *Major Barbara* and *Misalliance*, the subjects of Chapters Six and Seven, gardens and libraries are less obviously present on stage. Stafford extends the concept of library in *Major Barbara* to include Cusins's books and learning, while the concept of garden encompasses both the yard of the Salvation Army shelter and the idyllic village of Perivale St. Andrews that houses Undershaft's Armament Works. The cold, bare Salvation Army yard contrasts sharply with the picturesque comforts of St. Andrews, yet Stafford connects them through their "potential for destructiveness and violence" (79). In *Misalliance*, the library and garden have moved off stage, in keeping with Shaw's experiment with dramatic form. The garden can be seen through a large glass pavilion, while libraries and books are an important topic of conversation. This garden, like the one in *Man and Superman*, is aligned with nature, sexual attraction, and the Life Force. The library motif is associated primarily with Tarleton, the capitalist obsessed with books—including books with the power to demolish capitalism.

Stafford's final chapters are devoted to *Heartbreak House* and *Back to Methuselah*. The garden in *Heartbreak House* is once again associated with natural, creative forces, and Stafford points out how the tone of the play shifts according to characters' access to the garden. The mood darkens in Act II when the curtains are drawn, blocking the view of the garden. But when the scene shifts to the garden in Act III, the mood becomes markedly more peaceful. Stafford reads the garden as a place of truth and natural creativeness that contrasts with the dangers of human invention. In the final chapter, he analyzes Shaw's treatment of the Garden of Eden in *Back to Methuselah,* particularly his apparent substitution of Lilith, a powerful woman, for God.

This book makes a valuable contribution to Shaw studies and to the scholarship of modern drama through its thoughtful exploration of the convergences, divergences, and resonances of a well-chosen pair of settings. Stafford locates his argument effectively within the field of Shaw studies, but he may have missed an opportunity to broaden the book's scope and potential impact by connecting it to studies of space or place in drama by such scholars as Anne Ubersfeld, Michael Issacharoff, Hanna Scolnicov, or Una Chaudhuri. There is, however, some benefit to carefully restricting one's scope in order to cover a subject systematically and in rich detail, as Stafford does here. Throughout the book, Stafford's knowledge of and enthusiasm for Shaw's work is readily apparent, and his lucid prose makes the book welcoming not only for more advanced scholars but also for students new to Shaw's work.

REBECCA S. CAMERON
DePaul University

Michael Y. Bennett, *Narrating the Past through Theatre: Four Crucial Texts.* New York: Palgrave, 2013. Pp. 98. Hardcover $65.

Michael Y. Bennett's recent monographs adhere to a recurrent formula, consisting of a thesis that marries theatre and philosophy, exemplified by readings of four or five dramatic works, at the rate of one per chapter. Where the claims are bold and the texts well chosen, the sample size appears sufficient. Broadly speaking, this is the case in Bennett's 2011 work *Reassessing the Theatre of the Absurd.* The controversial claim that in 1961 Martin Esslin misconstrued the nature of Camus's existentialism, when supplemented by Bennett's theory of "parabolic drama" and substantiated by interpretations of Absurdism's canonical works, makes for an engaging study. In *Narrating the Past*, however, which identifies the characteristics of *modern historical drama*, via an examination of Georg Büchner's *Danton's Death* (1835), Oscar Wilde's *Salome* (1893), Bertolt Brecht's *Life of Galileo* (1943), and Robert Bolt's *A Man for All Seasons* (1960), though Bennett makes some astute observations about the plays themselves, his formula breaks down.

The choice of three exemplary texts and one (*A Man for All Seasons*) that, according to Bennett, represents the emergence of a partially new sensibility spanning 125 years, seems problematic in a study with periodizing objectives; but Büchner and Wilde *are* conventionally seen as anticipating and/or originating various trends in twentieth-century theatre, so this is not necessarily untenable. The difficulty is rather that the argument exemplified by these three central (and one outlying) case studies is not sufficiently coherent to rest comfortably upon such unstable foundations.

Bennett's introduction summarizes the book's three major claims: firstly, "that the narration of the past is largely an act of translation" (4); secondly, "that we must understand these playwrights as acting as 'modern' historical translators who fuse the past with the future and, like a translation, say something about their moment in time, bringing past, present, and future together in the tense of *always*" (4). And thirdly, he asserts that "modern history plays depart from, especially, early modern history plays in that these modern reincarnations of the form do not focus on commemoration (as do those of the early modern period) but *use* history as a means of critique and a way to look at and act in the future" (4).

Bennett's "tense of *always*" sounds as if it entails transcendence—treating history analogically as a source of universal truths—but his study is dominated by a Brechtian historicism (ascribed, in one way or other, to all of the plays) which, as the author well knows, discourages dramatists and audiences from eliding historical periods. Bennett does not exactly misread Brecht, but the terminology he adopts misdirects the reader. Equally difficult to swallow is Bennett's conviction that only modern playwrights use history *critically* to address the concerns of the present and raise questions about the future. The critic's reliance on Benjamin Griffin's (admittedly excellent) argument, that the early modern period replaces the Eucharistic "real presence" of medieval saints' plays with the *commemorative* dramaturgy of Protestant history plays, causes him to ignore more conventional accounts of early modern historical drama. Whether one shares Irving Ribner's view of the "Tudor historical purposes" pursued by the Elizabethans or rejects this interpretation in favor of New Historicist challenges, the crucial point stands that, in dramatizing the Wars of the Roses or the political upheavals of Ancient Rome, Shakespeare is thinking about his own society's present *and* future (the destinies of dynasties and polities). These concerns are not the unique property of a modern historical understanding.

If Bennett struggles to distinguish convincingly between the plays under his scrutiny and those of the early modern period, he also has difficulty in properly distinguishing between modern and postmodern philosophies of history. He focuses on writers who subscribe to "the concept of a 'chronicle' that possesses some inherent 'transcript'" (by which Bennett means simply an agreed upon version of events), prior to the emergence of postmodernism's "notion of multiple truths" (6). But he then proceeds to invoke the works of Freddie Rokem (whose *Performing History* is an authoritative text on postmodern history plays) and Hayden White and Michel de Certeau (the dominant voices in postmodern historiography) in a tutelary capacity on numerous occasions.

This confusion is exacerbated by the fact that Bennett's title, subtitles, and prose are dominated by the idea of "narrative." History plays *dramatize, enact, stage,* or *reconstruct* history; they do not *narrate* it and though, of course, they can *contain* narrative and narrators (see William Gruber's *Offstage Space, Narrative, and the Theatre of the Imagination* or Claudia Breger's *An Aesthetics of Narrative Performance*), Bennett does not provide a convincing account of the relationship between mimesis and diegesis, as he sees it. The recurrent argument that the protagonist in question "does not know how to craft a narrative appropriate for his contemporary society" (65) presents history as a range of competing fictions. One only has to recall Hayden White's most celebrated works (for example, *The Content of the Form: Narrative Discourse and Historical Representation*) to see that Bennett has, perhaps unwittingly, aligned his study of modern historical drama with postmodern historiography.

In spite of these conceptual inconsistencies, Bennett has an excellent eye for the plays' imagery. He speaks eloquently of the "paradoxical, liminal state" (41) occupied by Salomé, who is always presented as "an approximation" (39), "like the shadow of a white rose in a mirror of silver" (Wilde), defying recognition. Discussing the significance of the card game with which *Danton's Death* opens, the staircase that Herod ascends in the closing moments of *Salomé*, and Galileo's telescope as a metaphor for historical understanding, Bennett is an insightful critic. When he turns his attention to the guillotine, eternally present in the language of *Danton's Death*, though surprisingly absent from its final scene, Bennett explains that "the focus on the nature of the machine (which, of course, has no nature) would distract the audience from the nature of the people who put the machine to use" (64). This is why Danton's death itself takes place outside of the play's action: "Büchner's sympathy towards Danton—by taking his dying out of his death—removes the terror from the Terror" (65), focusing the audience's attention instead upon the task of analyzing history. The value of this book is to be found in these thought-provoking reflections upon the plays' symbolic properties.

Bennett has been prolific in recent years—between 2011 and 2013 he has edited one book, co-edited another, and published three monographs. But in spite of *Narrating the Past*'s positive qualities, one cannot help feeling that the profession's "publish or perish" ethos has had a detrimental effect upon Bennett's scholarship. The book contains numerous factual inaccuracies, grammatical errors, and stylistic infelicities, indicating haste and carelessness on both Bennett's part and Palgrave's. (Perhaps the most bizarre example of this is the absence of all four principal playwrights from the index.) Including all of its paratextual material (notes, index, bibliography, chapter abstracts), *Narrating the Past* is a mere 98 pages long. Though Bennett certainly succeeds in illuminating a number of interpretative cruxes in these four seminal works, an inquiry into the modern history play demands a more careful, detailed, and theoretically sound analysis than he provides.

ALEX FELDMAN
MacEwan University

Kevin J. Wetmore, Jr. *Black Medea: Adaptations in Modern Plays*. Amherst, New York: Cambria Press, 2013. Pp. 343. Hardcover $119.99.

Kevin J. Wetmore's *Black Medea* invites us on a theatrical tour de force across three continents and three millennia, as Euripides's famous witch leaves Greece behind and finds new incarnations in Africa and (African) America from the eighteenth century to the present. The result is both intellectually and emotionally memorable—the Medeas and Jasons in this volume make a lasting impression on the reader even as their stories touch on the varied debates of the burgeoning field of *Classica Africana* (i.e., the study of African and African American appropriations of Greco-Roman antiquity). The editor hopes that his collection of six plays will inspire future performances, but considering the wide variety of issues this anthology addresses, it would certainly also make for a great classroom tool.

The volume opens with an introduction that is short but to the point. It provides a brief history of Euripides' play and its afterlife in works as diverse as Countee Cullen's *Medea*, Toni Morrison's *Beloved*, and Tyler Perry's *Madea*. Thus familiarized with the necessary contexts, we approach the plays proper, each of which Wetmore prefaces with a brief introduction. All except one also feature a follow-up interview with the author.

Structurally, Jim Magnuson's *African Medea* is closest to Euripides's original, but, nonetheless, the piece is rich in contemporary political implications. The play is set in Angola, Jason is Portuguese, and Medea African. Not unlike her *altera ego* in the Greek tragedy, this Medea is a marginalized "Other" demanding her due. When Jason leaves her and their sons for a white woman, Medea plots revenge, and amid a general uprising against European rule, she murders the children, the new wife, and the white father-in-law (Creon). The play thus reflects on the need to resist the bonds of racism and colonialism— Wetmore calls it "Fanonian" (9)—even as it meditates on the great moral cost of the resultant bloodshed. In the interview from 2013, Magnuson notes how far America has come since the play was first rehearsed during the Harlem riots of 1968. As I write this review in the wake of Ferguson, Missouri, I wonder if *African Medea* may be more relevant today than even its author suspected.

Father Ernest Ferlita, S.J., sets his *Black Medea* (1976) in 1810 New Orleans among the fugitives of Toussaint Louverture's Haitian revolution. Jerome (Jason), last in a line of French slave owners, leaves voodoo priestess Madeleine (Medea) for the daughter of a Louisiana businessman. While the ensuing revenge plot is familiar, its presentation is not. The play has us witness the voodoo ceremony that precipitates Madeleine's vengeance. The rest we learn through flashbacks. African religion is here impressively pitted against Christianity—a recurring theme of the anthology—and we are invited to reflect more on the role of capitalism in the oppression of blacks. Classicist readers may also find themselves reminded of ancient portrayals of witchcraft ceremonies, such as Theocritus's Second *Idyll*.

If Magnuson's *African Medea* was "Fanonian," then Steve Carter's *Pecong* (1981) is nothing short of Bakhtinian. The longest (and most fun) of the six plays, *Pecong* transports the reader onto a Caribbean island, "[w]ell in the past" (132) and in the midst of Carnival. Bakhtin's interest in the "material bodily lower stratum" is on full display as we experience countless acts of sorcery, a beating heart ripped out of an old witch's chest, sex on stage, fart jokes, and the gutting of a large jungle cat. While different audiences will reliably see the same drama through different lenses in different political climates, *Pecong* more than most other plays in the collection stages not a Battle of the Races, but a Battle of the Sexes. In the name of all women, voodoo priestess Mediyah and the ghost of her grandmother (!) revenge themselves on this Medea's hyper-masculine and yet oddly likeable lover, the appropriately named Jason Allcock. A particular plus is Carter's recreation of the island's sociolect, rich in rhymes and local color, particularly as Jason challenges Mediyah's brother to a contest of wits not unlike a modern rap battle (the "pecong" of the title). Where the play does address different skin tones, it singles out discrimination within the black community ["Strike me blue and Holy shite! Cleopatra think she white!" (144)]. Finally, I wonder if there could be a deliberate echo of the carnivalesque plots of Greco-Roman comedy in Carter's *Pecong*. After all, Mediyah first has sex with Jason in a vaguely religious context (i.e., on an enchanted island), then hides her pregnancy and eventually gives birth removed from the audience's view, all of which is common in the plays of Plautus and Terence. Of course, the sympathies of the play's interior audience shift as Mediyah murders the twins, and the comedy turns into a tragedy. Nevertheless, *Pecong* ends with a group of drunk revelers that reminded me of Menander.

The anthology's shortest play, Edris Cooper's *There Are Women Waiting: The Tragedy of Medea Jackson* (1992), shares many features with the longest. It captures the language of a different time and place as the songs of Aretha Franklin resound through late-twentieth century Oakland, California. *Medea Jackson* grew out of interviews that Cooper and Rhodessa Jones conducted with female inmates at the San Francisco County Jail, and the piece's originally all-woman cast (a notable reversal of ancient Greek practice) takes the Battle of the Sexes up a notch. When Jason leaves the mother of his children for the daughter of this play's Creon (their landlord), Medea remarks, "Shit, better just be dead or turn gay" (230). There is a comment on class here as well as on race and gender. Forced out of her apartment, she sees no way out of humiliation and poverty, and throws her children off a roof. She then dies mysteriously with the police in hot pursuit.

Silas Jones insists that his *American Medea* (1995) is not based on Euripides but re-envisions a myth that is older than Greek tragedy. This clarification forms part of the play's wider indictment against a slave-owning America that stylizes itself as an heir to Athens. Jones takes issue specifically with Euripides' portrayal of a murderous Medea (289), who—as a Colchian—is of African descent (if Herodotus 2.104 is to be believed, that is). By contrast, Jones's Medea is no infanticide: "You've been reading those Greeks again. African mothers do not kill their children" (279). Elsewhere, in a similarly strong rejection of white claims to moral superiority over Africa, there are clear echoes of Martin Bernal's thesis that Greek (and, therefore, American) civilization is descended from African roots. And finally, tying into another item of frequent discussion among Americanists and classicists, the play enacts a clash between Greek and American conceptions of slavery. In antiquity, human bondage was harsh but was not based on race. However, as a Greek Jason brings his black wife, Medea, and their two children to George Washington's Mount Vernon in the late 1700s, the lighter-skinned son suddenly starts thinking of his brother as a slave. In this respect, as well as in its biting portrayal of Washington's fawning servant Prince Whipple as the "first oreo," *American Medea* recalls the satirical style of Ishmael Reed. In its use of the "Quest for the Golden Fleece" as a metaphor for colonialist and imperialist aspirations, the play connects to similar imagery in Magnuson's *African Medea* or in W. E. B. Du Bois's *The Souls of Black Folk*. Jones himself best summarizes his message that black Medea was betrayed when she bought into stories of American liberty: she "went to bed with a myth and got fucked by a metaphor."

In the last play, Marianne McDonald's *Medea, Queen of Colchester* (2002), the volume tackles a topic so far somewhat subdued in (though not entirely absent from) *Black Medea*: homosexuality. This Medea is a transvestite from South Africa (hence the title) who settles in Las Vegas. She is also an immigrant with a criminal record of murder and drug dealing who could be deported if found out. She has internet, raps, and works as a drag performer at the Parthenon casino. However, she is not married to the man whose children she helps raise. When he leaves her for the casino owner's daughter, her bloody revenge brings truly contemporary issues to the fore, ranging from same-sex marriage to green cards. In the end, this gay male Medea faces the same conflicts as her straight, female predecessors. Pointing a gun at this play's Jason (James), Medea casts the rejection she is facing as a direct continuation of Western greed that plundered Africa. Seen another way, her violent response to perceived oppression makes her "the first terrorist, murdering innocents" (336). As such, Medea has truly arrived in the present.

My only serious point of criticism does not relate to the material but to its presentation: the plays, their introductions, and the interviews are all riddled with typos (especially in the first third of the volume). But in the end this does not take away from the value of six plays that raise tantalizing questions about Euripides's enduring appeal to audiences of all colors. One of this anthology's Medeas asks if we never "tire of standing transfixed, listening to a tale told and told again, ending each time the same way, litany of agony" (30). If new playwrights keep bringing new perspectives to the table, then the answer must be an emphatic "no."

MATHIAS HANSES
Columbia University

Marianne Novy. *Shakespeare and Outsiders.* Oxford: Oxford University Press, 2013. Pp. 203. Hardcover $84. Paperback $30.95.

Marianne Novy's *Shakespeare and Outsiders* is composed of five case studies, each focusing on a different manifestation of the "outsider" in Shakespeare's plays. Although there are many acute and a few startling observations made by Novy, this work does not really engage the category of "outsider" in any sustained way; it does not expand the conversation about "outsiders," because it takes for granted the narrow notion of the "outsider" that we are predisposed at present to retain.

To say that Shakespeare wrote plays that feature outsiders is simply to say that Shakespeare wrote plays. Animated by conflict, drama *ipso facto* deals with the struggle for power. Since power is always asymmetrical, there are those within the favor of its orbit and without. This dynamic is so fundamentally a part of the structure of drama that there are myriad theatre games used by directors and actors to establish in every scene, even in every beat, which characters are insiders and which outsiders.

So what is fundamentally *Shakespearean* about his representation of "outsiders"? What do they offer that might help us to understand the standing of outsiders in general or help us to crystalize the status of outsiders in other contexts? How are Shakespeare's outsiders like or unlike, for example, Medea, Tamburlaine, or Laura Wingfield? Novy explains:

> The book shows how often Shakespeare's plays break down oppositions and categorizations—they are structured by a juxtaposition of several kinds of outsiders or potential outsiders who may contrast in obvious ways but also have points of similarity. While, in varying degrees, the outsiders may resonate with stereotypes, they also break out of them [...]. This book aims to contribute to showing why those characters and their plays originally had resonance and why they still have it today [16].

Shakespeare's "resonance," Novy argues, is the result of a kind of nimbleness of characterization. The status of his characters is fluid. Yet Novy contends that this elasticity accomplishes something above and beyond dynamic representation. From "ambiguity and ambivalence" about outsiders, Shakespeare's audiences may experience ambiguity and ambivalence about their own status, which may lead them towards "tolerance."

Noting what Alexandra Walsham calls "the considerable reserves of tolerance embedded in early modern society," Novy situates Shakespeare among those carrying on a sustained conversation about equality:

> Anglican apologist Hooker writes that men are all 'of one and the same Nature,' and of the 'relation of equality between ourselves and them that are as ourselves.' The skeptical political theorist Machiavelli declares, 'All men, having had the same beginning, are equally ancient and have been made in one mode.' The founders of the United States did not follow the most universal implications of 'all men are created equal,' which they affirmed in the Declaration of Independence, but the idea was there to be developed. Similarly, the idea of human equality was available for development in Shakespeare's time [19].

Shakespeare, it appears, is engaging an "idea" floating out in the ether, "available" to be "developed." That Hooker, Machiavelli, and Jefferson each meant about equality and its consequences something radically different, particular to the argument that each was making for a specific kind of polity, is washed over. Novy is making a Whiggish historical argument about the unfolding of "ideas" over time—why else feel compelled to link Shakespeare so incongruously with the Declaration of Independence? And thus the reason that Shakespeare has "resonance" is that he has jumped the historical queue, that his plays may trigger in his audience, through sympathetic engagement with certain characters, a change in perspective about the world, bringing it closer in line with our own notions of equality.

To make this historically charged argument, however, Novy engages in some very tenuous historicizing. In Chapter 1, she focuses on Shylock's forced conversion at the end of *The Merchant of Venice*, the moment when, under duress, he moves from being a Jewish outsider to a Christian insider. Novy measures the importance of this moment by the effect, or potential effect, it has upon members of the audience: "Thus Protestants as well as Catholics in Shakespeare's audience might have in their literal or spiritual ancestry members who had converted under pressure [...] and might have been sympathetic to Shylock in the final section of the trial scene" (28). The evidence that audiences would have made such an association is remarkably thin. Yet the claim is made because it implies that identification with the "outsider" through the recognition of shared persecution will engender sympathy, and provides evidence, however scant, that that is what Shakespeare intended. Novy then reads *Merchant's* Antonio as many others have, as homosexual, and therefore as a member of a marginalized group. But what she fails to take up in any significant way, and which is really the most interesting question about the play's outsiders, is why, if the shared experience of marginalization can generate sympathy, do Antonio and Shylock persist in hating one another?

The remaining chapters veer in and out of such loose historicizing. Chapter 2, focused on *Twelfth Night*, raises many interesting points of similarity between Malvolio and Shylock; but then it presses the point too far, leaning too heavily on Malvolio as a confessional "puritan," and puzzling over why audiences have less of a problem with puritan-baiting than Jew-baiting. The chapter rehearses the many arguments that have been made by other scholars to establish Antonio's identity as homosexual, but once he has been conferred this outsider status Novy moves on to the women in the play. Having promised a look at the dynamic qualities of outsiders, this study is too often content to simply demonstrate that a character *is* an outsider without pushing further.

Chapters 3 and 4 expend most of their energy reminding us about the many ways that women and members of other races were marginalized in early modern England. We get a tangled mix of insider/outsider talk: "[Goneril and Regan are] at first apparently social insiders because they behave as Lear wants them to, although they know that he always loved Cordelia most. Having been given their halves of the kingdom, they make Lear into an outsider by challenging the behavior of his men. However, their development, especially their blinding of Gloucester, reveals them as moral outsiders and they die as social outsiders also in the competition over Edmund" (83). There are so many overlapping categories here, such breezy sliding back and forth, that the distinction between outsider and insider loses signification, eliding into confusion. Is there no distinction between social, generational, moral, political, or gendered outsiders? What, one may ask, is a "moral outsider"? Can a "moral outsider" be a social insider? The issues are infinitely more complex than who is *in* and who is *out*.

There are several characters in Shakespeare who puzzle out rather profoundly what it means to be an outsider, from Richard III's self-conscious (and self-serving) soliloquizing to Hamlet's pained self-scourging at the peripheries of Elsinore. There are also moments, such as Prince Hal's denial of Falstaff, that dramatize the forces that impel us to thrust others outside the circle of love/friendship/society. *Shakespeare and Outsiders* is at its most engaging when it thinks *with* Shakespeare, as it does best in Chapter 5 (on *King Lear*), about the meta-questions surrounding "outsiders." When it sticks with our current insider perspective on outsiders, it treads well-worn territory.

PETER KANELOS
Valparaiso University

Ryan Claycomb. *Lives in Play: Autobiography and Biography on the Feminist Stage*. Ann Arbor: University of Michigan Press, 2012. Pp. 261. Paperback $27.

Lives in Play: Autobiography and Biography on the Feminist Stage focuses on what it terms "life narratives" in the context of feminism from the 1970s to the present. The book brings together material on performance pieces, in which the writer is also the performer, and scripted plays, linking such disparate works as Carolee Schneeman's hallmark performance piece *Interior Scroll* (1975), Terry Galloway's *Out All Night and Lost My Shoes*, a 1998 solo performance piece that engages with disability and sexuality, and April De Angelis's *Playhouse Creatures* (1993), a scripted play about five Restoration actresses. Using a theoretical framework that combines narratology and feminist theory, the book bridges a considerable time period, in which theories of feminist performance moved from body-based conceptions of gender associated with Hélène Cixous and the ideal of *écriture feminine* to the performative conception of gender most notably articulated by Judith Butler. Claycomb's formulation weaves together aspects of both forms of feminist theory, arguing that body-based and performative approaches complement each other.

The first section of the book, dealing with autobiographical solo performances, provides the stronger part of the two-part study. It encompasses a history of feminist performance art, describing in brief terms major artists and works of the 1970s and 1980s, including Laurie Anderson, Rachel Rosenthal,

Karen Finley, Holly Hughes, Orlan, Carmelita Tropicana, and Split Britches. This history is enriched by the accompanying theoretical discussion, which offers insightful observations about the meaning of the body in autobiographical performance and the role of the audience in the specific context of feminist performance. Although the performances and the theoretical approaches discussed will be familiar to many, this readable section offers a valuable introduction to students or non-specialists seeking background in this particular field.

The second section of the book, which discusses a number of scripted plays, rests on less secure ground. Scripted plays dealing with autobiography and biography do not form a distinct artistic movement, compared with the feminist performance pieces of the first section. It therefore depends upon the author to create a context appropriate for discussion of the plays, identifying a practice, tradition, or set of conventions that are used or resisted by feminist playwrights. This section's failure to present such a context is exacerbated by the narrow selection of plays brought up for consideration. This group of plays is neither comprehensive nor representative of feminist autobiographical and biographical dramatic writing.

Much of the chapter on autobiographical plays is devoted to one piece: the fragmentary *4.48 Psychosis* by Sarah Kane. Those closest to Kane have stated that this piece, apparently written immediately before Kane committed suicide, does not refer to her illness or suicide specifically; nevertheless, Claycomb insists on reading it as such and carefully crafts a definition of autobiography that permits such a reading. While this seems dubious, Kane's inclusion in a discussion of feminist stage work also raises questions. Kane herself denied being a feminist, and her work took place in a climate of rejection of all "isms" by members of her theatrical cohort, famously known as the "in yer face" playwrights. Similarly, Claycomb's suggestion that Paula Vogel's *How I Learned to Drive* be considered autobiographical in spite of Vogel's explicit statement that it is not seems questionable in its refusal to accept the playwright's authority in regard to her own work. The choice of these plays for particular emphasis seems especially odd in light of the frankly autobiographical plays that could have provided a sound foundation for the discussion of feminist life narratives on stage.

Prominent among the scripted plays that could have provided a better starting point for a comprehensive examination of feminist autobiography on stage are two works of Adrienne Kennedy: *Sleep Deprivation Chamber* (1996) and *Mom, How Did You Meet the Beatles?* (2008). These plays consciously and explicitly present Kennedy in her social context, giving expression to events and issues that have importantly defined her life. Claycomb, however, places his brief mention of Kennedy in a chapter titled "Performing Race and the

Object of Biography." He justifies separating the works of African-American women from those of white feminists with the claim that race has not been established as performative with the same authority that the performative nature of gender has been articulated by Judith Butler and others. Such a claim ignores the decades of work by Adrienne Kennedy, beginning with *Funnyhouse of a Negro* in 1964; in this play and a number of later works, the performative nature of race forms a central theme. The well-known writer/actor Anna Deavere Smith has also made the performativity of race a consistent theme in her solo performances of *Fires in the Mirror* (1992) and *Twilight: Los Angeles* (1994). This failure to understand and acknowledge the performative nature of race in the context of American society, and the consequent separation of African-American playwrights from white playwrights constitutes a painful flaw in the book.

Lack of attention to social context, when English plays are discussed side by side with American plays, contributes to the seemingly arbitrary, rather than representative, set of autobiographical or biographical scripted plays. A few plays—*New Anatomies* by Timberlake Wertenbaker, *The Summer in Gossensass* by Maria Irene Fornes, *Venus* by Suzan-Lori Parks, and the previously mentioned *4.48 Psychosis, How I Learned to Drive,* and *Playhouse Creatures*—receive detailed attention. Since Claycomb provides no indication of why he chose these particular plays for extended discussion, they seem to serve merely as vehicles for Claycomb's ideas, which unfortunately tends to negate their meaning as feminist productions.

Feminist plays in English provide a rich body of work for additional analysis. A line of wholly or substantially autobiographical plays could be traced from the 1960s to the present, perhaps including Doris Lessing's *Play with a Tiger* (1964), Wendy Wasserstein's *Uncommon Women and Others* (1977), Wakako Yamauchi's *And the Soul Shall Dance* (1977), Gretchen Cryer's *I'm Getting My Act Together and Taking It on the Road* (1978), Andrea Dunbar's *Rita, Sue, and Bob Too* (1982), Tina Howe's *Painting Churches* (1983), Sharman MacDonald's *When I Was a Girl I Used to Scream and Shout* (1985), Velina Hasu Houston's *Tea* (1987), Jackie Kay's *The Adoption Papers* (1990), Jill Morley's *True Confessions of a Go-Go Girl* (1998), and Pamela Gien's *The Syringa Tree* (2005). Feminist biography offers a host of interesting plays, including the long-running solo pieces *Eleanor* (about Eleanor Roosevelt), written by Rhoda Lerman and acted by Maureen Stapleton, and *Love Arm'd: Aphra Behn and Her Pen* by Karen Eterovich, as well as works about historical figures such as *Mary Queen of Scots Got Her Head Chopped Off* (1987) by Liz Lochhead, and recent plays that re-examine the lives of women denied credit for their accomplishments, such as Anna Ziegler's *Photograph 51* (2008) about the DNA researcher Rosalind Franklin, and *Emilie: La Marquise du Chatelet*

Defends Her Life Tonight (2013) by Lauren Gunderson, about the eighteenth-century physicist who prefigured the theories of Einstein. Perhaps, then, *Lives in Play* will point the way toward a more comprehensive study of feminist biographical and autobiographical drama.

AMELIA HOWE KRITZER
University of St. Thomas

Andrew Sofer. *Dark Matter: Invisibility in Drama, Theater and Perform-ance.* Ann Arbor: University of Michigan Press, 2013. Pp. 229. Paperback $29.95.

Andrew Sofer's *Dark Matter: Invisibility in Drama, Theater, and Per-formance* proves a true *tour de force*. Its strenuous thoroughness even sent me to read several plays I had not known. While I doubt that its vastness of scope will make it so easily "accessible" as the book jacket claims, its immense schol-arly depth deserves much admiration.

In general I believe Sofer strives to achieve three different goals. The first seems to be to taxonomize (to some necessarily limited degree) various per-formative, dramatic, and theatrical phenomena, all involving the presence-in-absence of "*dark matter,*" or "incorporeal" motifs ["[n]ot there" but also "not not there" (Sofer 9)]. As a critic who is also an active poet, Sofer zealously draws analogies between unseen presentational elements and the "dark matter" postulated by physicists: the "nonluminous mass that cannot be detected by observation" and which yet perhaps composes 80–95 percent of matter in the universe (3). Although his scientific information surely seems well-researched, the Boston College critic disclaims any large-scale specifically scientific goals (11). Still, he provocatively categorizes (sometimes with what is a probably necessary randomness) different sorts of invisibility affecting drama, perform-ance, and the stage.

Sofer's second perceived goal for this volume looks to be exploration of a vast (albeit not total) panorama of literary history. As the book jacket admits, he has basically examined only dramatic writings that are "postclassical" (though a few references to *Oedipus Rex* do appear). Nevertheless, he definitely demonstrates highly impressive familiarity with much of European and Amer-ican theatre history, from medieval Corpus Christi plays to more than one very contemporary script.

Examining Christopher Marlowe's *Doctor Faustus* as one of two Renais-sance (indeed, specifically two 1590s) English plays, Sofer focuses on long-standing debates about Faustus's dramatized summoning of insubstantial spirits, which pit against each other the stigmatization of "hollow" verbal con-juring and the contrasting valorization of potentially "efficacious performativity" (25). He acknowledges, with much argumentative fairness, the attacks made by Calvinist condemners upon all likely Faustian "fraudulen[ce]" (34–35). Yet he also perceives, with relative clarity, the "potential embedded in *all* performative speech to conjure dark matter into visible reality" (37).

Especially interesting as literary history is Sofer's third chapter, "Unmasking Women: *The Rover* and Sexual Signification on the Restoration Stage." The "dark matter" explored here is the hidden specific identity of individual women (some of them well-bred and affluent ingenues, others professional prostitutes) who all playfully masquerade during a Neapolitan carnival behind facial and costuming disguises (some, for example, pose as gypsies). In a play publicly launched just after women were first allowed to appear on the English stage, and also a work whose female authorship Aphra Behn did not at first dare to admit, the playwright clearly examined what Sofer terms "an ongoing negotiation over the sexual politics of the female body and its representation" (72). Sofer forthrightly proclaims that Behn ultimately "champions female visibility" (86)—even though her drama only very gradually reveals both the openly identifiable visage and the personality of its heroine, Hellena.

Sofer employs speech act theory in his chapter on Marlowe, theories of the "gaze" in his chapter on *The Rover*, and, it appears, special interest in minority group theatre in his pages concerning "Invisible Wounds." Hence, his third, and really his principal, area of focus in *Dark Matter* is contemporary literary theory and criticism. When he points us in his book's opening pages to the "real presence" of motifs and themes that are technically "felt" as "absence" (2), he seems anxious to affirm critical approaches like deconstruction and dialogism, which do not look for (and certainly do not insist upon) stilted monological (and, hence, perhaps superficial) readings of texts or staged productions.

Sofer's most delightful chapter for me is the second, "Quantum Mechanicals," in which he appears, subtly, to correlate Heisenberg's uncertainty principle in physics (49–50) with humanists' deconstructionist and dialogical textual study. Perhaps much of what makes this portion of the book so appealing is simply its tantalizing multivalent speculation about what occurred offstage (sexually or otherwise) between Shakespeare's *A Midsummer Night's Dream* characters Bottom and Titania. Yet Sofer's general principles here are just as right-minded as are his pragmatic investigations of an individual work: he never fears confronting open questions, and he does so by being hermeneutically bold.

Therefore, while I do not concur fully with every emphasis that he makes in his fourth chapter concerning Tennessee Williams's *Suddenly Last Summer*, I cannot particularly censure his treatment of that script and its productions, in which he perceives a variant of Stanley Fish's "rhetoric of self-consumption"

(92). Sofer may perplex me when he calls Sebastian Venable, and not Dr. Cuck-rowicz or Catherine, the "protagonist" of this drama (90). To be sure, however, as a character who never appears onstage, Sebastian is definitely "dark matter" in the play, "offer[ing] the audience no safe or privileged point of view from which to judge him" (92). Sofer contends that Sebastian, like Blanche Dubois in *A Streetcar Named Desire*, belongs to a key thematic pattern in Williams's works. According to that pattern, characters regularly turn principally into *sparagmoi*, "consumed in the praxis of [their] performance" (94). As usual, Sofer is brilliantly analytical at many points in this chapter, albeit ultimately more monological in his focus on one central Williams pattern than he often is elsewhere.

In his fifth chapter, partially reflecting Foucault's theories of "power" (114) as they apply to Arthur Miller's play *The Archbishop's Ceiling*, Sofer dis-cusses the "dark matter" frightening an international group of writer characters when they convene in an Eastern European (likely a Czech) apartment and believe that a surveillance "bug" may be secretly housed above the drawing room (105). The chapter deftly chronicles Miller's transition from an Ibsenite champion of moral analysis (106–107), through the moral doubtings of *After the Fall* (108), and on to *The Archbishop's Ceiling*. There Sofer contends that Miller almost completely rejects Ibsen's "causal dramaturgy of motive" and instead evokes a "*prismatic* dramaturgy of power"—voicing a more Fou-cauldian view of ultimately unresolved, "variegated behavior in response to a common [power] stimulus" (110). Admirably, Sofer remains willing to inter-pret *The Archbishop's Ceiling* dialogically, as a work "hover[ing] between the causal and the prismatic," and as a production still making a "plea for personal responsibility" against a "wry" sense of such a quest's contemporary incoher-ence. Yet Sofer clearly wants to focus on the latter interpretation as more path-breakingly postmodern. Thus he avers that "by portraying [the character] Sigmund as a martyr to the cause of art—albeit a flawed, narcissistic one—Miller buys a redemptive ending at the risk of replicating the very artifice he critiques" (114).

Sofer's final chapter, "Invisible Wounds: Rehearsing Trauma on the Con-temporary Stage," contends that "dark matter" seemingly inevitably impinges itself upon those who suffer traumatic events, because those events are not bounded, but instead produce over extended time large degrees of "*psychic absence*," "black hole[s]" of experience that cannot regularly or fully be grasped (119–120). The ever-thorough Sofer deals not only with contemporary trauma theatre, but also with antecedent works from *Macbeth* to *Blasted*. Principally, though, he examines quite recent dramatic detailings of "unseen terror rather than graphic horror" (123): for example, Suzan-Lori Parks's *The America Play*, wherein he perceives a variant of "classic family drama" (124), but one confronting "the Great Hole of History" enforced repeatedly upon African Americans (124).

No reader should sneer at the vigor provided for this book by its scholarly integrity—seen, especially, within its author's full fifty pages' worth of marvelously deep endnote documentation. This supporting research, like the entire volume, provides criticism of the first order—informed, reasoned, careful, and inventive. The book is decisively rich—and especially strong in its poet-critic's sense of analogies between scientific and humanistic study. This publication, albeit daunting in its amazingly vast range, is surely also exciting for that very extensiveness of endeavor.

JEFFREY B. LOOMIS
Northwest Missouri State University

Philip C. Kolin and Harvey Young, eds. *Suzan-Lori Parks in Person: Interviews and Commentaries*. London and New York: Routledge Taylor & Francis Group, 2014. Pp. 240. Paperback $41.95.

By now Suzan-Lori Parks's prolific, innovative, and erudite contribution to dramatic literature is not only exemplary of Ronald Judy's notion of "ironic duplication"—or "signifyin'"—but is also unarguable to most within the American theatre-going sphere. Editors Philip C. Kolin and Harvey Young attest to this in the introduction to their ambitious, deftly-organized volume entitled *Suzan-Lori Parks in Person: Interviews and Commentaries*. Perhaps less familiar to audiences are the perspectives of Parks's collaborators on the intricacies of engaging with the breadth of her dramatic interventions: into the "great hole" in history; the paradox that constitutes the lives of the slave-descended; and the attendant modes of survival required to traverse that paradox—usually by way of improvisation (Parks would, of course, say "riffing")—from transatlantic slavery's debut in the Americas to its afterlife in modernity. From the volume's apt cover photograph by Walter McBride of Parks—hands posed in mirroring, meditative mudras, her smile simultaneously "signifyin' on" the very posture she assumes—across twenty-three chapters (comprising eighteen interviews and five commentaries), the book opens a portal into Parks's enduringly visionary mind, and into those of a select group of directors, producers, dramaturges, scholars, and reviewers who have engaged her work over the past twenty-five years. I will list but three aspects of the book's productive structuring.

First, the volume underscores Parks's unflinching commitment to the artful arrangement of language in its very dialogic conceit: as a series of interchanges with and/or about Parks, revealing how she and others *think* about her work, both in the process of doing it and in hindsight. This is perhaps one of the most outstanding aspects of the volume: its valuing of *thought* as a critical ingredient in theatre-making. As such, the interchanges unfold loquaciously, in the very *best* sense of that word. This is to say, Parks—in concert with those speaking with and/or about her dramatic excavation of lost history, her fashioning a made-up history-as-response, and ruminating upon how her characters execute and innovate these labors—reveals the ways in which her investigative rigor detonates the productions of her plays; and by extension, the vibrant interlocutions within these pages. Punctuating the dialogues are retrospective interviews with and symposia about Parks, wherein she is evoked rather than actually present. Beth Schachter's comprehensive account of directing Parks's seminal *The Death of the Last Black Man in the Whole Entire World* and the two-chapter entry documenting a Hunter College Symposium on Parks, moderated by Jonathan Kalb, are exemplars.

Second, the volume is assembled *both* diachronically and synchronically; a savvy nod to Parks's deployment of jazz-inspired linguistic syncopation, dissonance, and counterpoint. In other words, it unfurls chronologically, beginning with a comprehensive introduction by the editors surveying her production trajectory. That course moves from Parks's debut upon the New York experimental theatre scene in the late 1980s, in venues such as BACA Downtown (a space curated by the Brooklyn Arts Council Association) with *Imperceptible Mutabilities in the Third Kingdom*; to her 1990s tenure at the Public Theatre in Manhattan (where *Venus*, *The America Play*, *In the Blood*, *Fucking A*, and *Topdog/Underdog* all premiered); her post–MacArthur "genius" grant, Broadway debut of *Topdog/Underdog*, which garnered her the Pulitzer Prize for Drama in 2002; and her mid-2000s turn toward a more expansive reach—her *365 Plays/365 Days* project, which premiered off- and off-off-Broadway, and then proliferated into regional, college and university theatres around the country. All of this spawned Parks's increased focus on the development of both young and emerging adult playwrights, where a great deal of her focus lies today, as well as on the continuing evolution of her own work as a playwright, screenwriter, director, and novelist. Simultaneously, however, the volume never loses sight of Parks as *both* a voice that has taken indelible root within the dramatic canon across a quarter-century and one who is also unequivocally engaged with the present moment and its deeply troubled relation to its past.

Third, and one of the subtler triumphs of the book, is that in assembling a prism of interactions with the same subject, repetition is bound to emerge. In their structural replication of Parks's now-legendary use of this stylistic element (and which the interview with David Savran foregrounds), the editors compose a multifarious purview of Parks, rather than mere factual and historical redundancy.

There are no customary biographies of the contributors. Rather, their queries of and reflections about Parks introduce them. This formidable array of artists and scholars consists of the editors (Philip C. Kolin and Harvey Young); the interviewers (Patti Hartigan, Erika Munk, Han Ong, Michelle Pearce, Tom Sellar, Una Chaudhuri, Shelby Jiggetts, Ronni Gordon, David Savran, Kathy Sova, Lisa Colletta, Rick DesRochers, John Marshall, Joseph Roach, Kevin J. Wetmore, Jr., Shawn-Marie Garrett, and Dave Steakley); the commentators (Jonathan Kalb, Beth Schachter, Kolin, and Young). Other key players appear within these engagements, including Adrienne Kennedy (interviewed by Parks) and Liz Diamond and Bonnie Metzgar (two of Parks's closest collaborators). There are also the participants in the Hunter College Symposium, including moderator Kalb and respondents Robert Brustein, Shawn-Marie Garrett, Marc Robinson, Alisa Solomon, Leah C. Gardiner, Bill Walters, and Diamond. Along the way, their reflections and dialogues retrospectively and anecdotally invoke a range of other collaborators, thinkers, mentors, and influences, not least among them, James Baldwin, Toni Morrison, George C. Wolfe, and Amiri Baraka, to name but a few. This powerful assemblage yields insightful and dynamic deliberations about the performance and study of Parks's dramaturgy.

The book also traverses uneasy territory. Parks's conversations with Adrienne Kennedy and dramaturge Shelby Jiggetts comprise a kind of centerpiece to the interviews. The distinct, intramural timbre of these two conversations is striking, wherein Black women note, among other things, the insufficiencies and treacherous nature of language. This coupling sets into stark relief that the majority of Parks's preeminent interlocutors in the theatre are not Black. This is not to diminish their perspicacity; for their brain power and creative breadth are humbling. Rather, it is to underscore the persistence of this predominance, suggesting that the feeling Parks and Kennedy share, of not being "theatre people," may not be coincidental. Moreover, one of the most formidable demands made of Black dramatists who intervene in slavery's afterlife (for example, ghettoized poverty, mass incarceration, genocidal state violence, and the more nuanced micro-antagonisms that plague "upwardly-mobile" Blacks) is that they do so, not only deftly, but with an abundance of gratitude, joy, investment in existential universality, and no evidence of despair. That demand intricately haunts these pages. Parks's resistance to being thought an exclusively "Black" or "issues-oriented" playwright and, paradoxically, her unease with being eclipsed by prominent aesthetic imposition (Bonnie Metzgar recalls, for example, the collaborative challenges during Richard Foreman's production of *Venus*) both evince Parks's continual navigation of that demand. For there is yet another dimension to Parks's work that remains underexplored: the *political* gravitas that undergirds her signifyin' aesthetic(ally).

For these reasons and more, *Suzan-Lori Parks in Person: Interviews and*

Commentaries is an essential addition to dramatic literary scholarship, in that it provides a textured, critical—if penultimate—interactive means through which to meet Parks, as a dramatist, a thinker, and as a person whose work continues to probe human relations historically and presently, thoughtfully and dynamically.

JAYE AUSTIN WILLIAMS
California State University, Long Beach

Siyuan Liu. *Performing Hybridity in Colonial-Modern China*. New York: Palgrave Macmillan, 2013. Pp. xiv + 245. Hardcover $95.

In *Performing Hybridity in Colonial-Modern China*, Siyuan Liu investigates various facets of the hybridity of *wenmingxi* (civilized drama), a new form of Chinese theatre originating in the early twentieth century. A fusion of Western theatre, classical Chinese theatre, and a new form of Japanese theater called *shinpa* (new school drama), *wenmingxi* offers a rare insight into the early stages of the modernization of Chinese theatre. Nonetheless, as Liu has pointed out, *wenmingxi* has been largely neglected in modern scholarship. One possible reason for this lack of scholarly studies is the necessity of looking into materials in both Chinese and Japanese languages. Liu examines various materials such as play scripts, newspaper and magazine articles, posters, diaries, and official documents in both languages, and presents a comprehensive study of *wenmingxi*. Liu adopts Brian Stross's paradigm of hybridity, defined in Stross's article "The Hybrid Metaphor: From Biology to Culture," which applies biological hybridity to that of culture, as a model to examine various aspects of the development and nature of hybridity in *wenmingxi*. The six chapters of the book are structured according to the six components of the hybridity paradigm. Yet the book is not simply an application of Stross's theory, but a display of Liu's meticulous research, methodology, and insight. The comprehensive research brings to light the missing link in the study of modern Chinese theater—the emergence, production, and reception of *wenmingxi*.

In Chapter 1, "Emergence of a National Theatrical Discourse," Liu studies the environment that supports the need for a hybrid new theatre which is considered more effective in dealing with colonialism and modernization than traditional theatre. Liu investigates the different interpretations of the myth of Paris Opera by Chinese and Japanese elites, and how the Chinese came to the realization of the nationalist potential of theatre after Japan's success in building a new form of theatre.

Chapter 2, "Hybrid Sources: Western, Japanese, and Chinese," looks into the "parents" of the hybrid, European theatre and *shinpa*. Liu examines Chinese students' discovery and adaptations of the two sources. Drawing on students' productions in Shanghai's international settlement and the Spring Willow Society in Tokyo from 1906 to 1911, the chapter illuminates how the sources inspired the Chinese artists to realize the potential of a hybrid theatre. Liu's analysis of several productions by the Spring Willow Society is perceptive, and demonstrates his exceptional ability to conduct research on Chinese topics in Japan.

Chapter 3, "Hybridization in Shanghai," centers on the relationship between the hybrid theatre and the hybrid sources (parent). The chapter explores the two phases of *wenmingxi*'s development, the first from 1907 to 1913, and then during the mid-teens. The first phase features *wenmingxi* productions that were bound to the 1911 Revolution yet had no commercial success. Theatre artists, such as Wang Zhongsheng and Lu Jingruo, attempted to introduce elements from Western theatre, shinpa, and Chinese theatre, as well as adapted plays (for example, *Black Slave's Cry to Heaven*) to the Shanghai theatrical scene. Liu explicates the process of developing the hybrid forms and the reasons for the commercial failure. The next phase is marked by the "1914 Revival," during which *wenmingxi* enjoyed commercial success. Liu examines new troupes and their efforts in building the repertoire of the new theatre form. He elaborates on the melodramatic approach, such as that of the New People Society's *An Evil Family*, which enjoyed commercial success. Liu also evaluates other troupes, namely the People's Voice and the Enlightened Society. Japan's Twenty-One Demands in 1915, which includes special concessions and rights in China, had led to the upsurge of anti–Japanese feeling and prompted some *wenmingxi* companies to stage plays with nationalistic overtones.

The next chapter, "Literary Hybridity: Scripts and Scenarios," explores the issue of the literary achievement of *wenmingxi* scenarios. *Wenmingxi*'s lack of complete scripts and its adoption of scenarios and improvisation have hindered its recognition as the earliest modern Chinese theatre. Liu tackles the issue from various perspectives. He argues that scenarios and improvisation functioned well as an effective mechanism for *wenmingxi* as an emerging theater. Using a scenario and a script version of the play *Orchid of the Hollow Valley*, Liu demonstrates how the play started out with basic scenarios, and later developed into an excellent play with a solid script. He then illustrates a scripted play, *Family Love and Grievance, that showcases the dramaturgical hybridity of blends of Western theatrical themes and techniques and Japanese and Chinese aesthetic sensibilities for the Chinese audience.*

In Chapter 5, "Translative Hybridity: Acculturation and Foreignization," Liu looks at the methods employed in the treatment of foreign sources, "acculturation" and "foreignization," in script and performance. By examining various *wenmingxi* versions of Western and *shinpa* plays (such as *La Tosca* and *Othello*, and *The Echo of Cloud* and *The Tide*) as well as their respective receptions, Liu concludes that acculturation was the preferred hybrid form in *wenmingxi*.

The last chapter, "Performance Hybridity: Searching for Conventions," scrutinizes the challenges encountered in *wenmingxi* performances. As a new form of theater, *wenmingxi* could not avoid comparisons with traditional Chinese theatre, which has highly stylized performance conventions. Liu examines three areas of *wenmingxi*'s hybrid performance—movements, music and singing, and gender identity. Movement patterns, dance, and song might have been viewed as "evidence of *wenmingxi*'s evolutionary backwardness"; however, Liu argues that such performance hybridity shows *wenmingxi*'s "instinctive recognition of Chinese audience's preference" (173). The gender of female roles is more complicated. As the norm of cross-gender casting for female characters in traditional Chinese theatre was challenged, Liu states that the gender identity highlights *wenmingxi*'s performance and ideological hybridity. Indeed, with the emergence of actresses and the rise of the debate on women's rights in the early twentieth century, the gender identity issue in modern Chinese theatre deserves more scholarly studies.

As Liu argues in the Epilogue, the discussion of *wenmingxi*'s hybridity is inevitable in the study of *huaju* (spoken drama). He illustrates *huaju*'s long struggle to regain the commercial success that it once enjoyed when many hybridity strategies of *wenmingxi* were incorporated. Indeed, Liu's book offers a rare glimpse into Chinese dramatists' work on modernization within the realm of hybrid theatre during the early twentieth century. On that note, *Performing Hybridity in Colonial-Modern China* is a crucial contribution to the study of modern Chinese theatre and modern Chinese history.

Leo Shingchi Yip
Gettysburg College

Index